THE CONSCIENCE
OF THE VICTORIAN STATE

THE CONSCIENCE
OF THE VICTORIAN STATE

Edited by
Peter Marsh

SYRACUSE UNIVERSITY PRESS   1979

Library of Congress Cataloging in Publication Data
Main entry under title:

The Conscience of the Victorian state.

Bibliography: p.
Includes index.
1. Great Britain—Politics and government—
1837–1901. 2. Political parties—Great Britain—
History. 3. Political ethics. I. Marsh, Peter T.
JN216.C63   320.9'41'081   78-10614
ISBN 0-8156-2195-7
ISBN 0-8156-2196-5 pbk.

CONTENTS

THE CONTRIBUTORS

JOHN CELL is Associate Professor of History at Duke University. A recipient of fellowships from the Social Science Research Council, the National Endowment for the Humanities, and St. Antony's College, Oxford, his publications include *British Colonial Administration in the Mid-Nineteenth Century* (1970), and *By Kenya Possessed* (1976).

JOSEPH HAMBURGER is Professor of Political Science at Yale University. A recipient of grants and fellowships from the Earhart Foundation, the Rockefeller Foundation, the Guggenheim Foundation, the American Council of Learned Societies, and the National Endowment for the Humanities, he is the author of *James Mill and the Art of Revolution* (1963), *Intellectuals in Politics* (1965), and *Macaulay and the Whig Tradition* (1976).

RICHARD J. HELMSTADTER is Associate Professor of History at the University of Toronto and advisory editor for the *Victorian Periodicals News Letter* and for *Albion*.

PETER MARSH is Professor of History and Director of the Honors Program at Syracuse University. A onetime visiting fellow of All Souls College, Oxford, and of Emmanuel College, Cambridge, he is the author of *The Victorian Church in Decline* (1969) and of *The Discipline of Popular Government* (1978).

DAVID ROBERTS is Professor of History at Dartmouth College. An associate editor of *The Journal of British Studies* and on the advisory board of *Victorian Studies,* he is the author of *The Early Victorian Origins of the British Welfare State* (1960).

DERYCK SCHREUDER is Associate Professor and Chairman of the Department of History at Trent University. A research fellow at New College, Oxford, and more recently at the Research School of Social Sciences in the Australian National University, he is the author of *Gladstone and Kruger* (1969).

THE CONSCIENCE
OF THE VICTORIAN STATE

CONSCIENCE
AND THE CONDUCT OF GOVERNMENT
IN NINETEENTH-CENTURY BRITAIN
An Introduction

Peter Marsh

THIS DAMNED MORALITY will ruin everything!" exclaimed Lord Melbourne, the jaded Whig who was Queen Victoria's first prime minister. In its very heat, Lord Melbourne's response to the injection of moral passions into Victorian politics was typical of the age. That injection inspired some Victorians and exasperated others but left few unmoved. Even in retrospect it continues to move writers and scholars, once again by attraction or repulsion. The loss, during the massive, mindless slaughter in the first World War, of the civilized moral certainties of the nineteenth century still haunts people. Some historians[1] sustain the argument that there was far-sighted realism as well as ethical vision, for example in the policies advocated by that most idealistic of Victorian statesmen, William Gladstone. But the moral pretensions of the Victorians disgusted those in the succeeding generation for whom Lytton Strachey spoke. And the moral, progressive, eventually just short of democratic cast which Victorian politics acquired provokes some historians[2] to insist that, then as always, politics was really about power and that political history must be the story of those few who possessed it.

This book analyzes the ways in which a variety of Victorians combined the promptings of conscience with the pursuit of power and their fashioning of policies for the state to follow. No attempt will be made to sample the entire range of the ethical perspectives which Victorians brought to political action. The most glaring omission from that spectrum in the following essays involves the vast mass of Englishmen who lacked political power: the unenfranchised including all women and until 1885 most men, the workers or the unemployed who expressed their aspirations through trade union activity, peaceful agitation, or rioting. Though these people often couched their protests in a deeply moral framework, they will be dealt with indirectly, as they affected the sensi-

1

tivities or forced themselves upon the attention of the politically powerful. Many, though not all, of those studied in the following pages were Parliamentary politicians. Some held or contended for the highest offices of state. Some sat in Parliament but did not regard it as their primary forum, hoping instead to mold the minds of the educated classes through the great periodical journals of the century or to arouse and mobilize electoral opinion through public meetings in the provinces. Others were religious leaders. Some were senior civil servants. All were in a position to influence the conduct of state. This book, then, focuses on the moral concerns of the politically influential, on the particular values and virtues and the interests which the governing minority sought to foster, on their principles of conduct, and their performance.

Even within this range, the following investigations are not exhaustive. But they have been designed to include, either directly or through representative groups, the broadest bands in the spectrum of Parliamentary opinion: Whig and Tory, Liberal, Conservative, and Radical. They also include, in Nonconformity, one of the extra-Parliamentary *corps d'armée* which widened the arena of political warfare in the century. They include, too, in empire, one sphere of substantive public policy. That sphere was world-wide as well as century-long; and in order to avoid the distorted impressions which a specific case study would convey, "the imperial conscience" has been tackled to some extent bibliographically in chapter six. The other chapters are arranged in roughly chronological and also thematic order. They begin with the morally cool Whig party which was in power when Victoria came to the throne. Chapter three then deals with the Utilitarians, who brought the humane rationalism of the late eighteenth century to bear with great intensity in the first half of the nineteenth. Utilitarians and, in the religious vein, Evangelicals helped to raise the moral temperature of politics, which reached its height in the creed and career of Gladstone, the subject of chapter four. The fifth chapter analyzes the diminishing evangelical fire but more sharply defined ethical demands of the Nonconformists later in the century. After the chapter on the empire, the book concludes with a discussion of the Conservatives, whose wish to reduce the dictates of morality to a level compatible with maintenance of prosperity at home and of the national interest abroad won almost uninterrupted acceptance from the electorate in the concluding years of Victoria's reign.

If interest in the relationship between ethics and politics in the past depends upon the level of ethical feeling about political issues in the present, this volume is timely. Rarely has the bearing of moral standards upon the conduct of the state and of politicians been more heatedly argued than over the last dozen years, especially in the United States. The following studies reflect concern with that argument, and are presented in hopes of shedding upon it light from some pertinent past experience. But their primary intent is to stumulate thought about one of the most conspicuous and distinctive characteristics of Victorian England: the attention which it lavished upon morality, its penchant for moral rhetoric, the strong tendency of Victorians to analyze their society, to attack each other, and to defend their various interests in moral terms. Victorian England had no monopoly on morality, of course. Every age, in its social debate, refers to ethical principles, religious teachings, candid assertion of interests, abstract social analysis, and pragmatic marshalling of observed fact. But from age to age the mixture varies. Religion dominated the terms of argument until the seventeenth century; scarcely veiled assertions of interest characterized English politics in the eighteenth century; economic analysis bulks large in the twentieth. Morality was the dominant mode in the nineteenth, so much so that it still colors the implications of the word *Victorian,* often obscuring from memory the raw economic and armed power of nineteenth-century Britain.

One of the most effective ways of acquiring an understanding of the people of a bygone age is to penetrate their ethics, to put on the spectacles of right and wrong through which they looked out at and reacted to their world. But the ethical vision of a former age is singularly hard to assess. To do so requires some ability to detach ourselves from our own ethical beliefs. Assessment also requires a tolerant reaction when the moral viewpoints under investigation turn out, inevitably, to be entwined with interests. It may be, as Marxists are not alone in contending, that ethical systems are essentially rationalizations for individual and group interests. It is certainly hard to discover a group of people whose moral values do not in some way reinforce their interests. The group may not be entirely conscious of the entanglement. But with hindsight, the historian can penetrate at least some of those layers of unconsciousness.

It is particularly hard to separate interests from moral precepts in politics because the politician has a basic interest in power. Without power, he can accomplish nothing. Yet, as Lord Acton wrote in 1887 to Bishop Creighton, "power tends to corrupt and absolute power corrupts absolutely." Acton was thinking mainly about the possession of power. Most Victorians, however, were more concerned with the corrupting effects of the pursuit of power. The privileged position and influence of the propertied and educated classes in Victorian England gave a twist of condescension to their political ethics, as we shall see. But power was too widely diffused in the nineteenth-century British body politic to concentrate concern on its use and abuse. The Victorians were more worried about the ways in which men struggled to obtain and maintain power. The central character in Anthony Trollope's novel of 1874, *Phineas Redux,* is driven to

> doubt whether patriotism can stand the wear and tear and temptation of the front benches in the House of Commons. Men are flying at each other's throats, thrusting and parrying, making false accusations and defences equally false, lying and slandering,—sometimes picking and stealing,—till they themselves become unaware of the magnificence of their own position, and forget that they are expected to be great. Little tricks of sword-play engage all their skill.[3]

However high-minded, a Parliamentary politician would be powerless unless he managed to triumph in debate, outmaneuver opponents, and exploit opportunities. He also had to cultivate supporters, build an electoral organization, and keep it in good repair. These were Machiavellian skills. And if they did not necessarily corrupt their practitioners, they certainly put a premium on sharpness, a quality which could degenerate into sharp practice and did not seem readily compatible with pure commitment to high principle.

Acton's famous dictum as well as Trollope's bitter observation had to do with the behavior of politicians. But there is more to politics than that. It also has to do with the behavior of states. The policies which states adopt in their various departments of activity, the character which these public policies give to the conduct of different states, and their relations with each other, are also subject to ethical evaluation. It is in this impersonal sense that we can speak of the conscience of a state. The voice of conscience is usually thought of as residing in the individual breast, its promptings holding each person to account. But states are held to similar account, the prompting voices of conscience coming from their members and from each other.

Of the following chapters, the one on the empire concentrates largely on the conscience of the state in this sense. It deals with the moral concerns and defects, aspirations and insensitivities which characterized Great Britain's treatment and expansion of its overseas dependencies. The other chapters deal with the conscience of the state in this sense too, with the effect, for example, which Utilitarian propaganda had upon the moral assumptions of the state as a whole. But these chapters also deal with what may be termed conscience *in* the Victorian state. They focus on individuals and groups within Britain, and seek to identify the particular moral concerns which motivated them and to assess the weight which moral concerns possessed in their thinking on public policy and in their pursuit of power.

Even when dealing with the individual politician, the following chapters are concerned with public, not personal, ethics. But in no age can the line be drawn sharply. And in Victorian Britain the distinction was hotly disputed. Though most of the chapters say little or nothing about the sexual conduct of the politicians with whom they deal, the Nonconformists, as Professor Helmstadter makes clear, insisted upon what they called sexual purity as a prerequisite for public office. Even partisans who could tolerate deviations from sexual respectability but could not discern any integrity in the political conduct of their opponents tended to assume that they lacked personal integrity as well. Trollope once remarked that he would be delighted to hear that Disraeli had been caught shop-lifting.[4] Trollope mirrored his age in placing greater importance upon the strength of character with which a politician adhered to his political principles than upon those principles' abstract worth. The Victorian electorate, as Disraeli ruefully observed, preferred grave statesmen. It was not just a matter of taste, or a result, as Disraeli facetiously suggested, of the fog-bound climate. The Victorian preference for gravity reflected a more or less conscious middle-class assault upon the privileged citadel of the aristocracy, in which personal eccentricities had been complacently indulged, and the imposition instead of the disciplines by which the middle class had earned its place in the sun.

This insistence upon middle-class morality was applied to much more than the personal demeanor of political leaders. It extended to public policy in domestic and foreign affairs. A prime objective of much Victorian social legislation was to foster in the lower social orders the cardinal virtues of thrift and self-help with which the middle class associated its own ascent, and to encourage the working class to accept the patterns of work-discipline essential to the smooth functioning of mills and mines. There was much less agreement about the application of the criteria of personal morality to foreign affairs, and in the last half of the century Conservatives tended with increasing explicitness to reject the demand. But, under Gladstone's leadership, many Liberals refused to tolerate any other standard. As Canon Liddon impatiently explained in the wake of the agitation over the Bulgarian atrocities: "We wish our relatives to be good men in the first instance, and then successful men, if success is compatible with goodness. I cannot understand how many excellent people fail to feel this way about their country too."[5]

As with personal ethics, so with religion: though neither is the primary focus of these essays, both did much to fashion the political morality of Victorians. Religious commitments obviously formed the basis upon which the denominations of Protestant Nonconformity approached political matters. Religion was also the starting point for Gladstone. He embarked upon a career in politics as a vocation every bit as religious as Holy Orders, and his first institutional commitments were to the Church of England rather than to the state. The moral earnestness of Sir Robert Peel and Lord Salisbury, and of John Bright and Keir Hardie—to name only a prominent few among scores, indeed hundreds, in the leading echelons—had deeply religious roots. As for the electorate, its partisan affiliations were shaped if anything more powerfully than those of its leaders by denominational loyalties, and its willingness to support or resist new ventures in national policy depended heavily on their religious reverberations.

The bearing of religion upon political ethics was not as straightforward as in the case of personal morality. Religion was much more obviously a matter of interests as well as ethics, a fact of which secular Radicals like the Utilitarians were angrily aware. Though rival denominations invariably provided an ethical rationale for defense of their separate interests, interests were very much at stake in the Church of England's fight to preserve its privileges and endowments, in Nonconformity's crusade for religious equality, and in Roman Catholics' concern about Ireland. The entanglement of interests with ethics in religion was not confined to the arena of conflict between organized Churches, as Marx and Engels knew when they adopted a description of religion as "the opium of the people." Quite consciously the Victorian middle and upper classes relied upon religious ministrations and teaching to foster social contentment down below. Conservatives at home and imperialists abroad were not alone in employing religion to protect the institutions and policies upon which their security depended. Still, religion could be worked both ways. At the end of the century Keir Hardie used the teachings of Christ in attempting to persuade the wealthy to allow the working class its due.

Enquiry into the morality of a former age automatically activates our contemporary assumption of moral relativity. However valid that assumption may be, it must not blind us to the fact that most Victorians did not share it. The characteristic which most distinguished the moral cast of their age from ours was its assurance. Even their heated debates about the bearing of moral precepts upon public policy demonstrated their confidence in the power of morality. Its appeal was conceived to be universal, at least among Englishmen of their generation. And, in sharp contrast to our generation, the moral confidence of the Victorians was only strengthened by contemplation of earlier ages and other peoples. Earlier centuries they despised as morally barbarous or lax. Other peoples, even Continental Europeans and Americans let alone Asians and Africans, they regarded with proud or paternal condescension.

There was, nevertheless, a modesty or, to put it less kindly, a superficiality about the Victorian moral vision. It was rarely brought to bear upon the structure of society. The prophet of Christian Socialism, F. D. Maurice, and the philosopher who applied Hegelian idealism to British political analysis, T. H. Green, paid what seems in retrospect surprisingly little attention to the social and political ramifications of industrial capitalism. The lines of redemption or reform which these men envisaged would have left the economic system of their society largely undisturbed. Though, of the two thinkers, Maurice was perhaps the more searching, his discussion of social morality was aimed at the sanctification of existing, often preindustrial relationships among individuals. The subjects of public policy which specially concerned Green—public health, education, temperance—were primarily matters of personal well-being. The public moralists of Victorian Britain did not aim at a total reordering of society at home or, for that matter, abroad. Though they helped to dislocate and even shatter the structure of many non-Western societies within the Empire, this effect was to a great extent inadvertent and more than they intended.

There was little that was utopian about the Victorian political conscience. It was concerned not with the ideal society but with the preservation of old values or with moral betterment, with how to move toward a desired end rather than with what exactly that end might be. The concern was with conduct—the conduct of classes, the conduct of politicians, the conduct of government. The principle with which Utilitarians, for example, were most closely identified was a standard for assessing the worth of existing institutions and new legislative proposals: the greatest happiness of the greatest number, a standard of calculation rather than a concrete vision. Richard Cobden could describe his prescription for the ills of England and in international relations as "God's own method," but it was still just a method, and a very terrestrial one at that: free trade. The subject which turned Lord Salisbury into an angry moralist was the relationship between leaders and followers within political parties.

Preoccupation with the conduct rather than the ideal objectives of government made some politicians, in particular Whigs and such Conservatives as Disraeli, uneasy about the introduction in debate of any ethical criteria at all. Insistence upon moral absolutes was the earmark of the potentially explosive extremist, whether on the left or the right. The almost complete absence of genuine revolutionaries and reactionaries at the ends of the Victorian spectrum reflected a dearth of moral absolutists. Still, the fervor of which Ultra Tories or crusading reformers were capable was quite enough to make Macaulay apprehensive that they would disrupt the central political task of improvement and gradual adaptation to social change.

Even Gladstone agreed with that definition of the essential task of government; but Gladstone and most Victorians went on to invest the work with moral import. The disagreements within this large majority had to do with the level of political activity which should be invested with moral significance, with their assessment of the state's capacity to do good, and with their various, essentially psychological levels of moral intensity. The lower levels tended to produce Conservatives, the higher Liberals, Radicals, and later socialists, though idiosyncratic mixtures were more the rule than the exception.

About the degree to which any government could elevate the moral caliber of its citizenry, there seems, at first glance, to have been a wide consensus among the governing classes. Speeches disparaging reliance upon the state poured forth from all sides. But this rhetoric disguised critical differences which counteracted the consensus. Conservatives employed such rhetoric in order to uphold the institutions of the Established Church and the landed estate as the most efficacious agencies of moral and social betterment. Liberals and, more aggressively, Radicals used similar rhetoric to deprive these same agencies of their privileges, an effort in which they were largely successful. But the emancipatory Liberal side of the political spectrum included many, often antagonistic gradations. All placed their trust for the moral advancement of society ultimately upon the spontaneous strivings of individuals, voluntary philanthropy, or the variety of religious denominations, in a free economy and unencumbered social order. But they disagreed about how much governmental action was needed in order to bring about this happy state of affairs. There was a division, for example, in the ranks of those who campaigned for repeal of the Contagious Diseases Acts which, in order to curb venereal disease, made suspected prostitutes liable to compulsory medical examination. Some repealers opposed special facilities for the treatment of venereal disease as an encouragement to vice, while others favored them so long as their use was voluntary. Utilitarians opened up a still wider conception of the moral efficacy of state action with their talk of "making" men virtuous. Though this language was emancipatory in spirit, its application helped to lay the foundations of the welfare state, and it was open to great extension in the hands of socialists.

Beneath the conflicts about the level and scope of moral concern appropriate to politics lay a pervasive awareness of class conflict. Ethical argument was embraced as a weapon in this conflict, whether for class attack or defense or alliance between two classes against a third or for the penetration of one class by another. During the second quarter of the century, while the middle class was impressing its wishes upon Parliament, moral argument was a disruptive more than an eirenical force. Richard Cobden and the Anti-Corn Law League whipped up a burning sense of moral indignation among the middle and, to a much lesser extent, the working classes about the way in which the landed class used its ascendancy. The efforts of Young England and the Oxford Movement to ward off this attack by refurbishing the moral credentials of aristocratic, Anglican government, failed. Their one successful tactic was a counterattack, emphasizing the callousness of *laissez-faire* Liberals' opposition to legislation which would reduce the hours of labor of women and children in mines and factories.

But after mid-century, reflecting the gains which the middle class had secured, the social ethics of those who were politically influential— Liberal as well as Tory, bourgeoisie as well as squirearchy—became essentially preservative and paternalistic. This was true even of T. H. Green, though he had imbibed the Radical ideals of Cobden's partner, John Bright, and in turn inspired the socially advanced "New Liberals" of the turn of the century. Green abjured paternalism as it was normally thought of, on the model of the landed estate, and he traced the societal discontents of his day back to feudal sources. He praised fraternity instead of paternalism; he welcomed the removal of discriminatory privileges; and he advocated the creation by law of conditions which would encourage the individual working man to stand on his own feet—as the businessman had learned to do before him. That was the rub. The middle class was the model which working men were to be enabled, encouraged, and, on occasion, forced to emulate. Eventually, so advanced Liberals of Green's ilk hoped, the working class would assimilate middle-class values, and the distinction between the two classes would melt into insignificance. Though between 1832 and 1885 Britain enfranchised most of its adult males, willingness to recognize and respect the ethical sensibilities of the lower classes developed slowly. Until the most glaring forms of electoral corruption were proscribed in the 1880s, fastidious politicians

tended to think of frequent contact with electors as a contaminating experience rather than as a source of moral strength. Walter Bagehot
smugly opined that, "The lower classes in civilized countries . . . are
clearly wanting in the nicer part of those feelings which, taken together,
we call the *sense* of morality."[6]

The connection between political ethics and interests, whether of class
or party or country, was never severed and rarely even strained. Whenever it was strained, the cost was discouragingly high, as the fortunes of
Gladstone demonstrated. Gladstone was no pure altruist, as irritated
commentators have never ceased to point out. His eagerness to invest the
process of hearkening to the voice of more and more of the electorate
with ethical significance was, nonetheless, remarkable. So was his "persistent effort to enforce on England a Christian instead of a pagan conception of her duty to foreign peoples"[7]—remarkable, but politically
costly. The moral enthusiasm of "the People's William" alienated Whigs
and the men of urban property who had contentedly followed the previous
leader of the Liberal party, Lord Palmerston. In foreign and imperial affairs, Gladstone identified his party with crusades, over the Bulgarian
atrocities and Ireland, which were "unrelated to the standing
'interests' "[8] of Radical politics. His foreign and imperial policy may very
well have coincided with a wise assessment of British national interests,
but it was discredited by his failure during the Ministry of 1880–85 to
watch events overseas closely, culminating in the death of General Gordon
at Khartoum. These cumulative offenses inflicted wounds on the Liberal
party which crippled it for the rest of the century.

Still, the need to point out that class and national interests bounded
and shaped the dictates of conscience in Victorian Britain only under-
scores the remarkable prevalence and even power of that conscience. We
look for such limitations as inevitable. It is the persuasive influence of
moral argument in nineteenth-century British politics which needs
explanation.

So intangible and varied a phenomenon defies complete, definitive
accounting. But at least some of the main forces behind it can be identified. It was, obviously and perhaps at the deepest level, a product of the
stresses created by the transformation of Britain into the world's first industrialized society. Ethical argument, as we have seen, was a weapon in
the civil warfare between an expanded middle class, a larger more concentrated proletariat, and the old landed order. But their choice of weap-

ons indicated some faith, or at least hope, that their class warfare was not, or need not, be total. Moral appeals were not, of course, the only weapons they chose. They used strikes, riots and repression; they bought and intimidated electoral support; the specter of revolution hovered over the second quarter and revived faintly in the final quarter of the century. Coercion, threatened or actual, played a very large part in the relations between the propertied classes and the proletariat, and between Westminster and recalcitrant peoples in its dependencies. Still, at home, there was faith among all classes in the possibility of peaceful dialogue and moral suasion. Between the middle and the landed classes, this faith eventually reached the proportions of a consensus within which partisan disputes were about secondary matters of tactics.

The contrast between the main island and Ireland is illuminating here. Peel observed before the end of the Napoleonic wars, to his disgust, how much the relationship of the Irish including the ascendant Protestants to the state was a matter of patronage and raw power.[9] And later, whether through O'Connell's Catholic Association or through Parnell's use of Parliamentary obstruction, the Irish continued to *force* themselves upon the attention of Britain. In turn Englishmen as a whole, including even so insistently moral a politician as John Bright, never quite grasped the ethical case for Home Rule. In spite of the class conflicts exacerbated by industrialization, there was within Britain a degree of social solidity and hence of solidarity lacking between Britain and Ireland. Conscience in the Victorian state, the reliance upon and resort to moral suasion, rested upon that foundation.

The prevalence of moral argument was fostered also by some basic changes in the intellectual culture of Britain. After a pause in the eighteenth century, literacy began again to spread among the population until, by the death of Queen Victoria, it was virtually universal. Facilities for education multiplied, and the quality of the education provided by existing institutions at all levels was signally improved, particularly in humanistic rather than technological subjects. An increasing appetite for political news and commentary accompanied the spread of literacy and improvements in education. In response to this demand, Parliament was forced in the second half of the eighteenth century to allow publication of its proceedings; over the course of the nineteenth century techniques for producing and marketing newspapers on a large, eventually massive scale were developed; and periodical journals aimed primarily at the educated classes flourished as never before.

The character of political discourse was bound to be profoundly affected. In place of the veiled adjustment of interests occasionally interrupted by riot which had characterized politics in the eighteenth century, this set of cultural changes put a premium on public explanation. The governing elites had to articulate principles broad enough for the public to grasp and approve. There was some loss in sophistication of debate in Parliament once its members had to address themselves not just to their peers from families long familiar with the craft of government but also to an as yet untutored public. But political debate rarely degenerated into demagoguery, because the governing classes and the electorate were broadened by stages rather than at a rush. There was, as a result, a pedagogic quality to Victorian political rhetoric, a conscious attempt by insecure elites to instill as well as to appeal to common principles.

In the middle half of the nineteenth century, when the executive had been deprived of most powers of patronage and was not yet fortified by strong popular party organizations, its need for moral approval was especially acute, and gave rise to attempts, preeminently by the Peelites and by olympian civil servants, to act with nonpartisan, even altruistic disinterestedness. After the ideological murkiness of the maneuvering over the second Reform bill in 1866 and 1867, political debate assumed a more sharply partisan character, but without abandoning the appeal to principle. Now the desired quality was consistency rather than altruism. Gladstone took pains to prove his consistency in his next initiative, the disestablishment of the Irish Church. During the 1870s, the leaders of both parties displayed less concern than heretofore with the nuances of opinion among the men in Parliament, and more concern to satisfy the electoral desire for evident consistency. Gladstone and Disraeli met this demand by imposing markedly antagonistic policies upon their parties, particularly in foreign affairs. The man who eventually emerged as Gladstone's most successful rival, Lord Salisbury, made one form of consistency, loyalty by party leaders to followers, the centerpiece of his political ethics and statecraft.

Even more powerfully than the growth of a literate, reading public, two other cultural phenomena, both stemming from the eighteenth century —the Evangelical revival, and a surge of rationalistic enquiry associated with the Enlightenment—imbued Victorian political debate with a concern for principle. The Evangelical revival had spread far beyond its Wesleyan origins by the beginning of the nineteenth century. It revived the denominations of English Nonconformity from their moribund condition. The term "Evangelical" attached itself to a small but infectiously saintly group of members of the Church of England known as the Clapham Sect. The evangelical revival touched all classes: working and unemployed men in the economically distressed counties where Wesley found a response, earnest town-dwelling businessmen, upper middle-class men of assured income, and landed gentry active in politics. The revival continued to spread during the first half of the nineteenth century, and its influence extended far beyond its obvious adherents.

The evangelical revival impressed the British with a sense of moral obligation and accountability in their relations with their fellow men. That sense formed the heart of the civic conscience. It gave the Victorian polity its remarkable moral cohesion. It made the dialogue between rival elites and different classes easier. It fired a minority in the ruling classes with compassion for the powerless: for slaves, lunatics, women and children in mines, and street urchins. It strengthened the commitment of Peel in Parliament and of Sir James Stephen at the Colonial Office to administrative altruism. In its most diffuse form among the powerful, it reduced the thickness of their skin of indifference. It made the morality of the governors something subtler and gentler than a rationalization of economic and class interest. At the same time among the working classes, particularly through Methodism, it fostered an idiom of social thought which their would-be leaders could not safely ignore or slight.

The evangelical conscience was a plastic force. It could rarely do more than modify hard interests. Furthermore, as Melvin Richter has emphasized, it contained a "profound ambivalence." On the one hand, it quickened "a sense of obligation to those in need." On the other hand, it reinforced, at least among some of its adherents, a "belief in the economic virtues and the identity of poverty and sin, views more likely to proscribe charity than to encourage it."[10] Thus, while the evangelical conscience gave rich and poor a common moral language, it could not prevent them from drawing contrary conclusions from its promptings.

This ambivalence in the evangelical conscience extended, as David Roberts points out, to the main legatees of the British Enlightenment— the Utilitarians. The Utilitarians had still more in common with the evangelicals. Both had stronger hearts than heads.[11] But, true to their origins, the Utilitarians articulated and applied the major tenets of their creed— demands for the greatest happiness of the greatest number, for political liberty, an emancipated economy, and a reforming state—with enough intellectual clarity to elevate their creed into a theory. Their detachment from, indeed contempt for, the entrenched institutions and interests of Church, the existing political parties, and the land deprived them of social weight. But what they lacked in weight and numbers they more than made up in trenchancy of argument. However emotional themselves, the disciples of Bentham shaped the civic conscience more through the head than through the heart. Arguing in harmony with the appetite of the busi-

ness world for efficiency in the conduct of government, they equipped
Victorian England with principles of political judgment which were more
transparently rational than those embedded in the fervent religion of the
evangelicals. Though there were also differences between these two
creeds in substance as well as style, they were no more incompatible than
the ambivalent social impulses which both encouraged. The combination
of the Utilitarian appeal to the head with the evangelical appeal to the
heart injected principles powerfully into the center of Victorian political
debate.

    The character of that debate underwent searching changes in the
years immediately preceding and following the death of the Queen. The
earnest religious belief which had deepened the moral gravity of Britain
in the middle half of the nineteenth century decayed. At the same time,
the United States and Germany deprived Britain of its uniqueness as an
industrial power and then surpassed her. Likewise, Britain ceased to be
the only dynamic imperial power. The resulting loss of economic and imperial confidence helped to bring the social and political order of mid-
Victorian Britain into question. At no time static, that order was itself
subject to accelerating change and assault. The Reform Acts of 1867 and
1884–85 gave the country a thoroughly popular though not yet fully
democratic electorate, thus quickening the shift in the center of political
gravity from the elite to the rank and file. The Irish Land Act of 1881
marked, furthermore, not only a victory for a popular agitation, but also
a precedent-setting violation by government of "free" economic contract. As the young economic and social analyst, Arnold Toynbee, eagerly
pointed out, the act embodied two maxims capable of wide extension:
"First, that where individual rights conflict with the interests of the community, there the State ought to interfere; and, second, that where the
people are unable to provide a thing for themselves, and that thing is of
primary social importance, then again the State should interfere and provide it for them."[12]
    What Irish tenant farmers had won, English working men could also
claim. The extension of trade union organization from skilled to unskilled
workers in the last twenty years of the century, together with some successful industrial action, angry disturbances in Trafalgar Square, and the
birth of small socialist societies, heralded a new determination among the
forces of labor to impress a working-class rather than a middle-class bias

upon economic and political intercourse. The pressures which they were able to exert made social injustices harder to ignore, but also brought class antagonisms more candidly to the fore. Conscience in the late Victorian and early Edwardian state became increasingly a collective matter. While the moral sensibilities of some were heightened, others were hardened. And the suspicion which a few had always entertained—that the application of ethical ideals to politics was nothing better than self-serving rationalization of economic interests—spread.

But Victorian moral concern proved to be a surprisingly sturdy and adaptable plant, not finally uprooted until World War I, and even then not killed. The consolidation of the interests of industrial, mercantile, and landed property within the Conservative party, while politically advantageous, narrowed its social sympathies. Its leader in the closing years of the nineteenth century, Lord Salisbury, was a profoundly if pessimistically Christian statesman who pressed his party's commitments to the Established Church; but that legacy was submerged quickly after 1902 by the tariff reform campaign waged, as his son pointed out,[13] with frantic because religiously shallow fervor. Nowhere was the hardening of British political sensibilities in the first World War to be more evident than in the bitter chauvinism of the Conservative Parliamentary party and press.

The moral reflexes of mid-Victorian politics persisted past the turn of the century more vigorously, though in varying intensities, on the left. Among the Fabians, they assumed a secular form. Akin to the evangelicals with their sense of responsibility to discern and advance God's social purposes, the Fabians were gripped by a sense of obligation to identify what Sidney Webb called the "blind social forces" at work in Britain and to bring public policy intelligently into line. That effort was sanctified and fired in them by an emotional altruism; and Beatrice Webb was shocked by Shaw's "unmoral" argument in *Major Barbara* that self-sacrifice for the good of society was self-deceptive.[14]

Among no group were the middle-class blinkers on the moral vision of most nineteenth-century British political elites more conspicuous than among the Fabians, condescendingly conscious as they were of their intellectual superiority, and reliant upon their private access to highly placed politicians and civil servants. Keir Hardie and the popular working-class components of the nascent Labor party were much more candidly class-conscious in their appeals for electoral support. At the same time, the message of Keir Hardie, unlike the empirical science of the Fabians, was explicitly, pervasively moral. It arose from and spoke in the accents of the culture which Methodism and other Protestant sects in Scotland,

Wales, and England had fostered among the working class. And while Hardie could use the language of class warfare, he also appealed to moral injunctions which all Christians revered. Like the mid-Victorian moralists, he too desired a harmonious society, but he meant to place the working rather than the middle or landed class at its center and, with that end in view, to persuade the other classes to accept or at least respect working-class values.

The New Liberals of the early years of the new century could not go that far. They were, for instance, repelled by strikes timed to maximize discomfort to the consuming public: "the coal-porters no doubt deserve their extra money," L. T. Hobhouse commented on one occasion, "but were they justified . . . in catching London out in a cold snap?"[15] Nevertheless, studies by late-nineteenth-century social scientists of urban poverty, and economists' changing analyses of its roots, pushed the New Liberals closer than any preceding group toward a conception of social harmony based not upon permeation of other classes by the ethics of their own, but upon mutual sympathy. The New Liberals relied still, indeed more than ever, upon middle-class elites to furnish the country with competent and intelligent as well as beneficent governors. This increased reliance on the government which their class could offer compensated for their diminished faith in the economic system of private capitalism which had made their class prosperous, and in the attendant individualistic virtues of thrift and self-help. Revolted, meanwhile, by the imperialism of the 1890s which had culminated in the Boer War, the New Liberals wedded their emancipation from classical economics to the Gladstonian rejection of subservience in foreign affairs to reasons of state. They insisted that the costs of empire were "a direct financial threat to social reform."[16]

The vehicle of their vision, the Liberal party, was shattered by the first World War; and the moral loss was critical. Although the conscience of the Victorian state had been refracted throughout the spectrum of political opinion, the ideal of a society whose internal walls of class and interest were dissolved by a common ethic was its central light, and the Liberal party was the surrounding prism. The ideal never shone pure. It was always, inevitably, distorted by class. But the distortions tended to become more obvious, and the angles of refraction more oblique, wherever the commitment to class was most conscious and explicit. However illusory, however deceptive the Liberal party's claim to altruism transcending class, that claim matched the dictates of the Victorian ideal more readily than the often explicitly sectional commitments of the Conservatives and of Labor. Whether the relationship was symbolic or substantial, faith in the ideal flickered as its most congenial vehicle broke apart.

Notes

1. See R. W. Seton-Watson, *Disraeli, Gladstone and the Eastern Question* (1935), J. L. Hammond, *Gladstone and the Irish Nation* (1964), and J. L. Hammond and M. R. D. Foot, *Gladstone and Liberalism* (1966).

2. E.g., Maurice Cowling, *1867: Disraeli, Gladstone and Revolution* (1967), Andrew Jones, *The Politics of Reform, 1884* (1972), and A. B. Cooke and J. R. Vincent, *The Governing Passion: Cabinet Government and Party Politics in Britain, 1885–86* (1974).

3. The Oxford Trollope edition, II, 278.

4. Michael Sadleir, *Trollope* (1927), p. 330.

5. Quoted in R. T. Shannon, *Gladstone and the Bulgarian Agitation, 1876* (1963), p. 24.

6. *Physics and Politics* (1948), p. 122.

7. Hammond, *Gladstone and the Irish Nation* (1964), p. 727.

8. Shannon, *Gladstone and the Bulgarian Agitation*, p. 273.

9. Norman Gash, *Mr. Secretary Peel* (1961), p. 120.

10. Melvin Richter, *The Politics of Conscience: T. H. Green and his Age* (1964), pp. 292–93.

11. See *infra*, p. 12.

12. Quoted in Richter, *Politics of Conscience*, p. 288.

13. Lord Hugh Cecil, *"The Life of Gladstone,"* *Nineteenth Century and After* 59 (349) (Mar. 1906): 369.

14. Norman and Jeanne MacKenzie, *The First Fabians* (1977), pp. 115, 309.

15. Quoted in Richter, *Politics of Conscience,* p. 374.

16. P. F. Clarke, "The Progressive Movement in England," *Transactions of the Royal Historical Society,* 5th ser., 24 (1974): 165.

THE WHIG CONSCIENCE
Joseph Hamburger

THE WHIGS in the nineteenth century were usually regarded as the leaders of the popular party, as reformers, as sympathetic to the needs of the people, indeed, as liberals. This interpretation of Whig motives and policies was applied to the party both in its past and in the Victorian present. Lord John Russell, a leading party spokesman with an impeccably respectable Whig lineage, said of the historic Whig party that it "looked toward the people, whose welfare is the end and object of all government." Describing early eighteenth-century Whigs, and by implication those that followed, the historian Henry Hallam said "the whig had a natural tendency to improvement, the tory an aversion to it," and that the Whig "loved to descant on liberty and the rights of mankind." By the late eighteenth century the Whigs under Charles James Fox's leadership claimed to be for peace, economy, and reform. And during the agitated years immediately following the end of the wars against Napoleonic France the Whigs, we have been told, "associated themselves with the popular cause," indeed, that the events of 1817–20 "served to unite the Whigs with the democratic party—if not in general sympathy, yet in a common cause."[1]

This view of the Whigs as somewhat left-wing and as liberal had its origin in such things as the Whig legend about the Whigs being the architects of the Glorious Revolution of 1688; in the belief that Locke's ideas became part of Whig beliefs; and in Fox's somewhat sympathetic views on the French Revolution. Such things allowed historians to cast the Whigs in the liberal role. Thus the Whigs are said to have maintained their influence after the Reform Act of 1832 "by virtue of their special relationship to the Liberal forces in the community." And Halevy thought that "the epithet [Liberal] was accepted by those against whom it was directed [the Whigs], until it finally became the official designation of the

19

revived and reconstituted Whigs."[2] The implication of these judgments is clear—that there was a Whig conscience, and that it consisted of a moral concern for the well-being of the people and that it was made evident in proposals for liberal reform.

This was not a uniformly held view, however, for there were critics, including such varied persons as James Mill, the young Disraeli, and Karl Marx, who were skeptical about Whig professions of concern for the people. These critics took note of the aristocratic position and great wealth of most leading Whigs as well as their occasional enjoyment of political power and their unending participation in a system of privilege. Thus the Whigs were regarded as part of the aristocratic ruling class and therefore as having interests opposed to the people. Consequently these critics accused the Whigs of hypocrisy, of only pretending to be favorable to reform, and of using liberal rhetoric and offering petty concessions to the people in order to divert radical criticism from the established system of privilege from which the Whigs derived great benefits.[3] This analysis clearly implied that conscience played no role in Whig politics, for it held that expressions of moral concern for the people were manifestations of selfishness and cynicism.

In attempting to resolve the conflict between these two interpretations we are greatly helped by Lord Acton, who was one of the most thoughtful and most erudite of British historians in the nineteenth century. Acton's testimony is especially valuable, for he was hypersensitive to the phenomenon of conscience in politics. He also observed the juxtaposition of aristocratic privilege with professions of liberal sentiment and moral principle in the Whigs, and like ealier critics he reacted skeptically. However, he avoided the tendentiousness of the earlier critics by distinguishing between two different political outlooks—one liberal, in which there was a public conscience, and the other Whig, in which there was no place for conscience. Each represented different political traditions which at certain historical moments and in certain individuals came together, but they were analytically separate.

The Whig, Acton said, "acquiesced in the existing order"; he would destroy little and innovate little; he was willing to improve but anxious to avoid reconstructing. For him political change involved patching-up and improvising, and this was achieved by being pragmatic and flexible. The Whig thought of himself as realistic and practical and as not needing philosophy, including moral philosophy. Thus the absence of moral conscience in the Whig did not prevent him from being useful, for he contributed to the maintenance of the existing, and, from the Whig point of view, satisfactory political system. If moral values were served by this, by virtue of their being supported in the prevailing political order, it was not the result of systematic and self-conscious moral scrutiny by Whig politicians. The liberal, on the other hand, had principles; indeed, he had a moral vision, however blurred the light by which it was illuminated. For him the purpose of politics was to improve and to do so in the light of a moral ideal.[4]

In order to test the usefulness of Acton's distinction it is necessary to specify which of the various kinds of Whigs is most relevant to an inquiry into nineteenth-century politics. Evidently Acton had in mind a type of Whig that had played a prominent part in recent politics. But there were other kinds of Whigs that do not fit his description and which were not so important during the Victorian era. There were the so-called real Whigs whose inspiration came from the Commonwealth ideal; they believed in natural rights and republicanism, and they were inclined to criticize established institutions and old traditions. But this kind of Whig flourished in the eighteenth century and by the nineteenth faded from view, and when it did appear, as, for example, in the person of Godwin, Hazlitt, or Major Cartright, it was associated with Radicalism.[5] In addition, there had been a kind of Whig that during an earlier period was distinguished from other politicians by a doctrine that emphasized the importance of the constitution as it was formed after 1688, including limited monarchy, Protestant succession, religious toleration, and rule of law. However, by the nineteenth century this kind of Whig doctrine no longer distinguished Whigs, for it was an outlook shared by most politicians.

During the nineteenth century the most visible of the Whigs were the magnates—the aristocrats who usually were wealthy and who naturally followed political careers, men such as Grey, Russell, Lansdowne, Althorp and Holland. But these politicians are not the ones in whose words and conduct we should look for evidence of public conscience, for their explanations and reasonings, even in private correspondence, were not stated with that articulateness and fulness that reveals elaborate views on the relations of morality and politics.

It is to the Whig intelligentsia that we should turn—to Francis Jeffrey and Thomas Babington Macaulay, who were, respectively, editor and most notable contributor to the *Edinburgh Review,* which was acknowledged to be the pre-eminent Whig journal. Although they too were constrained by considerations of practical politics, as publicists they sought to provide reasoned explanations of their party's policies, and in doing so they revealed their views on the role of conscience in politics. Macaulay especially serves our purpose, for more than anyone else he became the spokesman for Whiggism, and not only in his time, for he be-

came a legendary figure in the Whig tradition, and by this means he continued to influence the interpretation of Whiggism long after his death in
1859. Acton said the Whigs had a policy but needed a philosophy (unlike
the Liberals who had a philosophy but needed a policy). Macaulay may
be regarded as one who provided such a philosophy—that is, a rationale
for the Whig party. This is how his party colleagues thought of him. E. J.
Littleton (later Lord Hatherton) said of one speech that it "had more of
argument and profound philosophy, given in the most appropriate
language . . . than I ever before witnessed." And Le Marchant thought
another speech had provided a "noble vindication of the policy of the
Whigs during their exclusion from office." Such was his success in providing justifying arguments that by mid-century Macaulay, who was
born a Tory, who had flirted with Radicalism, who was a "new man"
facing the famous cousinage, became the spokesman for Whiggism.
James Fitzjames Stephen said he "was the greatest . . . advocate and ex-
pounder of Whig principles since the time of Burke." And Henry Reeve
said of Whig principles that "these truths will be remembered in the language [Macaulay] gave them."[6] Thus in examining Macaulay's political
thought we are looking at a body of Whig argument in which the role of
conscience and moral principle is bound to be revealed.

What, then, was the role of conscience in Macaulay's—and to a considerable extent, in the Whig's—conception of politics? The result of our
inquiry might be surprising, for in Macaulay we find a fundamental rejection of public conscience. This is not to say that Macaulay was without private conscience. His generosity and his charities are well known.
And he was censorious and often expressed outrage at what he considered the misconduct of others. He even attended church. But in his discussions of contemporary politics it is difficult to find evidence that
moral or conscientious considerations influenced his deliberations. And
in his reflections on historical characters and events, and in his general
observations about politics, he indicates that moral considerations are an
undesirable influence on political decisions.

A clue as to the place of conscience in his political outlook can be
found in his attitude toward those in whom conscience most prominently
resided—religionists generally, and especially Nonconformists. His diary
and published writings provide innumerable expressions of disdain and
also ridicule for anything or anyone associated with religiosity. Quakers,
Muggletonians, Methodists, Swedenborgians, and Evangelicals—
especially Evangelicals, with whom his father was intimately connected—
they were all regarded as absurd, or malignant, or mad. He ridiculed "a

mad Swedenborgian" who pestered him with "his grievances and his rev-
elations." Methodists elicited a similar response: "the controversialists
[among them] . . . are so absurd and malignant that one is always
against the last speaker." This attitude is even evident in his observations
on the Evangelicals, especially those who formed the Clapham Sect, whose
members, in addition to leading the anti-slavery movement, also founded
the Sunday School Society, the Religious Tract Society, the Church Missionary Society, and the British and Foreign Bible Society. Evangelical
beliefs set the tone of Macaulay's moral and religious education, and
throughout his life he carried memories of the famous Evangelicals who
came to his father's home. But irritation was mixed with his admiration
for the Evangelicals. The preacher Buchanan, for example, along with
fine qualities, also demonstrated "a little or rather not a little fanfaro-
nade and humbug." Macaulay also ridiculed Exeter Hall, which was associated with manifestations of enthusiastic religion. His famous reference to the "bray" of Exeter Hall during the debates on the Maynooth
grant caused outrage among some of his Edinburgh constituents and
contributed to his electoral defeat.[7]

Macaulay's attitude also was evident in judgments of historical examples of religiosity. John Bunyan, author of *Pilgrim's Progress,* and
George Fox, founder of the Quaker sect, were described with the language of pathology. Bunyan had a religious sensibility which "amounted
to a disease." His excitable mind "was tormented by a succession of fan-
tasies which seemed likely to drive him to suicide or to Bedlam." Indeed,
"scarcely any madhouse could produce an instance of delusion so strong,
or of misery so acute." And Fox also suffered from "the constitutional
diseases of his mind."[8]

Puritanism, a great source of conscientiousness, not to say moral
fervor, in politics, also provoked Macaulay's hostility, despite his admiration for it as a source of strength and courage. The Puritans' austerity
was an obstacle to the cultivation of literature and the arts. Furthermore,
it was ridiculous, as was evident in his description of a Puritan household
at the time of the Restoration: there were "Geneva bands, heads of lank
hair, upturned eyes, nasal psalmody, and sermons three hours long." But
above all else, Puritanism was objectionable because of its association
with sectarianism and as a source of fanaticism which had dreadful consequences in politics. It gave men strong moral convictions, compared
with which, every other consideration, including politics, became unimportant. Solely concerned with their relation to the deity, the Puritans,
Macaulay wrote, felt "contempt for terrestrial distinctions. The differ-

ence between the greatest and meanest of mankind seemed to vanish
when compared with the boundless interval which separated the whole
race from him on whom their own eyes were constantly fixed." Although
the Puritan "prostrated himself in the dust before his Maker . . . he set
his foot on the neck of his king."[9]

Assertive Catholicism also attracted Macaulay's criticism, not because it was Catholic (he welcomed Catholic Emancipation and defended
the Maynooth grant), but because of its assertive, proselytizing character. He confessed feeling "the same disgust at Anglo-Catholic and Roman Catholic cants which people after the Restoration felt for the Puritan
cant"; and he confessed in his diary, "I hate Puseyites and Puritans im-
partially."[10]

There may have been biographical sources for Macaulay's readiness
to be irritated by religiosity, for he was exposed to a good deal of it in his
own family, in which there was much piety and strong commitment to religious causes. His father was an active member of the Evangelical movement and served as editor of the *Christian Observer*. However, there was
much more to Macaulay's religious views, for he also had a reasoned argument against religiosity. He objected to it because it generated strong
moral feelings and encouraged their development outside institutional
channels, and therefore it acknowledged no conventional restraints.
Such moral feelings became immoderate; from Macaulay's unsympathetic perspective, they produced zeal or fanaticism, and Macaulay used
no words of greater disapprobation than *fanatic* or *zealot*. Religiosity,
then, was objectionable because of its political consequences. It drove
men to extremes, made them intolerant and uncompromising, disposed
them to do battle with their ideological opposites, causing them to divide
the state and to be obstacles to conciliatory politics. Such fanaticism was
a kind of madness, a political disease. If it spread, its consequences were
dreadful, for it could convulse nations, cause revolutions, and sustain
fierce civil wars.

On the other hand, if intense religiosity did not exist, there would be
a better chance that discontents would be relieved by adjustments made
through the political process. Then the political realm would be uncon-
taminated by hopes and enmities associated with religion, and politics
could be practiced without the distorting effects of utopian desires for
change and romantic dreams of restoration. Politicians could then debate, adjust, compromise. With religion kept moderate, conciliatory politics would become possible. But if it became extreme, religion was a
source of conflict and an obstacle to conciliation.

It should be said that Macaulay was not opposed to religion as such, but to religious fervor. Tepid, conventional religion was acceptable, for it was politically useful. It restrained appetites, consoled those in want and calamity, allowed one to go to the grave without despair, and restrained those "who are placed above all earthly fears." Thus he defended the Church of England for serving these purposes and for being a bulwark against fanaticism.[11]

Macaulay also was highly critical of secular factions that introduced moral feeling into politics, and these included many political radicals and social reformers. Indeed, he discerned a religious dimension to political and social radicalism, and thus he found it objectionable for the same reasons that he condemned religious sectarianism. In fact, in his thinking he assimilated political radicalism and religious sectarianism. When he encountered immoderate Radicalism, with it sweeping criticisms of established arrangements and its utopian standards of judgment, he interpreted it in the context of religious radicalism, especially Puritanism. Just as the old religious enthusiasts had generated political radicalism, he also thought that secular radicals in his own time stimulated moral passions that had a religious dimension. Both encouraged discontent, criticism, and in the end, separation and rebellion. Macaulay used the terms zealot, demagogue, sectarian, enthusiast for both. He described the seventeenth-century Independents, the root and branch men, by using, as he said, "the kindred phrase of our own time, radicals."[12]

This way of regarding radicalism is especially evident in Macaulay's observations on the Philosophic Radicals, who were the most intellectually serious and perhaps the most politically ambitious radicals of the 1820s and 30s. These heirs to Bentham's utilitarian philosophy—including James Mill, John Stuart Mill, George Grote, and John Roebuck— engaged in political journalism and most of them looked forward to Parliamentary careers. It is worth noting that Macaulay called James Mill a "zealot of a sect." Macaulay thought of the Philosophic Radicals as playing a role comparable to the Puritans in the mid-seventeenth century:

Even now [1827], it is impossible to disguise, that there is arising in the bosom of [the middle class] a Republican sect, as audacious, as paradoxical, as little inclined to respect antiquity, as enthusiastically attached to its ends, as unscrupulous in the choice of its means, as the French Jacobins. . . . Metaphysical and political science engage their whole attention. Philosophical pride has done for them what spiritual pride did for the Puritans in a former age; it has generated in them an aversion for the fine arts, for elegant literature, and for the sentiments of chivalry. It has made them arrogant, in-

tolerant, and impatient of all superiority. These qualities will, in spite of
their real claims to respect, render them unpopular, as long as people are satisfied with their rulers. But under an ignorant and tyrannical ministry . . .
their principles would spread as rapidly as those of the Puritans formerly
spread, in spite of their offensive peculiarities.[13]

Of course Macaulay was aware of the differences between the Puritans
and the Philosophic Radicals. But when he thought of the way in which
the radical intelligentsia of his day might lead the combined middle and
working classes in revolution against the government of the day, he pictured its leaders as being like the Puritans.

Macaulay was so opposed to strong moral feeling that he criticized it
even when it was not in the first instance political. For example, in 1857
when he witnessed the swelling demand for revenge against the mutineers
in India, he noted that the "effeminate mawkish philanthropy of the
Ewarts and Sturges . . . will lose all its influence," and, he added, "that
is a very good thing." And there was the slavery question, with which his
father had been greatly concerned, and which Macaulay himself had addressed. If there was any subject about which Macaulay had a political
conscience, this was it. "I hate slavery from the bottom of my soul," he
wrote in his diary; "and yet," he added, "I am made sick by the cant and
the silly mock reasons of the Abolitionists." After his niece had been at
an anti-slavery meeting at Exeter Hall, he wrote with satisfaction, "she
despised the nonsense as much as I could wish."[14]

Macaulay's criticism of moral feeling has meaning within the context of his general political outlook. According to it the main task of politics was to protect the center, which meant diminishing the extremes.
This meant the extreme Right as much as the Left; Macaulay was as severely critical of the Ultra-Tories as of the Left, and he also called them
"fanatics."[15] By reducing the extremes it would be possible for individuals and groups with diverse goals and beliefs to coexist, all enjoying
both order and liberty. On the other hand, if either extreme prevailed, it
would bring either order or liberty but not both. On the Left, radical politicians seeking liberty would bring anarchy. On the Right, extreme conservative politicians seeking order would produce despotism. The moves
to both Left and Right were fueled by moral views that made the spokesmen dogmatic and inflexible. Thus both were condemned.

In passing it should be said that Macaulay's political career can be
understood in the light of this outlook. It explains why he defended the
Canningites in 1827, why he was for the Reform Bill and against Chartism, why he acted like a classical Trimmer—trimming between Mitford's

attack on democracy and James Mill's defense of it, between Left and Right, Anarchy and Despotism, Radical and Ultra-Tory. In all this he was not seeking improvement as such but stability, and he defended as improvement only what promoted stability. This outlook also provided the main interpretive theme of his *History of England,* in which heroic status was given to George Savile, Marquis of Halifax, who was author of the classic "The Character of a Trimmer."

This trimmer's concern for stability implied opposition to the moral views that inspired those at the extremes between whom Macaulay wished to trim. And it was the Whig party that he most frequently cast in the trimming role. During the Reform Bill crisis when he thought the constitution was threatened by the extreme Tories, who in the name of tradition resisted change, and by the extreme Radicals, who advocated fundamental change in the name of popular rights and democracy, Macaulay thought the Whig party should have promoted moderate changes that would have separated the liberally minded middle classes from the Radicals who advocated universal suffrage. This policy, Macaulay calculated, would have sustained the Whigs as a center party, thus denying influence to both extremes.

That this policy was not Macaulay's alone can be shown by pointing to another member of the Whig intelligentsia, Francis Jeffrey, who was one of the founders of the *Edinburgh Review* and its editor until 1829, as well as having been a Member of Parliament and Judge Advocate for Scotland. He too thought the main function of the Whig party was to preserve the center against the extremes, thereby allowing the constitutional order to be perpetuated. As early as 1810 Jeffrey analyzed the political situation in these terms. "The great body of the nation," he wrote, "appears to us to be divided into two violent and most pernicious factions —the courtiers, who are almost for arbitrary power—and the democrats, who are almost for revolution and republicanism. Between these stand a small, but most respectable band—the friends of liberty and of order— the Old Constitutional Whigs." It was not only the size of the extreme factions that was worrisome, but "the acrimony of their mutual hostility is still more alarming," for it threatens civil war and revolution. "If the whole nation were actually divided into revolutionists and high-monarchy men, we do not see how they could be prevented from fighting, and giving us the miserable choice of a despotism or a tumultuary democracy." Jeffrey added, however, that fortunately, "there is a third party in the nation . . . composed of the Whig Royalists."[16]

Some years later Jeffrey made an even more explicit statement of this theme, in which he included clear allusions to Halifax's conception of trimming:

> We have frequently had occasion to speak of the dangers to which the conflict of two extreme parties must always expose the peace and the liberties of such a country as England. . . . We [Whigs] acknowledge that we are fairly chargeable with a fear of opposite excesses—a desire to compromise and reconcile the claims of all the great parties in the State—an anxiety to temper and qualify whatever may be said in favour of one, with a steady reservation of whatever may be justly due to the rest. To this sort of trimming, to *this* inconsistency . . . we distinctly plead guilty. . . . If there were indeed no belligerents, it is plain enough that there could be no neutrals and no mediators. If there was no natural war between Democracy and Monarchy, no true ground of discord between Tories and Radical Reformers—we admit there would be no vocation for Whigs, for the true definition of that party . . . is, that it is a middle party, between the two extremes of high monarchical principles on the one hand, and extremely popular principles on the other.[17]

To the extent that the Whig as portrayed by Macaulay (and Francis Jeffrey) was a Trimmer, he was not much of a Liberal (in Acton's sense, as one for whom the purpose of politics is to achieve a moral purpose). Of course there was collaboration and intermingling between Whigs and "liberals." But their cooperation conceals differences in motivation and rationale, which are the things we must look to if we wish to locate the phenomenon of moral conscience in relation to politics.

That there was something non-liberal in Whiggism as represented by Macaulay is evident in his rationale for reform. Whereas for the Liberal reform was a matter of improvement, of reducing the gap between ideal and reality, for Macaulay the purpose of reform was to reduce discontents, to undermine the extremes, to solidify the center, and thus to promote stability. The need to do this arose from what Macaulay called noiseless revolutions, such as population shifts, the creation of new kinds of property, and the transformation of small towns into large cities. Such irrevocable changes made alterations in political institutions necessary, for they created a disproportion between social institutions and the artificial polity, and this was the main source of the discontents which, if unattended, led to an erosion of legitimacy and a long-term risk of revolution. Therefore it was the main task of politicians to direct policy so as to eliminate abuses—not because they were morally offensive but because they might become worse and undermine the social order. If this was postponed until discontents reached critical levels, it was the politicians' responsibility to make even radical changes.

The Reform Bill crisis was such an occasion, and it elicited Macaulay's (and other Whigs') rationale for reform. Noiseless revolutions had created dissatisfaction with constitutional arrangements, and Macaulay thought there was a danger of "a complete alienation of the people from their rulers." Thus Macaulay's immediate purpose was "to soothe the public mind," to "avert civil discord, and to uphold the authority of law." The long-term purpose of the Reform Bill was for "the healing of great distempers, for the securing at once of the public liberties and of the public repose, and for the reconciling and knitting together of all the orders of the State." Or, as he (and other Whig leaders) said, "Reform that you may preserve." He also said, "a liberal Government makes a conservative people."[18] Reconciliation was the most prominent theme in his rationale for reform, for it prevented the kind of conflict that undermined consent and legitimacy. With this as the rationale for reform, Macaulay and those many Whigs who shared his analysis necessarily depreciated the conscientious and moral claims of those who justified reform because it would reduce the distance between a moral ideal and the existing reality.

The same emphasis on political utility rather than on morality is evident in Macaulay's occasional discussions of liberty. One would think that for a "liberal," liberty would have a moral status. But he justified liberty for its contribution to (among other things) the stability of government. First of all, it dissipated passion. "That governments may be permanent, nations must be free. That public opinion may not burst every barrier, it must be allowed an open channel. . . . It is when the destroying element is pent up within the volcano that it convulses the ocean and the earth." Liberty is important for another reason: it reveals discontents, which can then be dealt with by timely concessions. "The danger of states is to be estimated, not by what breaks out of the public mind, but by what stays in it." There is nothing "more terrible than the situation of a government which rules without apprehension over a people of hypocrites —which is flattered by the press and cursed in the inner chambers." A policy of restricting expression, instead of curing the disease, removes the outward symptoms that allow for diagnosis.[19]

The same subordination of moral to political considerations is to be found in Macaulay's rationale for toleration. Of course he considered persecution and religious disqualifications wrong. But the emphasis was on the imprudence of intolerance—on the fact that it alienated the victims and turned them into potential revolutionaries. Thus persecution was not only vicious, it was foolish. The Puritans were made dangerously rebellious by the cruelties of the church and the government.[20] The same

argument applied to the Jews in his own time. They still suffered disqualifications only because of their religion. "You make England but half a
country to the Jews, and then you wonder that they have only half
patriotism—you treat them as foreigners, and then wonder that they
have not all the feelings of natives." If their disabilities were removed,
their loyalty would be secured.[21]

If more need be said, we can turn to Macaulay's own testimony. In
making judgments he appealed "to the principles either of morality, or
of what we believe to be identical with morality; namely, far-sighted policy." Thus in criticizing he emphasized what was dysfunctional rather
than what was immoral; and in defending policies, he emphasized what
was useful rather than what was good. This was a shift in the Whig tradition, in which, in the eighteenth century, there had been a vague residue
of moral argument about such things as liberty and toleration. Macaulay, as spokesman for a new generation of Whigs, added the amoral,
functional argument. Indeed, the older moral position became subordi-
nated to the amoral argument. This was confirmed by John Morley, the
late Victorian liberal politician and intellectual, who complained about
the "present [1874] exaggeration of the political standard as the universal
test of truth," which, according to Morley, "has become an inveterate
national characteristic." The consequence of this, Morley argued, was a
proliferation of materialism and selfishness and a diminishing of motives
"which are generous, far-reaching, and spiritual; a deadly weakening of
intellectual conclusiveness, of clear-shining moral illumination"—in
other words, of the realm of conscience.[22]

Macaulay's reluctance to consider moral argument apart from its
political implications is evident in many additional ways. The regicides,
he said, "had committed, not only a crime, but an error." On the removal
of the sacred gates from Somnauth, he said, "Morally, this is a crime;
politically, it is a blunder." The Stamp Act was "unjust and impolitic,
sterile of revenue and fertile of discontents." The revolutionary Committee of Public Safety in France "was a tissue, not merely of crimes, but of
blunders." Jacobinism, he said, could not be justified—"we do not say
on Christian principles, we do not say on the principles of high morality,
but even on principles of Machiavellian policy."[23]

If the subordination of moral considerations to political usefulness
in Macaulay's judgments does not indicate sufficiently that he greatly diminished the role of conscience in politics, and if it does not cast sufficient doubt on his status as a Liberal (in Acton's sense), the following
facts may be mentioned. Generally he favored severe and strict enforce-
ment of the law, especially in political cases. He said he "would rather err

on the side of vigour than of lenity." He approved the severe punishments for rick-burners, who aroused fears of rebellion in some southern counties in 1830, and for the Bristol rioters, who were responsible for the most intense of the violence which occurred during the Reform Bill crisis (1831–32). He was unwilling to recommend mercy for the convicted leaders of the Newport rising (1839).[24] In addition, on the basis of conversation, it is reliably reported that "Macaulay thinks torture under regulations not so absurd as it has been thought," the reporter adding, however, that "he does not recommend it."[25] And, yet more, he held that "there are 100 cases which justify falsehood [and] one which would even extenuate the guilt of assassination."[26] These opinions add to one's doubts about his status as a Liberal; and their amorality is decisively important as we search for evidence of political conscience.

Perhaps it should not be surprising that Macaulay divorced conscience and appeals to morality from politics. He was without personal religious impulse and perhaps without religious conviction. G. M. Trevelyan has suggested that Macaulay probably never formulated his religious convictions but that most likely he was an agnostic. This gap was not filled by commitment to a philosophical position that might have given him confidence in a theoretical foundation for morals. He did not take philosophy seriously, and he even thought it harmful to politics and sometimes dangerous. With its emphasis on consistency it was an obstacle to the adjusting, trimming, and compromising that were necessary for the practice of conciliatory politics. "Logic admits of no compromise," he said, but "the essence of politics is compromise." In addition, he thought philosophy encouraged doctrinaire over-simplifications, as in James Mill's writings, and that it was utopian and unrealistic as with Plato. Most fundamentally, Macaulay found philosophy objectionable because it asked unanswerable questions. His sister Margaret has described how in conversation he would not allow her to adopt a "settled creed" but rather insisted on the inevitability of uncertainty. "He would go to the very bottom of the subject, talk it round and round on every side, and finding at last an impenetrable mystery . . . he would show me it was not on the question alone we might then be considering that this uncertainty remained . . . but on all questions or morals."[27]

Macaulay's expectations from philosophy are indicated in his contrast between Plato and Bacon. Plato was deprecated for his utopianism, whereas Bacon was admired for his common sense. Platonic philosophy encouraged men to reach for goals that were beyond their capacity. In contrast, Bacon was more practical. Although he treated moral subjects, "he indulged in no rants about the fitness of things, the all-sufficiency of virtue, and the dignity of human nature. He dealt not at all in resounding nothings. . . . The casuistical subtilties which occupied the attention of the keenest spirits of his age had . . . no attractions for him." Furthermore, and most revealing, Bacon did not "meddle with those enigmas which have puzzled hundreds of generations, and will puzzle hundreds more. He said nothing about the grounds of moral obligation."[28] This could be a description of Macaulay himself.

It also should be said that Macaulay was heir to that intellectual legacy from Locke in which the entire Victorian age increasingly shared— that is, the distinction between the jurisdiction of the magistrate, in which purely civil interests are protected, and the realm of conscience, which is private, and to which moral beliefs are relegated. By using this distinction the isolation of morality from politics is greatly facilitated, indeed, it is almost guaranteed.[29]

Macaulay's—and the Whig—position is strongly suggestive of Machiavelli. The concern about stability and the wish to reduce destructive divisions; the manipulative attitude to the people; the conception of a political leader as one who brings order out of chaos; the religious disbelief combined with the wish to use religion for political purposes; and above all the amorality (reduced in dimensions to make it appropriate to Victorian life), which was made evident in Macaulay's wish to define problems in political rather than in moral terms—all bear the Machiavellian stamp. It is not suggested that Macaulay's outlook originated with Machiavelli, for it was too much a part of the growing secularism and carefully cultivated political "realism" of the time. Yet it is worth mentioning that Macaulay admired Machiavelli: he thought him eminently practical and capable of using his experience to correct general speculations, giving them "that vivid and practical character which so widely distinguishes them from the vague theories of most political philosophers." In addition, he exonerated Machiavelli from the immorality of which he was conventionally accused. Acknowledging that Machiavelli's name was "generally odious," Macaulay, calling this view vulgar, thought Machiavelli's immorality "belonged rather to the age than to the man." And Macaulay added that he was "acquainted with few writings which exhibit so much elevation of sentiment, so pure and warm a zeal for the public good, or so just a view of the duties and rights of citizens, as those of Machiavelli. . . . And even from *The Prince* itself we could select many passages in support of this remark."[30]

It should also be said that the thought and conduct of Macaulay's greatest intellectual hero—Bacon—and his greatest political hero— Halifax—were infused with Machiavellian teachings. That Bacon was an important transmitter of Machiavellian ideas is widely known; and there is Bacon's acknowledgement that "we are much beholden to Machiavelli." As for Halifax, as Felix Raab has argued, he "had digested Machiavelli"; indeed, in all his published writings Halifax only once mentioned a political author by name, and that was Machiavelli.[31]

It should be emphasized again that by concentrating on Macaulay this account has a direct bearing on nineteenth-century Whiggism, for Macaulay, along with other Whig intellectuals such as Francis Jeffrey, had an immense influence on Whiggism. He re-shaped it, and, as Henry Reeve said, he created the language in which Whig principles and Whig precepts have been preserved. This was evident already during the debates on the Reform Bill. Macaulay spoke at each critical episode during the fifteen months of deliberations, and according to Francis Jeffrey, he defined the terms of debate: "the views of Macaulay, advanced perhaps at the fifth or sixth day's debate, formed the topic of discussion for the remainder of the time that the subject was under consideration." Since his rationale for reform confirmed the instinctive judgments of the Whig magnates and emphasized the important function of the Whig party, his aid was welcomed by the party leaders. The enthusiastic cheers for his speeches suggest that by providing his rationale for reform Macaulay was performing an important service. Lord Althorp thought most of his speeches "distinguished as beautiful philosophical essays, and for their splendid generalizations." Such a comment suggests that (as Acton said) the Whigs had a policy but needed a philosophy and that they looked to Macaulay as one who could defend their position by using political maxims and historical examples. It is not surprising that when, in 1833, Macaulay decided to go to India, Lord Lansdowne worried that no adequate successor would be found; and that in 1839, after his return, Sydney Smith said Macaulay was being "brought in [to Parliament] for the express purpose of speechification."[32]

Macaulay's influence continued and enlarged. In addition to his many notable speeches, there were his *Edinburgh Review* essays, which were frequently reprinted, and the more than 140,000 copies of his *History of England* which were sold during the twenty-seven years following the publication of the first two volumes in 1848. Many testifed to its great attractions, and Gladstone noted that Macaulay had established a "monarchy over the world of readers,"[33] which is significant, in view of the political teaching which was woven into Macaulay's historical narratives. This teaching most notably consisted of an exemplification of the trimming approach to politics and a rationale for it. Macaulay identified this way of conducting politics as the source of England's successes, most obviously the Glorious Revolution of 1688, and of her attractive political qualities, such as toleration, liberty, moderation, and continuity combined with change. But he also pointed to the failure to adopt this approach as an important source of shameful episodes of fanaticism, persecution, and civil war.

By virtue of his great influence Macaulay more than anyone else contributed to the process by which the Whig party and (what survived the party) Whiggism became associated with the idea of trimming. And this approach to politics, with its emphasis on moderation, stability, and compromise, and with its opposition to extremists, fanatics, and zealots as the villains who threatened to undermine moderation and stability, provided the context for Macaulay's criticism of those whose views were informed by moral ideas and by conscience.

Macaulay's political career and his extraordinary success as an author made him a legend in his own time, and this enhanced his influence. Anecdotes were repeated about his amazing feats of memory and his brilliant monologues, and his vast range of knowledge and his varied talents as administrator, politician, and author. The legend gave added authority to his ideas, so that, along with Francis Jeffrey and Sydney Smith, and a few others, he became something of an oracle whose words were repeated and remembered. This position is indicated in a description of the way a well-known churchman (Dean Milman) thought and spoke:

> His whole conversation was about the men who formed its [the Whig party's] leaders. It was Sydney Smith and Macaulay, Lord Holland and Lord Lansdowne, Tommy Moore and Rogers, at every word. You would have supposed from his discourse not only that the Whig leaders had been and were the greatest men of the age, but that they were the *only ones* who were worth thinking of or speaking about.[34]

Testimony of Macaulay's elevated, legendary status also was offered by later Victorian notables. Lord Acton said that as a young man he had been "primed to the brim with Whig politics," and he recalled that "it was not Whiggism only, but Macaulay in particular that I was so full of." And A. V. Dicey wrote that Macaulay was one of "the three authors [Mill and Burke were the others] to whom as far as I can judge I owe more than to any other teachers I could mention."[35]

An indication of Macaulay's influence on the shaping of the idea of Whiggism can be found in testimony from Herbert Butterfield, who has been the most authoritative commentator on Whiggism in relation to historiography. Butterfield was critical of Whig history for interpreting the past with perceptions, values, and a concern with issues that were contemporary to the historian, and consequently for misinterpreting past ages. However, this was not altogether a bad thing. "'Wrong' history," he wrote, "was one of our assets. The Whig interpretation, . . . whatever it may have done to our history, it had a wonderful effect on English politics."[36] And in explaining what in Whiggism made for good politics Butterfield pointed to the trimming approach to politics and the appreciation of historical continuities amidst great change that trimming made possible. His description of the trimming component in Whiggism, with its emphasis on avoiding extremes, on compromise, and generally on non-doctrinaire politics, could be used as a brief account of Macaulay's political outlook, yet Butterfield mentioned Macaulay only once and gives no indication that his analysis of Whiggism draws on Whig ideas after they received the imprint of Macaulay's trimming. The Whigs achieved their desirable influence on events, he said, by "standing in protest equally against diehardism on the one hand and mere lust for overthrow on the other." And Butterfield added, "Let us praise as a living thing the continuity of our history, and praise the Whigs who taught us that we must nurse this blessing—reconciling continuity with change, discovering mediations between past and present, and showing what can be achieved by man's reconciling mind."[37] This is a reflection of the ideas of the classic trimmer Halifax, and it is cast in the language given those ideas by Macaulay.

Finally, it may be suggested that the extent of Macaulay's influence on the way his own and later generations thought of Whiggism was not without deleterious consequences for the Whigs as a party. For by allowing so much room for Machiavellian themes, Macaulay also made it difficult for a Whig to express those moral impulses and principles that can never be quite driven out of the political arena. As a consequence, a gap was created that Liberals and Radicals were not slow to fill.

Notes

1. Lord John Russell, *An Essay on the History of the English Government and Constitution,* new ed. (1865), p. 105; Henry Hallam, *The Constitutional History of England,* 2nd ed. (1829), 3, 270; Donald Southgate, *The Passing of the Whigs* (1962), pp. xv, 4; Thomas Erskine May, *The Constitutional History of England since the Accession of George the Third* (1912) (1st ed. 1861), 1, 433.

2. Southgate, *The Passing of the Whigs,* p. xvi; Elie Halevy, *A History of the English People in the Nineteenth Century,* vol. 2, *The Liberal Awakening,* trans. E. J. Watkin (1949), p. 81.

3. James Mill, "Periodical Literature," *Westminster Review* 1 (January 1824): 218-19; Benjamin Disraeli, "The Spirit of Whiggism" (1836), in *Whigs and Whiggism*, edited by William Hutcheon (1913), pp. 351-52; "The Elections in England—Tories and Whigs" and "Lord Palmerston," in *Karl Marx and Frederick Engels on Britain* (1953), pp. 352-54, 395. The association of Whiggism with complacency is evident in William Morris' observation: "Before the uprising of *modern* Socialism almost all intelligent people either were, or professed themselves to be, quite contented with the civilization of this century . . . and saw nothing to do but to perfect the said civilization by getting rid of a few ridiculous survivals of the barbarous ages. To be short, this was the *Whig* frame of mind." "How I Became a Socialist," *William Morris. Selected Writings and Designs,* edited by Asa Briggs (1962), p. 35.

4. Gertrude Himmelfarb, *Lord Acton. A Study in Conscience and Politics* (1952), pp. 208-09.

5. Caroline Robbins, *The Eighteenth Century Commonwealthman* (1961), pp. 7, 20, 320-21, 357: see also the Foreword to the reprint (1968), p. ix.

6. *Three Early Nineteenth Century Diaries,* edited by A. Aspinall (1952), pp. 100, 346; J. F. Stephen, *The Saturday Review* 9 (7 January 1860): 9; Henry Reeve, "Lord Macaulay," *Edinburgh Review* 111 (January 1860): 273-76.

7. Journals, vol. 5, fol. 161 (2 November [1852]); vol. 11, fol. 115-16 (11 May [1857]); fol. 89 (22 February [1857]); vol. 3, fol. 64 (30 October [1850]): Trinity College Library. Diary of the 7th earl of Carlisle, vol. 36 (3 July 1858): Castle Howard. John Clive, *Thomas Babington Macaulay. The Shaping of the Historian* (1973), pp. 248-49.

8. *History of England,* edited by C. H. Firth (1913), 2: 876-78; 4: 1991-95; "Southey's Edition of the *Pilgrim's Progress,*" *Edinburgh Review* 54 (December 1831): 457-58.

9. *History of England* 5: 2402; "Milton" *Edinburgh Review* 42 (August 1825): 339-40.

10. Macaulay to Hannah Trevelyan, 17 January 1854: Trinity College Library.

11. "Church and State," *Edinburgh Review* 69 (April 1839): 278-79.

12. *History of England* 1: 101.

13. "Utilitarian Theory of Government," *Edinburgh Review* 50: 124; "Present Administration," ibid., 46: 260.

14. Journals, vol. 11, fol. 177-78 (19 September [1857]); fol. 342 (8 July [1858]); vol. 4, fol. 179 (22 July [1851]).

15. *Hansard* 51: 827-28, 830 (29 January 1840); 54: 1355-56 (19 June 1840).

16. Francis Jeffrey, "State of Parties, 1810," *Contributions to the Edinburgh Review* (1846 [2nd ed.]) 3: 258-59, 267, 269. In 1846 Jeffrey added a note saying that these "observations on the vast importance and high and difficult duties of a *middle party* . . . seem to me as universally true, and as applicable to the present position of our affairs, as most of the other things I have ventured, for this reason, now to reproduce" (p. 258 n).

17. Francis Jeffrey, "Middle and Extreme Parties" (December 1826), ibid. 3: 293, 295, 298. Jeffrey was responding to James Mill's accusation that the Whigs, as "the opposition section of the aristocracy," engaged in "a perpetual system of compromise, a perpetual trimming" between the aristocracy and the people: "Periodical Literature," *Westminster Review* 1 (January 1824): 218, 221. That Jeffrey's defense came to be shared is indicated by Lord Hartington's statement in 1883 that the traditional function of the Whigs was "to direct, and guide, and moderate . . . popular movements. They have formed a connecting link between the advanced party and those classes which, possessing property, power and influence, are naturally averse to change": in Southgate, *Passing of the Whigs,* p. 417.

18. *Speeches* (London, 1854), pp. 2, 11, 28–29, 54, 61, 69; "Hallam," *Edinburgh Review* 48: 168–69.

19. "Essay on the Life and Character of King William III," *Times Literary Supplement*, 1 May 1969, p. 469; "Southey's *Colloquies*," *Edinburgh Review* 50 (January 1830): 552.

20. "Hallam," *Edinburgh Review* 48: 102, 104; *Hansard* 72: 1183 (19 February 1844).

21. *Mirror of Parliament* 21 (17 April 1833): 1274. Also see "Civil Disabilities of the Jews," *Edinburgh Review* 52 (January 1831): 367–69.

22. "Warren Hastings," *Edinburgh Review* 74 (October 1841): 225–26; John Morley, *On Compromise* (1874), pp. 4, 14.

23. *History of England* 1: 110; *Speeches*, p. 281; "Chatham," *Edinburgh Review* 80 (October 1844): 574; "Barère," *ibid.* 79 (April 1844): 311, 313.

24. *Hansard* 15 (28 February 1833): 1326–27; 15 (6 February 1833): 260–61; 84 (10 March 1846): 893–95; *Mirror of Parliament* 16 (9 March 1840): 1650.

25. Diary of the 7th earl of Carlisle, vol. 28, fol. 64 (7 May 1852).

26. Marginal comment in vol. 1, p. 49 of Thomas M'Crie, *Life of John Knox* (1831), Macaulay's copy at Wallington.

27. G. M. Trevelyan, *Sir George Otto Trevelyan, A Memoir* (1932), p. 15; *History of England* 3: 1277; Margaret Macaulay, *Recollections by a Sister of T. B. Macaulay (1834)* (1864), p. 2.

28. "Lord Bacon," *Edinburgh Review* 65 (July 1837): 86.

29. The clearest evidence that Macaulay adopted this Lockean view, and in this instance a Lockean formulation as well, appears in his review of Gladstone, in which he noted that although there was no agreement on religious matters, all could agree that the ends of civil government were to protect persons and property, to compel men to avoid rapine to satisfy their wants, to decide disputes by arbitration not force, and to provide for the common defense. Regardless of religion, all had an interest in these things. "Gladstone on Church and State," *Edinburgh Review* 69 (April 1839): 236.

30. "Machiavelli," *Edinburgh Review* 45 (March 1827): 259, 261, 289. Lord John Russell used a passage from Machiavelli as an epigraph and also claimed that "the leaders of the Revolution [of 1688] knew, with Machiavel, that nothing so much tends to give stability to a change of government, as an adherence to old forms and venerated institutions": *An Essay on the History of the English Government and Constitution*, pp. 64–65. This was a favourite theme of Macaulay's. Professor Herbert Butterfield has said that "Machiavelli even became part of the political heritage of the Whigs": *The Statecraft of Machiavelli* (1940), p. 149. The Machiavellian parallel is developed more fully in Joseph Hamburger, *Macaulay and the Whig Tradition* (1977), Chap. 7.

31. Felix Raab, *The English Face of Machiavelli* (1965), pp. 73–76, 239–54. For Macaulay's appreciation of Halifax see *History of England* 1: 234–35; 3: 1050–51, 1232; and "The Life and Writings of Sir William Temple," *Edinburgh Review* 68 (October 1838): 169–70.

32. Edward L. Pierce, *Memoir and Letters of Charles Sumner* (1878), 1: 364. *Three Early Nineteenth Century Diaries*, edited by A. Aspinall (1952), pp. 100, 346. Lansdowne to Brougham, 17 December [1833]: University College, London, Brougham Papers. *The Letters of Sydney Smith*, edited by Nowell C. Smith (1953) 2: 693.

33. William Gladstone, *Gleanings* (1883) 2: 315.

34. Archibald Alison, *Some Account of My Life and Writings: An Autobiography,*

edited by Lady Alison (1883) 2: 331. Alison also described "the extraordinary *identity of thought*" in the Whig party and "the subjection in it of the many to the judgement and opinion of the few."

35. Himmelfarb, *Lord Acton,* p. 25. A. V. Dicey to Miss Wedgwood, 27 January, 1893: Wedgwood Archives, University of Keele.

36. Herbert Butterfield, *The Englishman and His History* (1944), pp. 78-79. In an earlier work, *The Whig Interpretation of History* (1931), Butterfield had unequivocally criticized the Whig interpretation.

37. *Englishman and His History,* p. 138. Butterfield traces trimming influence on the Whigs to the early eighteenth century and associates this with Rapin, but it may be doubted that as a matter of dating that this is correct: see p. 92 and Hamburger, *Macaulay and the Whig Tradition,* pp. 138-39. Butterfield mentions Macaulay at pp. 4-5, and he notes that the Whig approach became a national attitude: pp. vii, 73, 137.

THE UTILITARIAN CONSCIENCE
David Roberts

J EREMY BENTHAM published *An Introduction to Morals and Legislation* in 1789. In it he proclaimed the principle of utility, a principle that judged a law or an act morally good that brought the greatest happiness to the greatest number. It was not an entirely new idea. To act in terms of the public advantage, to be expedient and practical, to talk in terms of political arithmetic, and to calculate social well-being lay deep in the mentality of the eighteenth century. Bentham himself praised the philosophers David Hume and Joseph Priestley for realizing that happiness was the criterion of the good, a position that also formed a fundamental premise of William Paley's *Moral and Political Philosophy*. Published in 1781, Paley's book won great popularity. Utility had become a widely accepted yardstick for the measurement of the public good.

For most, of course, it was but one of many yardsticks. There was also religion, tradition, and natural law. These three sources, along with the philosophy of utility, supplied some of the major criteria that defined the public conscience of the ruling class. In 1815 that conscience was largely Tory. Few dared dispute the ethical truths so powerfully and theoretically expressed in Edmund Burke's *Reflections on the Revolution in France*. Neither did most MPs oppose the practical expression of the Tory conscience in the stern rule of Lord Eldon as Lord Chancellor, Lord Sidmouth as Home Secretary, and Lord Liverpool as Prime Minister. The Tory conscience valued hierarchy and authority, the status quo, and established institutions. It defended these values by appealing to religion, history, natural law, and utility. Burke employed all four though he particularly valued a society's history, seeing in its customs, institutions, and traditions the wisdom of the past.

The Whig conscience also valued history, but less as the justification of present institutions than as a revelation of those developments that promised greater liberty, toleration, and constitutionalism. The Whig conscience was eclectic and latitudinarian. It did not despise religion, particularly the rationalist and deistic Christianity of the eighteenth century Anglican Church. Neither did it call natural law nonsense since such a law formed the basis of the writings of the great Whig philosopher, John Locke, and the great Whig lawyer, William Blackstone. Natural law underlay that liberty, toleration, and constitutionalism that the Whigs valued so highly, developments that they also justified by appealing to their utility.

The public conscience of two powerful groups, the Evangelicals and the Radicals, challenged the Whig and Tories at the turn of the century. The Evangelicals, who represented the rising middle classes, found their greatest spokesman in William Wilberforce, orator, organizer of societies, and Parliamentarian. The leading Radical was Thomas Paine, author of *The Rights of Man* of 1791, a book whose powerful plea for democracy made it so popular among the emerging working classes that the Tory government repressed it. Paine and the Radicals rested their arguments on an appeal to reason and natural law. Wilberforce and the Evangelicals based their conscience on religious experiences and the commands of the Bible. Yet as far apart as were these two outlooks, Wilberforce could still plead utility and natural law as arguments for ending the slave trade, while Thomas Paine could invoke Anglo-Saxon history and the sayings of Jesus on behalf of equality. In the morality of the Evangelicals and the politics of the Radicals, as in those public consciences of Whig and Tory, one finds, though in very different combinations, appeals to religion, history, natural law, and utility.

Bentham's originality lay in the bold claim that these various criteria only confused the issue and that there was but one yardstick for the public good, namely, did an act or law bring about the greatest happiness to the greatest number. One should avoid all reference to religion, one should refuse to worship dead tradition, and one should never indulge in metaphysical nonsense about natural law; such avoidance is the first step to becoming a Utilitarian. If one then insists that all moral judgments be based on a sound understanding of human nature and on a rigorous concern for practical consequences, one has then become a thorough Utilitarian.

It is the purpose of the following essay to study the impact of this form of utilitarianism on the public conscience of England in the generation following the passage of the 1832 Reform Act. It will do so by examining the opinions of twelve MPs, four newspaper editors, and four civil servants, all believers in utilitarianism, all acquainted with Bentham. The intensity of their utilitarianism varied as did their acquaintanceship with

Bentham. Not all were his disciples. But a search for disciples or for
Bentham's influence is not the purpose of this essay. Its purpose is to
analyze the Utilitarian conscience by examining the ideas of both disciples and more distant admirers, both those MPs that were called Philosophical Radicals in the 1830s and those on the periphery.

The Philosophical Radicals were a group of young MPs who self-
consciously held Utilitarian principles. One of them was Charles Buller,
of a landed family in Cornwall and fortunate enough to have as a tutor
Thomas Carlyle. "I have adopted utilitarianism," wrote Buller in 1828,
at age twenty-two, to his tutor; "it provides the best explanation of men's
morals."[1] Also Philosophical Radicals were John Arthur Roebuck,
Henry Warburton, George Grote, William Molesworth, and Edward
Strutt. Their respect for Bentham was great, particularly so in the case of
George Grote, the London banker and historian of Greece. Grote, who
was the oldest of the Philosophical Radicals, knew Bentham well in the
1820s. For the younger men it was often James Mill and his son John
Stuart who won their admiration. "James Mill," said newspaper editor
F. Knight Hunt, "had on the active minds of the time a greater influence
than any other man in London."[2]

The Philosophical Radicals did not include all Utilitarians. They did
not for example include MPs like Poulett Thomson, editors like Albany
Fonblanque, and civil servants like James Kay Shuttleworth. One of
those on the periphery was John Black, editor of the *Morning Chronicle.*
John Stuart Mill praised him "as the first journalist who carried criticism
and the spirit of reform into the details of English institutions." A self-
educated Scotsman, Black was twenty-seven before he came to London
and met Bentham. He also met James Mill and enjoyed his advice on political matters. Self-willed and obdurate, he was no man's disciple, not
even his publisher's. His publisher after 1833 was Sir John Easthope.
James Grant, editor of the *Morning Advertiser* in 1840, said that Easthope was not part "of the utilitarian sect of philosophers who acknowledged the late Jeremy Bentham as their head; but he is a thoroughgoing
utilitarian in practice."[3]

The same might be said of Robert Rintoul, Albany Fonblanque, and
John Wilson, editors respectively of the *Spectator,* the *Examiner,* and
the *Globe.* Along with Black they propounded Utilitarian ideas of reform and enjoyed the friendship of Bentham, but they were too complex,
idiosyncratic, and independent to be part of a sect. The correspondence
of John Stuart Mill with Rintoul, Fonblanque, and Wilson makes it clear
that their basic political assumptions were Utilitarian. The correspondence in the late 1830s between Mill and Fonblanque also makes clear

that they could differ. When the *Examiner* chastized the Philosophical Radicals in Parliament for not supporting the Whigs, Mill grew piqued with Fonblanque, and they had a falling out. But there was no indication that Fonblanque was any less Utilitarian in his basic assumptions about the need of reform on pragmatic and rational principles. In 1841 Mill told Fonblanque that he agreed with him on all matters of importance, a fact Fonblanque underscored by having Mill write for the *Examiner* on behalf of the rational reform of society.[4]

In the development of utilitarianism Cambridge University played a role. It was from Cambridge that Charles Buller wrote Carlyle he had become a Utilitarian. After Buller came Sir William Molesworth, bart., like Buller heir to a landed estate in Cornwall. Also attending Cambridge were four other Utilitarians who would sit in Parliament—Perronet Thompson, Henry Warburton, Charles Villiers, and Edmund Strutt. Thompson became a colonel in the army, Warburton a timber merchant in London, Villiers (the younger son of the Earl of Clarendon) a barrister, and Strutt a partner in the family's cotton firm in Derby. At Cambridge they were required to read Paley's *Moral and Political Philosophy,* probably their first introduction to utilitarian ideas. They of course read much more. "My residence in Cambridge," wrote Molesworth, "fell in with a period of remarkable intellectual activity." Molesworth went on to enumerate other experiences that moulded his outlook: "my Scottish experience was favorable to sceptical thought, my German 'entourage' kindled democratic sympathies." Molesworth was also expelled from Cambridge for challenging his tutor to a duel, an event which led to his hatred of constituted authority.

Roebuck shared the same hatred. Raised in Canada, he read Locke in the Quebec City public library and learned democracy from observing America. "I was very romantic," he later confessed of his youth. He was twenty-two before he knew the name of Bentham.[5] Poulett Thomson, John Bowring, John Temple Leader, and Joseph Hume also had well-formed opinions before they met Bentham.

The presence of these men in the Commons brings to twelve the number of MPs who could easily win James Grant's description "thoroughgoing utilitarians." Some might doubt Thomson's thoroughness particularly since he was President of the Board of Trade in a Whig government, but Bentham, in 1827, left his retired life at Queens Gate to canvass personally for Thomson's election. There was no rigid Utilitarian orthodoxy, no unified group of disciples. John Bowring, for whom Bentham had a great liking, was detested by the Mills. Bentham made

Bowring the executor of his estate, editor of his papers, and his biographer. A Unitarian, merchant, world traveler, and ardent champion of Greek independence, his outlook reflected the religious impulses of liberal Christianity and the romantic radicalism of European nationalism as well as the idealism of Bentham's visions. The same manysidedness and independence characterized John Leader, son of a wealthy London merchant and the only one of the twenty Utilitarians educated at Oxford, and Joseph Hume, the doyen of Parliamentary radicals. Hume, a Scotsman and son of a shipmaster, had fought repressive Toryism in the Commons since 1812.[6]

The civil servants who brought the utilitarian conscience to the heart of the Victorian state were also manysided and independent. The most famous of them, the formidable Edwin Chadwick, was Bentham's secretary in 1831. He was secretary of the Factory Commission of 1832, secretary to the Poor Law Commission from 1834 to 1847, author of the Sanitary Report of 1842, and a Commissioner of the General Board of Health from 1848 to 1854. After retirement he insisted that his administrative ideas were largely his own and not Bentham's.[7] His friends James Kay Shuttleworth, Frederick Hill, and Southwood Smith could make the same claim. Kay Shuttleworth, an assistant Poor Law commissioner until 1839 when he became secretary of the Committee in Council on Education was a close friend of Chadwick and associate of utilitarians. He brought to his work the scientific attitudes of medicine learned at Edinburgh and the first-hand experience in investigating and writing on conditions in Manchester's slums. Southwood Smith, a Commissioner on the General Board of Health was, like Kay Shuttleworth, a doctor, and like Bowring, a unitarian, and like Chadwick an intimate of Bentham. Frederick Hill's intellectual background was his father's school, an experimental one run on enlightened principles that so impressed Bentham that he aided it. Bentham also entertained at Queen's Gate the father, Thomas Hill, and his sons, whom he introduced to the Utilitarians of London.[8]

The brief introductions to the twenty Utilitarians who form the basis of this essay should make two facts clear: first, that the sources of the Utilitarian conscience were more numerous than the teachings of Bentham and, second, that these Utilitarians were more than simply "Benthamites." They were independent, intelligent, widely read, and complex personalities. Most had read the thinkers that had moulded Bentham's thought: from British empiricism, Bacon, Hobbes, Locke, Hume, Hartley, and Priestley; from the European enlightenment, Voltaire, Helvetius, Condillac, and Beccari; and from political economy, Smith, Ricardo, and Malthus. Utilitarian ideas were inherent in eighteenth century thought.

So were many other attitudes—deistic, radical, romantic, historical, paternalist, and liberal. Many were the strands making up these reformers' thoughts. It is a fact which raises doubts about a too easy use of the term "Benthamite." To use that term tends to two errors: first it exaggerates Bentham's influence on particular persons, on a Roebuck, Buller, Black or Thompson, men that come out of a rich intellectual world; and secondly it underestimates how far reaching Bentham's ideas might have been by narrowing his influence to his votaries.

Bentham was important. He was read by many. His ideas were much debated. He was admired, though more often by those already tending to utilitarianism. Indeed the very variety and diffuseness of the many sources of utilitarianism was a deficiency that Bentham, the great systematizer, could meet, and in meeting it he excited the admiration of reformers of various kinds. Bentham was astonishingly fertile in schemes, original in imagination, and searching and detailed in exposition. Systems of morality, consolidations of laws, constitutions for every land, pauper management schemes, Chresthomatic schools, panopiticon prisons, the springs of human action, political economy—all were analyzed, defined, classified, systematized, and all were subsumed under one grand, sweeping, humane, and above all rational principle. Such a comprehensive statement of ideas that these reformers were inclined to believe in won their applause. It also strengthened their resolve to propagate utilitarianism. It led John Bowring to finance and partially edit the *Westminster Review,* a journal that Colonel Perronet Thompson bought in 1829, featuring articles by Warburton, Chadwick, Grote, Roebuck, and the Mills. Sir William Molesworth founded the *London Review* in 1835 and fused it with the *Westminster* which he purchased in 1836. In 1840 Henry Chapman bought the journal but he did not pull down its utilitarian flag. The journal was still the spokesman of utilitarianism. In Wilson's *Globe,* Fonblanque's *Examiner,* Rintoul's *Spectator,* and Black's *Morning Chronicle* utilitarian ideas received a broader and looser expression, but they reached a larger audience.

The Utilitarians in Parliament addressed a smaller audience. But it was an important one. Though only a dozen in a House of 658, they were not intimidated. They were indeed garrulous beyond the average, hammering away, in speech after speech, at the irrationality and injustice of English institutions. In their speeches, as in the journalism of Black, Fonblanque, Rintoul, and Wilson, they advocated a new political pro-

gram, one that was secular, rational and practical, one tied to no Tory interests or weakened by Whig compromises. The program rested on three
basic principles: the virtues of liberty and democracy, the wisdom of
laissez-faire economics, and the need of a reforming state. And underlying these three principles was the most fundamental assumption of all,
the greatest happiness principle. These fundamental assumptions were
abstract and philosophical. Bentham could expound them with an imagination and fecundity not inhibited by the vicissitudes of day to day politics. Utilitarian MPs, editors, and civil servants enjoyed no such luxury.
It was their task to make these principles a working part of the Victorian
state. In doing so they tested both the strength and weakness of these
ideas. They also revealed on occasion, how qualified was the adherence
to them. Such was certainly true of the first and most basic of Utilitarian
principles, the greatest happiness to the greatest number.

The Greatest Happiness Principle

In telling Carlyle that he had become a Utilitarian Charles Buller
added that utilitarianism provided "the best framework on which we
may form and instruct the natural feelings of men to do that which pro-
duces peace and good will among men." Buller carried this conviction into
the House of Commons. In urging municipal reform for Ireland he in-
voked "the principle of public utility," and in urging the creation of a
Poor Law Board he implored the House to consider the "happiness and
social condition of the poor." His Utilitarian colleagues agreed with his
standards, though their phrases differed. Edward Strutt spoke of "the
welfare of the public," Roebuck cited "the benefit of the majority,"
Grote pled for "the happiness of the people," and Hume appealed to the
Commons to "see the people happy."[9] Warburton told the House that
"the public good was the only test," and Bowring asked "Was it not the
duty of the legislature to provide for all the community the greatest possible sum of enjoyments?" Molesworth would have answered absolutely!
"The happiness of each individual," he exclaimed, "and consequently of
the whole, is the grand object of legislation."[10] The greatest happiness to
the greatest number, and not the Tory's wisdom of the past, the Evangelical's Bible, or the Whig's prudence, was to be the yardstick for designing
and passing acts of Parliament. MPs were not only to calculate felicity
but to teach the young to do so. Colonel Perronet Thompson, in arguing
for the ballot, asked which decision "would produce the greatest *maximum* of good and which the least *minimum* of evil," while John Roe-

buck, who believed that "the business of government . . . is to increase
. . . the happiness and well-being of its subjects," thought that could be
done through government schools that taught children "to consult their
own happiness consistently with the happiness of others."[11]

Outside Parliament liberal journals repeated the same refrain. The
Morning Chronicle in 1841 wanted political alignments that brought "the
greatest happiness of the greatest number," an axiom the *Westminster
Review* in 1844 said should be the aim of all legislation. Seventeen years
earlier, in 1839, in an article entitled "The Greatest Happiness
Principle," Colonel Perronet Thompson had argued that "the object of
good government was the "increase of happiness to its maximum." That
government should minimize pain and maximize happiness won much
ridicule—but it had also sunk deep into the mentality of Victorian
England.[12]

It is clear from Parliamentary speeches and Radical editorials that
the greatest happiness principle played a part in the growth of a Utilitarian conscience. But these speeches and writings also make it clear that the
greatest happiness principle was only a part of that conscience. References to the greatest happiness did occur, but not as frequently, and with
lesser intensity, than references to justice, fairness, equality, or rights.
Charles Buller called the Corn Laws (laws which put a heavy duty on the
import of grain) a "monstrous and palpable injustice." A monstrous injustice was also the judgment of Henry Warburton to any depreciation
of the currency.[13] Colonel Thompson condemned church rates as "clearly
unjust," and considered that the giving of a portion of the property of
the Church to Dissent an act of "whole justice." To Bowring it was "a
case of great injustice" that an elder of the Scottish Church was dismissed and to Hume it was a flagrant injustice to put a man in prison for
four months for selling pheasant. George Grote told the Commons that
"they were bound, on every principle of justice, to deal fairly and impar-
tially" with Ireland. Again and again the Utilitarian MPs appealed to
justice, not happiness, to argue their case.[14] Both Rintoul's *Spectator* and
Fonblanque's *Examiner* did the same, both being quick to condemn the
arbitrary and unfair judgments of England's many justices of the peace.
"Our motto in everything," said the *Spectator,* is "fair play."[15]

These appeals to justice were in many ways far more effective, and
probably more genuine, than appeals to the general happiness. Though it
is obvious that legislators should consider the general happiness, it is in
fact exceedingly difficult to calculate that happiness with any precision.
It was difficult enough in the 1830s to measure the utility of an income
tax or tariff, but what schedule of utilities could possibly be contrived

concerning the unequal incomes of the Church of England, grants to Church schools, the regulation of beer shops, or the imprisonment of the Dorchester farm laborers for administering oaths? Utilitarian MPs denounced all these as unjust. They denounced them for being unfair, tyrannical, coercive, and unequal—but seldom as not maximizing happiness. For a few bishops to enjoy sumptuous incomes and palaces while hundreds of clergy lived in poverty struck Bullers as "a cruel and immoral system of inequality."[16] But that a more equal division of Church wealth would maximize happiness was dubious; it might very well pain more Anglicans than it pleased while the Dissenters might remain indifferent. Grants to Church of England schools from local taxes might even increase happiness by increasing education, but the thought of one penny of a Dissenter's income going to an Anglican school struck the utilitarians as unfair. The regulation of beer shops, which had mushroomed after the 1830 Act establishing them as alternatives to Public Houses, might also please more than it displeased. The imprisonment of the Dorsetshire laborers might bring more happiness to literate property owners who feared unions based on oaths than unhappiness to the illiterate poor who neither read about nor cared about them. But it was still a monstrous injustice to arrest laborers for administering oaths when rich Anglo-Irish landowners did the same in Orange lodges. The Utilitarian MPs protested this unequal treatment as unjust.[17] They were, in fact, constantly and vehemently protesting injustices however isolated and singular. Joseph Hume was a veritable gadfly on the conscience of the House: at one time it was two poor persons sent to prison for not paying poor rates, later it was the flogging of a soldier.[18] They were about as important, quantitatively, to the greatest happiness of the greatest number as Bowring's dismissed Scottish elder. For Hume and Bowring, for Buller, Roebuck, and Molesworth, it was no calculation of happiness that prompted their protests, but a sense of injustice. Grote felt the same way about denying voters a secret ballot—it was unjust because it denied voters the right to "a free conscience" and a "rational determination."[19] It is unlikely that Grote considered the felicity lost in drinks, bribes, and entertainments which would occur when the ballot took away a vote that could be more easily bought because done openly.

Grote's mother was a zealous Calvinist; the young Bowring, author of Christian hymns, learned virtue from the famous Unitarian minister Lance Carpenter; Buller's tutor was Carlyle; Roebuck was inspired by Byron; Colonel Perronet Thompson was a protégé of the Evangelical Wilberforce; Strutt was raised in Nonconformist Derby; Rintoul, Black, and Hume were Scotsmen trained in its universities, the home of the common sense school of ethics; Southwood Smith was a Unitarian; and Chadwick and Kay Shuttleworth had Nonconformist parents.[20] In virtually all of these Utilitarians there exists a lingering puritan morality, one no less serious for having floated away from its theological moorings.

The Utilitarians' judgment of justice also reflected the rationalism of the enlightenment and the interests and aspirations of the middle classes. This rationalism and these interests, in the hopeful atmosphere of the reformed Parliament, sharpened their desire for justice—or rather their indignation at injustice. They represented those who had suffered many wrongs from a proud aristocracy, an exclusive Church, and Tory monopolies. Of the twenty Utilitarians of this study, only Villiers, Buller, and Molesworth came from the landed classes; the rest were from the mercantile or professional world. They wanted justice and equality of opportunity. The Reform Act itself was a middle-class charter. It denied power to millions of adult males in Britain and gave it to only 800,000 voters, most of whom came from the middling classes. The Utilitarians attacked on their behalf the many monopolies and privileges of the aristocracy, whether they involved Corn Laws, the Church, justices of the peace, or the military. The greatest happiness principle tends to be democratic and socialistic—it suggests greater equality in the distribution of the fishes and the loaves. Justice and fairness is more middle class and capitalist—they mean only equality of opportunity in seeking the fishes and the loaves. Though the Utilitarian conscience was not merely a class conscience—both the elder Bentham and Roebuck were out and out democrats—middle-class aspirations were its paramount concerns. It was a concern that inspired Fonblanque's *Examiner* to tell its middle-class readers, "In all legislation the first thing to be considered is justice, the second is the advantage of the nation."[21]

The self-conscious preference of the *Examiner* and the semiconscious choice of Utilitarian MPs for justice as a firmer measure of the public good than calculations of happiness agrees with a recent critique of utilitarianism, John Rawls's, *A Theory of Justice*. It is not calculations of maximum happiness or utility, argues Rawls, that support a public morality, but a sense of justice as fairness. Rawls bases this sense of justice on reason. He asks what theory of justice would rational men adopt if they were, hypothetically, meeting to draw up a social contract. They would, he argues, develop a theory of justice as fairness, one that would assert two principles: "First, each person is to have an equal right to the most extensive basic liberty compatible with a similar liberty for others. Second: social and economic inequalities are to be arranged so that they are both (a) reasonably expected to be to everyone's advantage, and (b) attached to positions and offices open to all."[22]

To ask what rational men would do when drawing up a hypothetical social contract may appear fanciful, but it is in fact not far removed from what some Utilitarians felt when the first reform Parliament met. While no one believed that England was a *tabula rasa,* one free of the House of Lords, the Church of England, and law courts, there was a sense that England's oligarchies had lost their sovereign veto on further reform and that now rational men could end irrationalities and injustices. John Stuart Mill in 1845 wrote that the Reform Act "was to politics what the Reformation was to religion. . . . It made reason the recognized standard, instead of authority."[23] It was time to draw up a new charter, one that would bring happiness to the greatest number, but perhaps more importantly, bring justice to the new elements of society, to commerce, dissent, the professions, the captains of industry—even to trade unions and Chartists.

The new charter should also preclude cruel and acute suffering, and it should do so not merely because of the greatest happiness or the fairest justice, but because flagrant cruelty violated the feelings of humanity. Such feelings form a third element defining the ethical responses of the Utilitarian conscience. Utilitarians did not simply calculate felicity and weigh justice. They were not merely impersonal, unfeeling, and unpoetic rationalists, but men of emotion and sympathy. They could not, for example, think of the flogging of soldiers with equanimity. Even the hanging of murderers disturbed them. Utilitarians in Parliament and the press condemned flogging and hanging and many other cruelties whether in prisons or lunatic asylums. News of the death of a soldier from flogging in 1846 led John Bowring to confess that he "could not restrain his feelings," at this "horrid system at which humanity recoiled." Joseph Hume agreed. A stern opponent of a ten-hour day for factory labor, he was also the indefatigable opponent of flogging. His pleas for its abolition reflect more than a sense of its uselessness; they also reflect a deep empathy with the utter degradation that this "soul breaking, spirit destroying" punishment inflicted.[24] A similar empathy—sensitive, compassionate, and ardent—characterizes Molesworth's exposure of the sufferings of convicts transported to Australia.[25] It was an empathy that explains why the Utilitarian MPs voted so consistently for the end of corporal and capital punishment. It is a record far more generous and humane to unruly soldiers and erring criminals than is revealed in the speeches and votes of Disraeli's Young England or the Peelites—most of whom were admirers of Coleridge, Southey, and Wordsworth.[26] The utilitarian MPs were men of feeling and imagination. Grote wrote effusive poetry and played the violoncello; Roebuck was a fine water colorist and was from childhood passionately fond of poetry; Molesworth was widely read in literature and a person of strong emotions; Thompson gave Bentham's ideas a literary expression as vivid, concrete, and compassionate as any romantic of the day; Buller imbibed not a little of Carlyle's passion for the right; Bowring translated the poetry of many languages; Rintoul filled the *Spectator* with news of the arts; and Frederick Hill was the most humane and sensitive of British prison inspectors, far more compassionate than the Evangelicals Whitworth Russell and William Crawford.[27] No greater error can be made than to dismiss these Utilitarians as men of no feeling.

These feelings included a dash of hate. It was a hate aimed largely at the aristocracy. It quite dominated John Roebuck. His series, *Pamphlets for the People,* published in 1835, and his many speeches in the Commons abound in invective and vituperation, mostly directed at those who support tyranny and injustice. Vain, pompous, self-righteous, irritable, he soon became one of the more unpopular members of the House. The milder Molesworth had the same antipathies. "I vow," he told Harriet Grote, "to pull down this haughty aristocracy of ours."[28] Class jealousy was not absent from the Utilitarian conscience. But these feelings were outweighed by sympathy, a quality Bentham deemed necessary to a Utilitarian ethic. No other quality, he said, was more likely to coincide with the dictates of utility. Sympathy, along with a revulsion against pain, were feelings that lay behind Bentham's passion for the greatest happiness to the greatest number, a formula he insisted should include animals. Sympathy, including revulsion to pain, also informs his admirers and forms one of the lynchpins that enabled the greatest happiness principle to serve as the conscience of the state. Without it would the *Spectator* have told its readers, "The real good of society has never yet been promoted by the infliction of injustice upon any individual"?[29] It is a moving sentiment, but more compassionate than rational. It recalls Christ's "If ye do it unto the least of them, ye do it unto me." It is not a calculation Machiavelli would have made. It is not an assessment of maximum utility. It is rather a sympathy with individual suffering not unlike that which Bowring and Hume felt for flogged soldiers.

It was a sympathy that in fact was deeply characteristic of Robert Rintoul's *The Spectator,* a magazine whose humanity few journals could rival. It was a humanity that led Rintoul in 1844 to propose that utilitarian radicals and evangelical Tories form a new party, one based on a

"New Faith"—a faith in a more collectivized, protective society. However generous socially it was naive politically. It fits precisely with Charles Buller's judgment of that same year, that "Benthamites had very good hearts but wanted intellects."[30]

Buller was right about their hearts. He was also partially right about their intellects, particularly as reflected in earlier attempts to form a Radical party and in their optimism about the refashioning of an entire society. They failed to realize that a system of ethics cannot provide the basis of a political party—for a party one needs numbers, powerful interests, and money. Ethical principles alone cannot form a basis for the transformation of society—colonels will still insist on flogging, judges will demand murderers be hanged, and politicians will call the voting by secret ballot unEnglish. In their schemes for a third party and for vast reforms the Utilitarians of the 1830s were sectarian, doctrinaire, and naive, in some ways not unlike the Levellers of the seventeenth century. But they were much more. In the ferment that followed the Reform Act they were able to help form a public ethic, a state conscience, one that others had increasingly to meet. In the 1830s and 1840s the Utilitarians brought to Parliament, the press, and the government a new set of moral demands and a new moral theory to justify them. They asked, they insisted, they demanded, they clamored that all public institutions be judged by the standard of the greatest happiness for the greatest number.

That measurement of the average utility of an act of Parliament is next to impossible, that in fact they judged from a sense of justice, from feelings of compassion, and from middle-class biases only added, in a Parliament with few philosophers, to the strength of their demands. The greatest happiness to the greatest number has rhetorical intensity. It fits the political fact that a greater number, some 800,000, were now to rule. It was not even that sharp a break from tradition: William Paley had taught it to generations of Cambridge men and it was part of eighteenth century thought. Furthermore, many matters of legislation are quantitative and require estimates of maximum utility. The Corn Laws did affect all. "Millions," said Charles Villiers, were "cruelly affected by this law." Since millions did eat bread Villiers was correct.[31] The Utilitarian concern for the "greatest number" is a most proper one for legislators. That happiness is not a very precise measure is true, but that in no way lessens the affective power of demanding "the greatest happiness." It was also frequently a reflection of the intensity of the benevolence of the Utilitarians themselves. In the 1840s it was a principle that even some Tories used. Two of them, Lord Francis Egerton and Baillie Cochrane, had long defended the Corn Laws. In 1846, along with Peel, they came out for their repeal. Both claimed as a reason for their conversion the belief that repeal would increase "the general happiness of the people."[32]

The greatest happiness principle was a potent one. It was also a simple and vague one. Society could not be transformed by it alone. It only supplied the ethical rationale for other more substantive principles—principles such as liberty and democracy.

Liberty and Democracy

Early Victorian Utilitarians were passionate defenders of liberty. It was a passion that most had imbibed before reading Bentham. Bentham's writings indeed have little of the Promethean zeal for liberty of Shelley or Byron. A love of liberty was part of that English radicalism that began with Elizabethan Puritans and found glorious expression in writers as varied as John Milton and Thomas Paine. But though Bentham's passion for liberty was not Promethean, few could equal him in his hatred of "tyranny" or the avidity with which everywhere he exposed its baleful influence. For Bentham tyranny was an evil more than liberty was a good. Liberty was open ended; not so tyranny, which invariably brought pain. It must be extirpated wherever it existed.

The Utilitarian editors, administrators, and MPs sought to extirpate tyranny with a Benthamite avidity. They let few tyrannies pass unopposed. The Irish Coercion Bill of 1833 brought Grote and Warburton to their feet in order to denounce its suspension of *habeas corpus,* its trials by military tribunals, and its outlawing of public meetings.[33] The transportation of six Dorchester laborers for using oaths to form a union moved Roebuck, Hume, Warburton to eloquent pleas for the rights of laborers to form unions.[34] The impressment of Englishmen into the military struck John Bowring as sheer tyranny. The denial of the counsel of their own choice to prisoners at court aroused Joseph Hume's ire, as did most every legal obfuscation that denied the poor the due process of law.[35] For Roebuck that constant flow of bills for the strict observance of the sabbath meant only one thing, the invasion of the workers' one day of freedom and pleasure.[36] Bills for the stricter regulation of the sale of beer brought the question from Henry Warburton, "Why shouldn't the working class drink the beer at the place of sale?"[37] Religion, whether in the form of sabbatarian laws, Church privileges, or penalties on dissent, was particularly offensive to Utilitarians. Colonel Perronet Thompson, who avowed that "he had been born among the supporters of religious liberty," was a stout defender of the rights of Dissenters and Jews.[38]

Charles Villiers was just as stout a defender of a free press, a position which led him in the early 1830s to oppose that high tax on newspapers which made it impossible to publish journals cheap enough for workers to purchase.[39] For Edward Strutt the lack of a secret ballot at elections meant the tyranny of landlord and master. His attack on that form of despotism paled when compared to the attacks of George Grote.[40] All the Utilitarian MPs were for the secret ballot just as all fought for an unstamped press, an open sabbath, the rights of Jews and Dissenters, and the liberties of Irishmen and beer drinkers.

The secret ballot in the 1830s was the Utilitarians' preeminent cause. It was an issue of liberty against authority, of the freedom of voting for whom one wished against what Grote called the "sway of landlords" and Strutt called the power of "tyrannical landlords and tyrannical masters." Only the secret ballot, Grote told the Commons, would give the voter "his own free choice and conscience."[41]

Landlords and masters at election time were not the only tyrants. The law courts, as Bentham had tirelessly pointed out, were full of them, whether judges or lawyers. The great cost involved in pleading a civil case, because of legal technicalities, denied, said the *Westminster Review,* even the middling sort the freedom to contest with the rich.[42] Hundreds of statutes, loosely written, gave justices of the peace a vast array of arbitrary power. Bentham's friends Rintoul and Fonblanque filled the columns of the *Spectator* and *Examiner* with cases of the justices' despotic sway.[43] They also attacked the Church of England and its ecclesiastical courts. Formally the English Constitution guaranteed its subjects liberties far beyond those enjoyed on the Continent, but in the interstices of society freedom did not always flourish. On landed estates, in justices' petty sessions, at the hustings, in cotton mills, in church courts, in workhouses, prisons, and lunatic asylums freedom frequently yielded to oppression. The England of the 1830s was a deferential, paternalist, and authoritarian society.

John Stuart Mill was sensitive to this fact. It led him, in an article in the *Edinburgh Review* in 1845, to criticize that revived paternalist thought which had such a strong influence on the Tory conscience of Young England, on the Oxford movement, and on the Conservative party. Paternalists looked above all to property, the Anglican Church, and the magistracy for remedies to England's pressing social problems. The church would manage schools, landowners would care for the poor, millowners would regulate labor, and magistrates discipline the erring. Coleridge wrote of a church whose clergy would educate and supervise the nation, Southey urged property to resume its feudal duties, and Disraeli asked for the revival of almshouses. Even Carlyle indulged in medieval dreams. The revival of paternalism won even the applause of Whig patriarchs and Christian Socialists. Paternalism was easily the most popular and pervasive social outlook in England when Victoria ascended the throne.

Paternalism, however, did not win the applause of John Stuart Mill —or the other Utilitarians. The Utilitarian conscience was too deeply individualist. This revived paternalism, said Mill, required too much obedience and deference and too little self-reliance and independence. Paternalism, he said, was for the Russian boors; the slaves of the West Indies, and the subjects of Austria. "Obedience in return for protection." he wrote, "is a bargain only made when protection can be had on no other terms. Men now make that bargain with society, not with an individual."[44] The utilitarian conscience wanted liberty, and for all, not deference and dependency.

The Utilitarians also embraced democracy, though some had doubts about adopting it before the working classes were educated. Bentham had been a late convert to democracy, though when converted he went all the way to universal male suffrage. In 1820 James Mill, in his famous *Essay on Government,* argued that universal male suffrage would produce a government whose rule would be the most identical with the interests of the community. Thomas Babington Macaulay, the future historian of England, reviewed Mill's work in 1829 in the *Edinburgh Review.*[45] He said Mill's analysis was unduly deductive and abstract, the work of a narrow Utilitarian who was historically blind to the varying circumstances governing differing ages and psychologically blind to the richness and subtlety of human nature. Colonel Perronet Thompson answered Macaulay in the *Westminster Review* of July 1829.[46] Thompson's article was Bentham simplified and a very light rejoinder to the heavy barrage of Macaulay's learning and wit. It was, however, an argument for democracy that the working classes of Western Europe and America would eventually insist on—and successfully insist on. Thompson said that wherever a few rule the many, the few will pursue their own interests rather than the interests of the many. The rich, he said, are more apt to pursue selfish policies than the poor. Hence only the many can represent the interests of the community at large. There should thus be universal suffrage.

In 1835 John Stuart Mill repeated this argument in the *Westminster Review.* In his article Mill fully supports the proposition that "Men will, in the majority of cases, prefer their own interests to that of others," and concludes that the rule of the few will not lead to the public good. To achieve the public good "Every member of the legislature [must be] under the most complete responsibility to the community at large." It was a compelling argument. Who could possibly know better what would bring the greatest happiness to the majority than their elected representatives? But the argument worried the young Mill. He therefore hedged. He said that this democratic rule should be applied only when the "state of civilisation of the country renders it consistent with other necessary ends."[47] Other Utilitarians were equally ambiguous, being both persuaded of its logic and fearful of its consequences. Charles Buller told the House that "the most complete democracy is the only rational principle of municipal institutions."[48] On the rationality of complete democracy for the British Parliament, he was reticent. So were men like Strutt, Villiers, Leader, and Hume when, in January 1837, Roebuck proclaimed himself a democrat and attacked the Radicals for abandoning it for a compromise with the Whigs. Roebuck said the real struggle was one between aristocracy and democracy.[49] The *Spectator* reported that Roebuck was heard in silence. "Never," said a witness, "did men of all parties look more uncomfortable. . . . Even the radicals, with few exceptions, turned their backs."[50]

The courageous Roebuck was premature in his demands. But he was never one to be diffident. He had, in his *Pamphlets for the People* of 1835, called for "Democracy to raise her front" and insisted that those who governed "must be representative of the general will."[51] Roebuck supported the Peoples Charter of 1839 with its demand for universal suffrage.[52] In 1842 he urged that they be heard at the bar of the House of Commons, as did Hume, Leader, Villiers, and Bowring.[53] Whatever the reservations of the Utilitarians about immediate universal suffrage, they were, on the Municipal Corporations Act of 1835, the Irish Municipal Act of 1837, the resolution to hear the Chartists, the secret ballot, and the Canada Bill, in the vanguard of those working for democracy. On June 20, 1848, Hume even moved to widen the franchise for electing Parliament. Bowring, Molesworth, Thompson, and Villiers supported him.[54]

For championing an extended franchise, for advocating a secret ballot, and for planning to build a Radical party the Utilitarians have been called sectarian and doctrinaire. In a way they were. But in 1867 and 1884 adult male householders won the vote, and in 1872 Parliament adopted the secret ballot. In 1918 women over thirty won the vote, and in 1928 it was given to women between twenty-one and thirty. John Stuart Mill had proposed female suffrage, prematurely, in 1867. No historian can measure the influence of Roebuck's pleas, Grote's endless speeches,

Villiers' motion, or Mill's proposal on the events of 1867, 1872, 1884, and 1918, but none of these gains would have come without someone at some time having the boldness to propose them. An important part of the utilitarian conscience was the audacity to expound ideas whose time had not yet come.

Their advocacy of liberty and democracy was not, in fact, that utopian. The two principles fused in a practical manner in the Canadian crisis of 1837–40. A Legislative Council of Englishmen who were appointed by the Crown for life terms had increasingly vetoed the measures of an elected assembly representing the French Catholics of Lower Canada. The French rebelled in 1838. Lord John Russell and the Whigs suspended the Constitution in Lower Canada. Parliament was angered and perplexed. The Utilitarian MPs pleaded the cause of colonial liberty and democracy. Sir William Molesworth called the rule of an English Governor General and an appointed Legislative Council over a French majority "a grievous tyranny" and insisted that the representatives of the people alone should determine how their taxes should be spent.[55] Roebuck told the House, "If we desire the people to be well governed, we must allow them to govern themselves."[56] Buller in fact went to Canada as Lord Durham's secretary and wrote much of the famous report that recommended the Canadians be given far greater rights of self-government. *The London and Westminster Review,* with John Stuart Mill as its authority on Canada, joined Rintoul's *Spectator,* Fonblanque's *Examiner,* and Black's *Chronicle* in advocating greater liberty and democracy for the Canadians.[58] The government even sent out Poulett Thomson as Governor General to carry through the new constitution. Thomson, in politics a Whig and not a Philosophical Radical, could still remember the days when Bentham helped canvass for his election to Parliament. Bentham's influence was not limited to the Philosophical Radicals alone. All who read him, all who knew him, all even who criticized him, could not but see things a little differently thereafter. His ideas were too bold, too original, too imaginative to be lightly dismissed. The men most important in the settlement of Canada were largely men of a Utilitarian conscience, men persuaded of the value of liberty and democracy. It was their most practical and effective achievement. The Utilitarians' passion for liberty and democracy clearly helped to bring happiness to Canadians, and in considerable numbers. But their individualism and passion for liberty did not always have so fortunate a consequence. It certainly did not invariably prove salutary when fused with their belief in political economy. It led them to be strong advocates of the laissez-faire principle.

Laissez Faire

Among the more dramatic social issues that divided the English into warring camps in the 1840s were the New Poor Law and the Ten Hour Bill for factory workers. For many support of the first and opposition to the second were acts of inhumanity. Charles Dickens felt so. In his caricature of Alderman Cute in the *Chimes* and Mr. Gradgrind in *Hard Times* he satirized those whose political economy and utilitarian calculations forced the poor into cruel workhouses and satanic mills. Dickens' caricatures have provided multitudes with a picture of economists and Utilitarians as hard and unfeeling. Though Dickens exaggerates, his criticisms are not without foundation in fact. Most Utilitarian MPs, editors, and administrators opposed the Ten Hour Bill and supported the New Poor Law, though Charles Buller among MPs and Robert Rintoul among the editors supported measures that would limit workers in factories to a ten-hour day. As a result, Fonblanque's *Examiner* branded Buller a subversive, comparing him with the fifteenth-century rebel, Jack Cade. John Wilson's *Globe* denounced Rintoul's *Spectator* for departing from the laws of political economy.[59]

Buller, who wrote in 1844 that he had left utilitarianism, was not really that subversive. His support for the New Poor Law was consistent and orthodox and it won him the Presidency of the Poor Law Board in a Whig government. All the Utilitarian MPs and journals supported the New Poor Law and had done so since 1834 when that Law was passed.[60] In one sense the law brought more, not less, government. It established a Poor Law Commission in London with enough power and enough Assistant Commissioners to set up and supervise some 550 new poor law unions. The commissioners ordered most of the guardians who ran these unions to deny able-bodied paupers any relief except that given in the unions' workhouses—houses critics of the law likened to bastilles. Justices of the peace and parish overseers could no longer give workers a few extra shillings a week to augment their sparse wages or grant outdoor relief to paupers in their cottages. Instead it was the workhouse or no relief. Property owners, Tory and Whig, liked the new law since it meant less relief and lower rates. Political economists, a category which included most Utilitarians, rejoiced in the law since it made all workers part of a free labor market, one no longer prey to the meddling interference of over-generous justices and overseers. It made the laborer stand on his own feet. From an economic point of view it thus accorded squarely with the principle of laissez faire.

The Utilitarians were not shy in praising the wisdom of laissez faire.

To let the economy alone was to maximize its energies and productive-
ness. This principle was based on the inexorable laws of supply and demand, laws that converted the self-interest of each into the public good
of all, laws that Adam Smith discovered and that Bentham and Bentham's friends David Ricardo and James Mill expounded with a rigorous
logic. These laws were harmonious and self-acting. For government to
intervene with them was mischievous.

The Utilitarians in Parliament felt the same way. Few were the proposals for the regulation of labor that they did not oppose. They called
bills for controlling the hours of work in print works and lace mills unnecessary and mischievous.[61] Bills to set rents and prices for hand-loom
weavers and frame-work knitters were considered delusory.[62] To regulate
the hiring of men to unload coal in the port of London was "objectionable and injurious," a "departure," said Bowring, "from the sound principles of political economy."[63] Even the outlawing of dog carts and of
small boys as chimney sweeps won not a single vote from the Utilitarians
and some protests against these measures.[64] It was a record that would
have appalled Charles Dickens.

The Utilitarians' support of a stern Poor Law and opposition to the
protection of labor reflects their belief in the harsh doctrines of political
economy. Yet the Utilitarians were idealistic men. How can these facts be
squared? Part of the answer is to be found in the age in which they lived.
There were four characteristics of the age that made their arguments sincere and plausible: (1) past government regulations of the economy had
been vexatious, irrational, and harmful; (2) government had been repressive and extravagant; (3) a free economy did encourage individual
self-reliance; and (4) the laws of political economy were not without some
impressive truths, even concerning the practical benefit of laissez faire.

The first of these characteristics was an inheritance from centuries
of mercantilism and took a myriad of forms ranging from Navigation
Acts filled with ancient rules to customs regulations that were vast and
detailed. "Melancholy is the result," said the *Westminster Review* in
1840, "of centuries of mischievous and often wicked legislation."[65] Parliament was still at it in the 1830s, anxious to limit the use of omnibuses
and the hours of beer shops, regulations that led Bowring to protest
against such "frivolous legislation." They would, he added, "interfere
with the comforts of the poor while leaving the rich alone."[66]

The government could be politically oppressive as well as economically vexatious. It was a fact that loomed large in the minds of Radicals.
Memories of Pitt's gagging acts of 1793, of the Peterloo Massacre of
1819, of the Six Acts of Lord Sidmouth that followed, and of Oliver the

Spy were as fresh to Hume, Warburton, and Grote as were memories of a government still, however reformed, full of extravagant sinecures, pensions, useless functionaries, and red tape. The vivid sense of government as the repressive and extravagant instrument of the aristocracy persuaded many of the rising middle classes to look with greater confidence to the principle of laissez faire. The extravagance of a government bloated with sinecurists, redundant officials, and an inflated military bothered Joseph Hume in particular. From 1812 to 1850 he became famous in Parliament and the country as the inveterate advocate of retrenchment. Fierce and constant were his attacks on every item of the budget. He and his fellow Utilitarians wanted an economical and small government, one that would let the economy and society alone.

Letting society alone also encouraged individualism and self-reliance, virtues that, having proved so beneficial to the middle classes, could not but be of value to the working classes. John Roebuck and Joseph Hume were the staunchest advocates of laissez-faire principles among the Utilitarians; they were also the stoutest defenders of Chartism, universal suffrage, and the workers' rights to liberty and equality. They opposed the Ten Hour Bill and supported the New Poor Law not from ill will toward the laborer but from a desire that labor prosper. "The only way to aid labor," said Roebuck in opposing a ten-hour day, "was to give full, free, and complete employment to his powers."[67] An easy and generous poor law was an evil, said Hume, because it "would destroy that habit of self-dependence and that spirit of self-reliance, upon which alone they could depend for the wellbeing of the people."[68]

The beliefs of Roebuck and Hume touched on many truths—the old poor laws did demoralize many; the workers, particularly through trade unions, would win much by their own efforts, and those most self-reliant would gain the most. But Roebuck and Hume and the other Utilitarians were in error on some crucial points. They were doctrinaire in their uncritical belief that reduced hours would mean precisely the same reduction in productivity and wages. They accepted the famous formula of the economist Nassau Senior: a 5/6th cut in hours meant a 5/6th cut in productivity and wages. The formula was wrong. Factories that had cut hours had kept up production. The Utilitarians were also elitist in their condescending and patronizing view that they knew best what the laborers wanted. What the laborers wanted, and gained, was the ten-hour day and a more generous administration of the New Poor Law. They gained it not because of the conscience of the Utilitarians but because other radicals, men like Thomas Wakeley, Thomas Duncombe, John Brotherton, and John Fielden, knew what the workers wanted and led them in that struggle. Nothing reveals the split between the Philosophical Radicals and what John Stuart Mill called the demagogic radicals more than the many divisions over the passage of the Ten Hour Bill and the renewal and continuance of the New Poor Law. In those votes the demagogic radicals were much closer to the desires and feelings of the working classes. They were much freer from the dogma of laissez faire.

The fourth characteristic of the age that caused the Utilitarians to believe so firmly in laissez faire was the impressive findings made by the political economists. Political economy from Adam Smith to James Mill was not without exciting truths, truths that John Stuart Mill expounded in his *Principles of Political Economy* of 1848. Utilitarian MPs and editors who condemned legislation that set wages and prices for weavers, knitters, and bakers had sound arguments. No government intervention could save the weavers from the power loom; no legislation could keep the wages of bakers from reflecting the laws of supply and demand, or if perchance they could, it would raise the price of bread. A more expensive loaf, of course, was an evil—an evil produced by the landed interest's Corn Law. It was above all in their attack on the Corn Laws that the Utilitarians fused together two of their guiding principles—the greatest happiness principle and the doctrine of laissez faire.

The repeal of the Corn Laws was the crowning achievement of the utilitarian conscience, the supreme example of how laissez faire could be beneficial. Sir Robert Peel was merely the last of converts. To veteran Utilitarian critics of the Corn Laws even Cobden and Bright were newcomers. Since 1824 the *Westminster Review* had been its fiercest opponent. In 1837 Charles Villiers met with Grote, Warburton, Hume, Buller, and had pledged himself to fight for the total repeal of the Corn Laws.[69] Roebuck, Strutt, and Thompson also joined in that battle. Colonel Perronet Thompson, of course, was a veteran, having exposed in 1827 in his popular *Catechism on the Corn Laws* the laws' fallacies—fallacies he again attacked in the 1830s in the *Westminster Review.* Throughout the late 1830s the *Examiner, Spectator, Chronicle,* and *Globe* conducted an increasing war against these laws.

The arguments which the Utilitarians used against the Corn Laws rested on sound theory, mixed facts, and an appealing ethic. The theory was that free trade throughout the world would encourage each country to use its capital and resources in the production of the particular goods it could produce the most efficiently. If each country did so the total production would bring the greatest number of goods to the greatest number of people. The theory was an integral part of the political economy of Adam Smith, David Ricardo, and the Utilitarians, and it proved a formidable weapon. It was laissez faire at its most logical and benevolent. The facts of the case, however, were uneven. England imported considerable grain when its harvests were poor—in 1831 and 1832 some 2.5 million quarters a year. The utilitarians were right that the duty did make bread more expensive. But the Corn Laws did not cause the depression of 1839–42. The repeal of the Corn Laws would have had only a marginal, not a decisive effect on the economy, a fact the Utilitarians obscured in their exaggerated claims that these Laws caused distress.[70] From 1839 to 1842 that distress was deep and pervasive. It was the result of fluctuations of a laissez faire capitalism, a fact which the utilitarians did not perceive. They did not know why the depression occurred and so blamed it on the Corn Laws. But their main arguments against the Laws were ethical. They were simply unjust because they taxed the poor to help the rich. It was unfair to tax that bread which constituted nearly half of the diet and a third of the budget of the poor, and to do so in order to raise the rents of landowners already wealthy. "It puts," said Villiers in 1838, "the interests of the few . . . on one side and those of the community on the other."[71]

However logical and benevolent was the Utilitarian argument against the Corn Laws, it did little good when espoused by only a handful of utilitarians. In 1838 Villiers' motion for repeal won only 95 votes. The opponents numbered 300. The utilitarian conscience limited to the Philosophical Radicals never became a powerful political force, either in its espousal of liberty and democracy, or in its desire to reform the law and end capital punishment. But its insistence on a higher ethic helped persuade other, more powerful political forces, to adopt juster positions. The political power of the North and Midlands, the power of cotton, wool, and iron, created the Anti-Corn Law League, and that League forced the repeal of the Corn Laws. The landed interest was no match for industrial and commercial wealth and its many friends among the 40 shilling freeholders and 10 £ householders, particularly when armed with the doctrine of laissez faire and the principle of the greatest happiness to the greatest number. A public conscience cannot alone rule a nation, but neither can raw political forces rule alone. Political forces need moral arguments to give their cause a popular appeal. In the 1830s the Utilitarians provided some logical and benevolent arguments for the repeal of the Corn Laws. They were the first to claim that repeal would bring happiness to millions in the form of cheaper bread. They were also the first to claim that the millions might benefit from better education and health. But these were matters that could not be left to laissez faire; they were matters that demanded a reforming state.

The Idea of a Reforming State

From 1832 to 1850 Joseph Hume objected strenuously to Parliamentary bills that would give the government power to interfere in the following activities: lace mills, framework knitting, print works, adult labor in factories, omnibuses, London bakers, chimney sweeps, dog carts, coolie labor in Mauritius, tenants' rights, labor rates to rural workers, unloaders of coal in London, and merchant shipping.

In the same eighteen years he also supported Parliamentary bills that would give the government the power to interfere in the following activities: prisons, poor laws, charities, education, public health, the property of the Church of England, medicine, emigration, police, justices of the peace, railways, mines, ejectment of tenants, passenger ships, tithes, and enclosures.

He was for laissez faire on thirteen issues and for a reforming government on sixteen other matters. Similar lists could be drawn up for the other Utilitarian MPs and for the *Examiner,* the *Spectator,* the *Morning Chronicle,* and the *Westminster Review.*

Were the Utilitarians inconsistent? They would deny it. They claimed to be devotees of laissez faire in economics, in favor of government intervention in social matters. "Laissez faire," said the *Westminster Review* in 1840, "should be the fundamental axiom of commercial policy." But there are, it added, higher objects than the pursuit of wealth. In subsequent issues they urged that the government promote education, public health, better prisons, emigration, reformatories, lunatic asylums, improved poor laws, and a sounder medical system.[72] These were objects above the pursuit of wealth. But the formula, laissez faire in commerce, government intervention in social matters, did not work. Economic and social activities were too intertwined. Public health demanded that government control water companies just as public safety necessitated regulating railway companies. Railways in fact posed the greatest challenge to laissez faire as "the fundamental axiom of commercial policy." Joseph Hume and John Roebuck, whose dedication to laissez faire few could exceed, insisted, when debating railway bills, that the government interfere —"for the benefit of the public," said Roebuck in 1844, "for the greatest amount of benefit for the community," said Hume in 1846.[73] The Utilitarian Edward Strutt, who became a Railway Commissioner in 1846, urged that Parliament set and revise fares and tolls and do so "with regard to the welfare of the public."[74] Utilitarians believed both in the axiom of laissez faire and the power of government to reform, and this belief involved them in inconsistencies. By 1842 the *Westminster Review* had to admit that on occasion the economy itself should be regulated. "Legislation to control industry expressly on behalf of humanity and public morals," it wrote, "marks a new era in our social life."[75] It then urged government intervention in railways, water companies, mines, real property, the sale of land, and highway tolls.

One explanation of that inconsistency can be found in the paradox that more government meant less government, that government interference would create an educated, industrious, and independent peoples not reliant on government. While not as apocalyptic as the Marxists who envision a socialism leading to the withering away of the state, the Utilitarians did argue, in their pleas for national education, a centralized poor law, and a board of health, that these measures would produce educated, self-reliant, and healthy individuals, sturdy peoples scornful of depending on government. Behind their desire to use government to make men free of government lay both a hidden authoritarianism and a sanguine rationalism. The authoritarianism was a reflection of that impatience to reform that is found in men as different as Bentham and Cromwell. The rationalism was a reflection of the enlightenment. Both contributed to their nearly utopian belief in the creation of a society of free and independent individuals.

Utilitarians, like puritans, wished to make men free by making them virtuous. The Utilitarian MPs constantly used the phrase "to make men good" or "to make men responsible" in pleading for schools, workhouses, boards of health, reformatories, and prisons. They even used it in arguing for the secret ballot and open museums. Joseph Hume told the Commons that opening the British Museum on Sundays was "one of the best means . . . for making men better."[76] George Grote said the ballot will "make" voters responsible to the public.[77] The surest way to raise the moral character of the laborer," said Charles Villiers in defending the New Poor Law "was to make him independent."[78] "The object of government," said Molesworth, was "to make good men, good citizens, industrious members of society."[79] Education, said Roebuck, will "make the [individual] a good child, a good parent, a good neighbour, a good citizen, in short a good man."[80] There were indeed no limits to what the state could do in molding men's character. The psychology of Utilitarians was associationist. Like David Hartley, Joseph Priestley, William Godwin, Robert Owen, and Jeremy Bentham, they believed that by associating pleasure with the virtues of industry, sobriety, thrift, honesty, and self-help, and by associating pain with laziness, drunkenness, improvidence, deceit, and dependence, one could produce good and independent persons. Government should thus build attractive schools that taught girls homemaking, gave boys industrial training, and inculcated both with deeply rooted habits of morality. The government should also give relief only in workhouses because only by that test could the destitute be given an adequate diet, clothing, and lodging, and yet a relief that was not more attractive than the life of the working poor. Reformatories and prisons would also discipline the poor, associating pain with crime and pleasure with reformed habits.

This belief in using government institutions to refashion society by reforming individuals is central to the Utilitarian conscience. It was a belief that found its fullest and most energetic expression in the reports and the work of Kay Shuttleworth, Secretary of the Committee in Council on Education, and Chadwick, Secretary of the Poor Law Commission and Commissioner on the General Board of Health. It also led the *Westminster Review* to propound far more collectivist measures in its pages than any Tory or Whig journal. In June of 1844 the *Westminster* argued that Edwin Chadwick and not England's poets best typified the spirit of the age. They found Chadwick's reports distinguished by benevolence and beneficence. In September of 1844 it said, "We live in an age of Benthamites."[81] It also moved so far toward collectivism in 1848 that it had good words for socialism. It said that Louis Blanc "was right in pointing out the evils of disorganization" and it called socialism in the France of 1848 "a valid security for the general stability of existing institutions."[82] The *Westminster,* like the Utilitarians in Parliament and the Civil Service, were so anxious to create a free and rational society of independent and happy people that they welcomed any government interference that they felt would further that end.

The paradox that more government would mean less government was, in fact, a deception, another case perhaps of utilitarians having good hearts and weak intellects. Edwin Chadwick in some ways was most deceived by its lures. His hopes that a poor law which combined the stern deterrence of the workhouse with the educative work of district schools and the healthy effects of good medical care would turn dependent paupers into independent workers proved too optimistic. The New Poor Law produced more reports than reformed paupers, reports calling for more government and holding out the promise that it would make people free of government. Chadwick found that disease was the chief cause of pauperism. Create, then, boards of health, clean the towns, and paupers will become fewer.[83] The result again was no significant diminution in pauperism but a significant expansion of government. That larger government was not to be a welfare state so much as a reforming one—one that would improve all sorts of institutions and all sorts of people.

There is no doubt that the Utilitarians believed that the expansion of government in the fields of education, poor relief, and health would produce a healthy, self-reliant, and educated peoples fit for a laissez-faire society. But that belief—which proved deceptive—was less deeply rooted and pervasive in their consciences than a more fundamental trait, their enthusiasm for the greatest happiness to the greatest number. "The business of government," said Roebuck, "is not merely to prevent evil, but also, by the concentrated force of the social system, directly to promote good, to increase, by all the means which its powers confer on it, the happiness and well-being of its subjects."[84] "Much had been already done for the ruling few in the way of legislation," said John Bowring, "it was now time that something should be done for the subject many."[85] These demands for government to increase happiness and to help the many reflect that social benevolence which forms one of the main characteristics of the utilitarian conscience, one that led to collectivism. It certainly lay behind Jeremy Bentham's *Constitutional Code,* that remarkable blueprint of a democratic and collectivist state. The *Code,* to be sure, announces that "Government is evil," being inherently costly and oppressive, but the *Code* then announces two rules pregnant with collectivism—first that when the evil that government removes is greater than the evil of a larger government, the intervention is good, and, second, that the end of all government is the greatest happiness of the greatest number.[86] The *Code* then outlines the elaborate and detailed functions of thirteen ministries. Six of these—the ministries of education, health, indigent relief, interior-communication, preventive service, and domain—were unknown to the England of 1834. The first four were adopted in the nineteenth century.[87] The *Constitutional Code* makes clear Bentham's deep belief that government, whatever its inherent evils, can augment happiness. It also suggests that behind his belief in government as an instrument of reform lay an enthusiastic and deep-seated benevolence. That same benevolence led Utilitarians in Parliament, the press, and the administration to clamor more persistently than other groups for a larger government.

This expanded government, to be effective, had also to be rational. The Utilitarians were not for a diffuse benevolence. They wanted hard-headed, efficient, rational planning. Rationalism was the second characteristic leading the utilitarian to a more collectivist state. They wanted to be social engineers. Benevolence was not sufficient unless guided by reason—and a hard, probing reason at that. Benevolence alone led to an easy poor relief that corrupted the poor, a soft prison discipline that did not deter, factory hours too brief to meet foreign competition, ragged schools that did not teach—in short the uncritical welfare world of the humanitarians, of Lord Shaftesbury the factory reformer and of Charles Dickens. The Utilitarians insisted benevolence be rational even if stern and calculating, and, given their belief in political economy, it led to a profound ambivalence within their conscience, one that continued throughout the nineteenth century.

Elie Halevy, in *The Growth of Philosophical Radicalism,* shows how that ambivalence reflects a basic ambiguity in Utilitarian thought. Bentham taught that to promote the greatest happiness legislators should use the government to achieve that artificial identification of interests that is necessary in a world of powerful, selfish, and conflicting egos. But the political economy of the Utilitarians—of Ricardo, Mill, and Bentham —assumed a harmony of egos, a harmony insured by economic laws which translated self-interest into the public good. It was an intellectual ambiguity that heightened the conflict between the doctrines of laissez faire and the idea of the reforming state.[88]

This ambivalence became even more acute when industrial and urban growth created problems that demanded the intervention of government and when the rise of the middle and working classes created a political force that insisted on greater liberty and equality. "A new social state," said Charles Buller in 1844, "such as we have become, . . . required new principles of legislation." "The very proximity of these masses of labouring population," he added, "placed them more completely under the control and direction of government."[89] These same urban masses were also demanding a say in society. The same realization that an industrial society presented new challenges appeared in the *Spectator* and the *Examiner* and the speeches of Utilitarian MPs.[90] Benevolent and rational still, and still dedicated to the greatest happiness, they moved warily but steadily toward the creation of a reforming state.

Benevolence and rationalism, though dominant qualities of the Utilitarian conscience, were no monopoly of that school. The Tory Gladstone, the Whig Lord Morpeth, the Evangelical Lord Shaftesbury, the Nonconformist John Bright would protest, and rightly, against any cornering of the market of benevolence and rationalism. Gladstone's *The State in its Relations with the Church* is no less benevolent and rational than Bentham's *Constitutional Code,* just as John Bright's speeches are as trenchant and humane as Mill's *Political Economy.*

How then does the Utilitarian conscience differ from these other outlooks? The answer lies both in the intensity of their dedication to these two qualities and in their freedom from vested interests and religious dogmas. Their intensity distinguishes them from that amiable *noblesse oblige* that marked the Whigs. The Whigs in the 1830s and

1840s had in fact a reasonably good record on reform, far better in matters of education, health, factory labor, prisons, reformatories, mining, and the poor law reform than the record of the Tories. But they were reforms which Utilitarians drew up and which political pressures drove through Parliament. Whig benevolence and rationality was latitudinarian and compromising. Only when circumstances demanded it did the Whigs transfer the easygoing *noblesse oblige* from their paternal estates to government. If the electors did not want the ballot or a national system of education the languid Whigs would not clamor for it.

The Tory Gladstone, the Evangelical Ashley, and the Quaker Bright were more intense. They were willing to clamor, but not for national education, which was to Utilitarians the *summum bonum,* the sovereign remedy. Gladstone, Ashley, and Bright all opposed the idea of public education: Gladstone and Ashley because they were tied to the Church of England and wanted it to manage schools, Bright because of a Nonconformist jealousy of the state. Disraeli too, in his novels, was as compassionate for the amelioration of the poor as any Utilitarian. Unhealthy towns led him to join the Health of Towns Association. But when the Public Health Act and the Mines Act came before the House in 1848 and 1849 he opposed both, even though diseased towns and mine accidents took the lives of thousands. He opposed them because he needed the support of the Protectionist Party, who hated the centralization of the Health Act, and he needed the friendship of Lord Londonderry, a great mine owner. Tories like Disraeli and Gladstone faced an array of vested interests that ranged from the Church of England and landed property to tithe owners and Tory justices. In the 1830s and 1840s there was no question of adopting social security laws or nationalizing coal or steel. The crucial questions involved education, health, poor relief, the care of prisoners, juvenile delinquents, the insane, and the regulation of industry and commerce. In these fields Tory and Whig were deeply bound by vested interests while Evangelicals and Nonconformists were bound by some strong beliefs.

The Utilitarians were freer of these constraints. They were bound neither by political parties nor by class loyalties, neither by vested interest nor by religious dogmas. That their public conscience was so free floating explains why their attempt to form a Radical party was so pathetic. In terms of party politics these Utilitarians were too uncompromising. But it was not as a political party that the Utilitarian conscience played so powerful a role. It was rather as political moralists that they were important. Tireless advocates of more rational ethics, they criticized all that was irrational, oppressive, and unfair. Gadflies commis-

sioned to sting blunt consciences, they called every institution into question. Writers of endless speeches, editorials, and reports, they burrowed
into the smug assumptions of the Victorians. And philosophers in possession of the ultimate moral yardstick in the greatest happiness principle, they imposed on all other parties—Whig, Tory, Evangelical,
Nonconformist—a stricter standard, a more comprehensive measuring
rod, a more practical ethic, one that simply could not be set aside. In the
years of great promise that followed the Reform Act, a period that saw
the decline of Toryism, the ineffectiveness of Whiggery, the atrophy of
evangelicalism, and the continued isolation of nonconformity, the Utilitarians were in a position to set those basic standards that were to define
the state conscience of later Victorians. With administrators as powerful
as Chadwick, Kay Shuttleworth, Southwood Smith, and Frederick Hill,
and with decided convictions about the mission of a reforming government, they brought their new standards to the very center of the Victorian state.

That the greatest happiness principle itself is less philosophically de-
fensible than a theory of justice built on fairness did not disturb the early
Victorians since they used the rhetoric of justice and fairness inter-
changeably with appeals to the greatest happiness. Those two principles
that John Rawls considers as basic in *A Theory of Justice*—that "each
person is to have an equal right to the most extensive liberty compatible
with a similar liberty for others" and that "social and economic inequalities are to be arranged so that they are both (a) reasonably expected to be
to everyone's advantage, and (b) attached to positions and offices open
to all"—are principles that would have delighted the early Victorian Utilitarians. The first of these principles, indeed, received its classic expression in John Stuart Mill's famous essay *On Liberty,* published in 1859. It
also inspired the Utilitarians in Parliament and the press to argue for the
largest possible amount of liberty. They wanted beer shops open on Sunday, Irishmen able to hold public meetings, the poor to be free of paternalism, and the Canadians free to rule themselves.

The Utilitarians also wanted an economy and society in which inequalities were to everyone's advantage. They were for private property
and laissez faire and the inequalities these involved because they led to
the greatest production of goods and services. They were against the
Corn Laws because the Corn Laws involved an inequality that diminished the goods available for all. They were for using inequalities in administering poor relief because such inequalities would help the most
people. They used the inequalities of the less eligibility principle, arguing

that it would rescue the poor from pauperism by making pauperism a bit less eligible than the lot of the industrious poor.

And lastly, they were for "positions and offices open to all." Equality of opportunity was a great desideratum with the Utilitarians. Their passion for education was inordinate. They led in the field of civil service reform, advocating appointment to office by merit, not favor. They argued for reformed law courts that would give the poor a better break and for cleaner, more civilized cities that would assure them of better health and opportunities to gain culture. All museums were to be open on Sundays.

They also wanted these schools and clean cities and open museums simply because they made the English happier. The Utilitarian conscience does fit Rawls's two principles of justice—but it goes beyond them. It also reflects a more emotional element. Stern and rational as they prided themselves on being, they often espoused the greatest happiness to the greatest number from sentiment, from humanitarian feeling, from sympathy. Charles Buller was right about their good hearts. Jeremy Bentham's greatest happiness principle as a theory for calculating the average utility of legislative and administrative measures may be a delusion if considered as a precise yardstick. But if not considered as a precise yardstick, it does provide a rough measure, one not lacking in fairness, and one whose rhetorical appeal is powerful, a fact which in an early Victorian England still romantic was not unimportant. There was, after all, a poetic element to Bentham and the Utilitarians. They abounded in feeling and sympathy. It was a feeling and sympathy which, when combined with their constant concern with justice and fairness and with their rational insistence on the practical and efficient, would impose on the Victorian ruling classes a most formidable public conscience. And when the Utilitarians also insisted that these standards alone be the measure of the public good and not tradition or authority or special interests or religious dogma, then there was truly born a new public conscience. The Utilitarians left this conscience as a legacy to the later Victorians. It was a challenging legacy, one that could never be set aside by those whose task it was to define and redefine the conscience of the Victorian state.

Notes

1. Charles Buller to Thomas Carlyle, August 31, 1828, Carlyle Mss, National Library of Scotland, Edinburgh.

2. L. G. Johnson, *General T. Perronet Thompson* (1957), p. 121.

3. *Dictionary of National Biography* (henceforth cited as *DNB*), (1921) II, 569;

James Grant, *Portraits of Public Characters* (1841) I, 82. There are *DNB* entries for all twenty Utilitarians who form the basis of this essay.

4. Francis E. Mineka, *The Early Letters of John Stuart Mill* (1963), see index for Rintoul, Fonblanque, and Wilson; E. B. Fonblanque, ed., *The Life and Labours of Albany Fonblanque* (1874), p. 32.

5. Harriet Grote, *The Philosophical Radicals* (1866), pp. 51–53; Robert E. Leader, *Life and Letters of John Arthur Roebuck* (1897), pp. 14–27.

6. For Thompson, Leader, and Bowring see *DNB*, II, 984; XIX, 716; *DNB Twentieth Century*, p. 431; L. B. Bowring, *The Autobiographical Recollections of Sir John Bowring* (1877).

7. Samuel Finer, *The Life and Times of Edwin Chadwick* (1952); R. A. Lewis, *Edwin Chadwick and the Public Health Movement* (1952).

8. Frank Smith, *Life and Work of Sir James Kay-Shuttleworth* (1923); Gertrude Lewes, *Dr. Southwood Smith, A Retrospect* (1898); Debby Gorham, unpublished paper on the Thomas Hill family.

9. T. C. Hansard, ed., *Parliamentary Debates of Great Britain,* 3rd Ser. (henceforth cited as Hansard), XXIX, 290; XC, 712; LXXXIX, 1188; XCIII, 731; XX, 166; LXV, 376.

10. Ibid., XXX, 954; LX, 409; XLI, 927.

11. Ibid., XXXIV, 827; LXIX, 530–31.

12. *Morning Chronicle,* January 26, 1841; *Westminster Review,* September 1844, pp. 3–4; July 1829, p. 260.

13. Hansard, LXI, 350; XVI, 957.

14. Ibid., XXXVIII, 1340; 1415; XXXV, 573–74; LXXX, 1094; XXXIV, 318.

15. *Examiner,* September 20, 1840; February 26, March 5, 26, September 17, 1842; January 7, April 15, August 5, 1843; *Spectator,* February 13, September 18, 1841; Margaret Oliphant, *William Blackwood and His Sons, Their Magazine and Friends* (1897) I, 514.

16. Hansard, XXXVIII, 1009.

17. Ibid., XXI, 816, 818.

18. Ibid., LXXVIII, 1394; LXXX, 1094.

19. Ibid., XXVIII, 371.

20. W. MacIlwraith, *Life and Writings of George Grote* (1884) pp. 2–6; Bowring, *Recollections,* pp. 1–3, 39–43; G. L. Nesbit, *Benthamite Reviewing* (1934), p. 30; Leader, *Roebuck,* p. 40; L. G. Johnson, *General T. Perronet Thompson, 1783–1869* (1957), pp. 14–38; *DNB,* V, 107; X, 230; *Spectator,* May 1856, pp. 463–66.

21. *Examiner,* February 7, 1846.

22. John Rawls, *A Theory of Justice* (1971), pp. 60–61.

23. *Edinburgh Review,* April 1845, p. 502

24. Hansard, LXXXVIII, 395, 691.

25. Ibid., p. 459; XCIII, 63–92.

26. Ibid., LII, 946; LV, 1101; LVIII, 1418–20; LXII, 538; XCVII, 591; XVII, 49; XXII, 256.

27. George Grote, *Poems* (1872); Leader, *Roebuck,* pp. 27, 40, 63; H. Grote, *Philosophical Radicals,* pp. 3, 7, 53; Johnson, *Thompson,* pp. 132, 144; Charles Buller to Carlyle, August 31, 1820, March 14, September 12, 1831; Carlyle Mss; *DNB,* II, 984; Mary C. Hill, ed. *Frederick Hill: An Autobiography* (1894).

28. H. Grote, *Philosophical Radicals,* p. 6.

29. *Spectator,* November 21, 1840, p. 1123.

30. *Spectator,* April 13, 1844, p. 346; Sir Henry Cole, *Fifty Years of Public Works* (1884) pp. 16–18.

31. Hansard, LX, 656.

32. Ibid., LXXXIII, 55, 571.

33. Ibid., XV, 1242–46; XVI, 472, 852.

34. Ibid., XXII, 730, 945; XXIII, 114–17; XVI, 818.

35. Ibid., XXXI, 1144–45.

36. Ibid., XVII, 1329–31.

37. Ibid., XXX, 558–59.

38. Ibid., XXXVIII, 544, 1837.

39. Ibid., XV, 1112–13; XXXV, 117, 127–29, 285.

40. Ibid., XXVIII, 409–14; XVII, 608–29; XXVIII, 369–400, 429–40, 471–72.

41. Ibid., XVIII, 374, 385.

42. *Westminster Review,* July 1825, pp. 60–88.

43. *Examiner,* September 20, 1840; February 26, 1842; April 15, August 5, 1843; April 27, 1844; January 9, June 5, 1847; *Spectator,* February 13, 1841, p. 904; December 30, 1843, p. 1233; April 5, 1845, p. 325; September 20, 1845, p. 927.

44. *Edinburgh Review,* April, 1845, p. 507, 513, and 498–525.

45. Ibid., March, 1829, pp. 159–89.

46. *Westminster Review,* July 1829, pp. 254–67.

47. *London Review,* July 1835, pp. 342, 370, and 341–71; Mineka, *Early Letters of J. S. Mill,* II, 434.

48. Hansard, XXXVI, 699.

49. Ibid., XXXVI, 29–31.

50. Leader, *Roebuck,* pp. 92–93.

51. "On the Means of Conveying Information," *Pamphlets for the People* (1835), I, 9; "Trade Unions," ibid., p. 9.

52. Leader, *Roebuck,* pp. 125–36, 142.

53. Hansard, LXIII, 28, 33, 52, 83.

54. Ibid., XCIX, 879–906, 222, 226–30.

55. Ibid., XXXVI, 1331.

56. Ibid., XXXVI, 13335.

57. Ibid., XL, 255–57, 516–25.

58. *The Westminster Review,* January 1838, pp. 503–33; *Spectator,* August 4, 1838, p. 731; October 27, 1838; November 23, 1839, p. 1111; November 30, 1839, p. 1133.

59. *Examiner,* March 30, 1844; *Globe,* March 22, 1844; *Spectator,* April 12, 1844.

60. Hansard, LIII, 1199; LVIX, 1086; LVI, 451; XXIII, 842; XXIV, 1062.

61. Ibid., LXXXVI, 928–29; LXXVII, 660.

62. Ibid., XCIII, 275–76; XXIII, 1096–97.

63. Ibid., LXXI, 86–87.

64. Ibid., LVIII, 1357; LIII, 1093; LV, 109–10.

65. *Westminster Review,* September 1840, p. 384.

66. Hansard, LXII, 867; XVI, 1119.

67. Ibid., LXXXIII, 405–406.

68. Ibid., XCVII, 658.

69. Anon., ed., *The Free Trade Speeches of the Right Hon. Charles Pelham Villiers* (1883), p. xvi.

70. Donald G. Barnes, *A History of the English Corn Laws* (1930) pp. 220–22.

71. Hansard, XLII, 922; LX, 657.

72. *Westminster Review,* September 1840, pp. 384–86; April 1834, pp. 296, 469; October 1836, pp. 207–209; July 1842, p. 86; May 1843, p. 488; August p. 150; September 1844, pp. 3, 44, 134; March 1845, pp. 163, 167.

73. Hansard, 1844, LXXII, 244; 1846, LXXXIV, 1259.

74. Ibid., 1847, LXXXIX, 1185.

75. *Westminster Review,* July 1842, p. 86.

76. Hansard, LXXXVIII, 728.

77. Ibid., XXXVII, 25.

78. Ibid., XXXV, 730.

79. Ibid., XCI, 1183.

80. Ibid., XX, 142.

81. *Westminster Review,* June 1844, 358–60; September 1844; p. 101.

82. Ibid., April 1848, pp. 110, 183.

83. Finer, *Chadwick,* pp. 85–95, 147–53, 229.

84. Hansard, XX, 148.

85. Ibid., LXXXI, 352.

86. John Bowring, *The Works of Jeremy Bentham* (1844), IX, 5, 24.

87. Ibid., pp. 428–48.

88. Elie Halevy, *The Growth of Philosophical Radicalism* (1955), pp. 508–24.

89. Hansard, LXXIII, 1434–36.

90. *Spectator,* April 13, 1844, p. 346; *Examiner,* August 20, 1842; April 6, July 13, 1844.

GLADSTONE
AND THE CONSCIENCE OF THE STATE

Deryck Schreuder

> Mr. Gladstone has said the State ought to have a conscience—
> but it has not a conscience. Can *he* give it a conscience? Is he to
> impose his own conscience on the State? He would be very
> glad to do so, if it would thereby become the State's con-
> science. But that is absurd. He must deal with facts. It has a
> thousand consciences, as being in its legislative and executive
> capacities, the aggregate of a hundred minds—that is, it has no
> conscience.—*J.H. Newman to W.E. Gladstone, 18 April 1845*[1]

GLADSTONE was never slow in drawing moral lessons out of political
practice. Yet the manner in which moral idealism actually came to shape
political practice was often far less clear. There were, however, two notable occasions in his extended public career of more than sixty years
when he offered something like a systematized explanation of his views
on morality and the workings of politics, suggested how conscience was
to apply to the actual constitutional processes of the Victorian state, and
indicated the fundamental importance in his own thought of an ethical
political philosophy which went beyond that of party–political program
alone. "Do not let us suppose this is like the old question between Whig
and Tory," as he characteristically informed the electors and non-
electors of Midlothian in his great campaign of the later 1870s. "What we
are disputing about is a whole system of Government."[2]

Gladstone's first declaration on the moral character of government
came in 1838 when he drafted *The State in its Relations with the Church*,
at the age of 29. The second occasion arose in 1868, some thirty-five
years after he had first entered the House of Commons, when he was
now aged 59—and Prime Minister for the first of four times—and took
the form of *A Chapter of Autobiography*. His first statement consisted
of 750 pages of diffuse language, in two volumes, in which he argued for
the very high ideal of a union of church and state to produce the Anglican utopia of a moral polity in the United Kingdom. His mature reflections were contained in a brief, lucid, and highly readable, best-selling

pamphlet of 54 pages. In this document, published on the occasion of Irish Church disestablishment, he eschewed the abstraction of his earlier declaration, offering instead the highly practical political credo of a man who had completely inverted his firmly announced views on the conscience of the state, while still holding earnestly to fundamental ideals concerning the moral purpose and function of the state.

I would like to explore those two points in his thought, particularly as they related to his evolving political ideas, together with the changing meaning which Gladstone gave to the phrase common to this volume of essays, "the conscience of the state." My aim is a general essay of synthesis and summary which speculates on the major conceptual underpinnings of Gladstone's mature "conscience politics" as revealed in Gladstone scholarship, Morley to Matthew. Only indirectly will it comment on the manner in which the image of the young Anglican idealist of 1838 dissolved into the familiar, craggy features of the powerful politician and single-minded prophet of Christian liberalism of 1868.

1838: Anglicanism, Toryism, and the Condition of England

Gladstone's initial answer to the "Condition of England Question" was his publication of *The State in its relations with the Church* (first edition August 1838; fourth enlarged and revised edition, April 1841). This verbose work was an integral part of his early and stern conservatism. "The work attempted to . . . inquire and determine whether the existing state of things was worth preserving and defending against encroachment from whatever quarter," he recalled in 1868. "The question it decided emphatically in the affirmative."[3] The tone of the volumes was set by the dedication: "Inscribed to THE UNIVERSITY OF OXFORD; tried, and not found wanting, through the vicissitudes of a thousand years; in the belief that she is Providentially designed to be a fountain of blessings, spiritual, social, intellectual, to this and to other countries, to the present and future times; and in the hope that the temper of these pages may be found not alien from her own." The ten chapters which followed duly reflected the mind of an intense and romantic young Anglican idealist confronting—or at least reacting to—the massive political and social changes taking place in early Victorian England.

It is interesting to notice the different responses of father and son in the Gladstone family to the public scene at the time. The reaction of John Gladstone, as the wealthy Lancashire merchant and Tory head of the family, was to concede such reforms as were absolutely necessary to preserve the status quo, and then to qualify them as much as possible. The response of "son William"—as the father docketed the letters of his fifth child and third son—was implacably to oppose the currents of change, regarding the potential victory of the liberal reformers as tantamount to the victory of the forces of the anti-Christ. Eton and Christ Church had removed the young Gladstone from the immediacy of sociopolitical realities he might well have absorbed in Liverpool. He made a name for himself in the Oxford Union by the purity of his conservatism and by the vehemence of his opposition to reform. Among his earliest political documents were two anti-reform handbills (23 April 1831) in which he happily conflated *reform* and *revolution,* and listed the effects of constitutional change in South America, France, and Belgium as "Confusion . . . Disorganisation . . . [and] Starvation." He called on all voters to support candidates "who are solemnly pledged . . . TO RESIST REVOLUTION TO DEATH. And may God send a happy issue."[4]

Gladstone duly entered public life as the pious, earnest and priggish MP for Newark—a convenient and corrupt Tory seat. As he later frankly recalled: "I had in me more fanaticism than piety: [and] the fanaticism in me was not held in check by such piety as there was to hand" (1896). His initial involvement in the life of Westminister merely appears to have propelled him further along his own lines of development, which took him even further from practical politics. His private journal (now published to 1868 as *The Gladstone Diaries*) well reveals just how brittle and excitable, how emotional and idealized, was his response to the era. He steeped himself in Anglican dogma and literature—Hooker, Paley, Warburton, Arnold, Coleridge, and Palmer—as he contemplated the ideal moral order in the state, and most especially on the role of the church therein. He yearned to devise a systematic, Anglican response to the march of events. He also interested himself in spiritual movements, such as the Irvingites, with millennarian tendencies; at the height of the reform crises he speculated on the apocalypse soon—"surely the actual signs of the times are as should make us ready for the coming of our Lord."

It was this intense religious sensibility which drew Gladstone intimately into Tractarianism and into close association with certain leading divines in the Oxford Movement.[5] The stress on personal holiness, and the theological concern to revivify the Roman Catholic Church by a new emphasis on teaching the Divine Truths of Scripture, made the Oxford Movement deeply attractive to Gladstone. He was also fascinated with the idea of the church as a moral society, which further moved him to consider the possibilities of England as a Christian community. Gladstone was not, however, a typical Tractarian. Most important of all, he rejected Hurrell Froude's proposition that the state was too evil to deserve the Church. In the eyes of the young Gladstone, the state desperately needed the visible church to redeem it from its secular tendencies. And even going beyond that, he felt it vitally necessary that religion be established in the workings of government. He could accordingly write to a clerical friend, "I . . . find myself recognising with you a conscience of truth in governments, and an attested Divine commission as the basis of the powers and functions of the Church."[6]

So determined was he in this view that he came to insist on the "incalculable advantages of an Establishment," which gave a conscience to the state. It was the church which alone could "consecrate the functions of the governors considered as individuals"; for the governors acted "as the vital organic principle of that society which we term the nation, which, acting in and by them, must hallow that action by religion, which religion must have a definite form, and I need not say a definite form of State religion is a Church Establishment." In short: "in the best polity, [and] the polity which would be best, we must have a State religion."[7]

Manning and some Tractarians tried to press upon Gladstone the practical problems which this high establishment theory raised: toleration of Dissenters and the growing number of English Nonconformists; Ireland and Roman Catholicism in the United Kingdom as a whole; and the fallen state of the Anglican Church itself. Gladstone preferred not to see these difficulties in their full import. It would, after all, have left his moral ideal without a means of advancement. Instead, he continued to argue that if the private conscience of devout Anglicans was "the inner citadel of the Church," as he indeed believed, then the established Church was in turn to supply the inner soul of the state. His ultimate aim was "the greatest holiness of the greatest number."

Richard Hooker had in the 1590s provided the classic Anglican establishment ideal, in his *Of the Laws of Ecclesiastical Polity,* when he had written of how "with us one society is both Church and commonwealth," an estate which was "according to the pattern of God's own ancient elect people."[8] Gladstone provided a variant on that ideal, in almost as lofty language, in his *State and Church:* "The State and Church have both of them moral agencies. But the State aims at character through conduct: the Church at conduct through character: in harmony with which, the State forbids more than it enjoins, the Church enjoins more than it forbids. The Church brings down from heaven a divine principle of life, and plants it in the centre of the human heart to work outwards to leaven the whole mass."[9]

It was not very difficult to see what was wrong with the prescription of *State and Church* as it related to the immediate, practical ills of the body politic in the later 1830s. As an answer to the politics of the "Condition of England Question" his book was largely irrelevant. And indeed even before it had been subjected to hard public scrutiny, Gladstone had already admitted, to Pusey, the limits of his establishment-conscience thesis as a strategy to confront the march of events: "I told him, for himself only—I thought my own Church and State principles within one stage of becoming hopeless as regards success in this generation."[10] In E. R. Norman's phrase, even as Gladstone published *State and Church,* he became aware of the need "to scramble back to constitutional realities."[11]

Within a few years, through a combination of realities absorbed in his role as a junior minister in Peel's great administration (1841–46) and intellectual assaults on his treatise—not least by Macaulay in a famous article for the *Edinburgh Review,* April 1839—Gladstone was in fact moved to admit the utter futility of his early abstract ideals. It was simply impossible to create a confessional Christian state in England by the agency of a reformed Anglican Church acting in alliance with the Tory party. "The State cannot be said now to have a conscience, at least not by me," he wrote bleakly to Newman in April 1845, "inasmuch as it acts, and acts wilfully, and intends to go on acting, in such a way as no conscience— that is no personal conscience (which is the only real form of one)—can endure."[12]

In the strain of moving to that honest conclusion, Gladstone gave some consideration to a withdrawal from politics. He admitted that his initial conception of the political process had been archaic, and had reflected a "fanaticism" of religious outlook, as well as an "ideology" which was "feeble and inconsequent."[13] Moreover, his involvement in politics had, from the beginning, been hedged about with delicate considerations of private conscience. In *State and Church* he had warned that the pious Anglican in public life "ran a thousand hazards of sinking into a party man, instead of a man employing party instrumentally for its ulterior purpose"; and in his formal proposal of marriage to Catherine Glynne in the next year, 1839, he had thought it proper to alert her to his own very particular and qualified connection to politics.

In fact, Gladstone's instincts were fundamentally political. He had vast energy and considerable ambition to fulfill himself by manipulating men and events. And while he cared little for the closed society of party politics *per se,* he was absolutely absorbed with the possibilities of the state as an ethical polity, an agency of moral progress in a God-given world, and with the role of the visible church therein. It was for this reason that Gladstone was always inclined to view his early work, *State and Church,* as a noble error, rather than a contemptible one.

July 14, 1894 Some of my errors

> . . . It may perhaps be thought that among these errors I ought to record the publication in 1838 of my first work. Undoubtedly that work was written in total disregard or rather ignorance of the conditions under which alone political action was possible in matters of religion . . .
>
> But I think there is more to be said. The land was overspread with a thick curtain of prejudice. The foundations of the historic Church of England . . . were obscured. The Evangelical movement with all its virtues and merits had the vice of individualising religion in a degree perhaps unexampled and rendering the language of Holy Scripture . . . little more than a jargon. . . . [There was also] the antagonism of Protestantism to Popery which had been taken up by Dr Chalmers in his recent lectures on Church Establishments, the wretched error of which confounds Church and world, and introverts their positions. . . .
>
> To meet the demands of the coming time it was a matter of vital necessity to cut away through all this darkness to a clearer and more solid position. Immense progress has been made in that direction during my lifetime and I am inclined to think that my book imparted a certain amount of stimulus to the public mind, and made some small contribution to the needful process in its earliest stage.

Moreover, not only did the young Gladstone perceive a positive moral role for the visible church in the public scene, but he wished to draw the state into his scheme for Christian regeneration. Thus while his *State and Church* may well have contained all the wrong answers for the immediate ills of the nation, he in fact still possessed the capacity to ask the central question: what was to be the nature and the range of the moral authority of government in the modern state? It is certainly revealing that as early as 1837 Gladstone could remark to Manning that a critical question of the hour was "how the principle of Catholic Christianity" was to be "applied in these evil and presumptuous days to the conduct of public affairs."[14]

Not so surprisingly, therefore, in the aftermath of the collapse of his youthful and idealist thesis, Gladstone decided to remain in politics. His journal also now clearly shows a mounting fascination with departmental and cabinet administration, and with the nuances of power in executive government. At the time he tended to explain his continued political role on the grounds of "the actual relations of State to Religion" which still subsisted, and which accordingly offered "opportunities for good." Indeed, he could even legitimize his political role to Newman essentially on church-state grounds: "I think public life is tolerable, and in my case at present as it stands, obligatory. But it is like serving Leah afterwards to win Rachel." If this was so, then Gladstone was to serve Leah all his life, not to win Rachel. As Alec Vidler has rightly observed, the mature Gladstone "never thought out a doctrine of the relations of Church and State to take the place of the original one."[15]

Yet Gladstone's whole career presumed the existence of a conscience within the state—a moral deposit of Christian values which could be quarried for the building of a moral nation. His politics were in fact increasingly to witness to this, as he attempted to mobilize the forces of righteousness in a variety of enthusiasms, initiatives, and missions in the public life of the state; and as he attempted to "work the institutions of the State" in a manner progressive by the lights of the new political economy *and* the ancient traditions of Christian dogma, toward what he termed "the moral government of this world." Above all, he wished to moralize the political culture of the state.

How then is this historical transformation in his thought and method to be explained? If he had been forced to abandon his early Anglican and Tory ideal of a conscience "established" in government, where now lay the conscience of the state? And if it was no longer possible to speak of the state expressing the moral personality of the nation, what did conscience imply in his political thought?

Conscience and Politics: The "Experiments in Truth"

"Faith proves nothing but its existence," a modern biographer has observed, "but in biography it requires to be allowed for."[16] In Gladstone's case this is more than usually true. It is not necessary to presuppose that his version of Christian conscience in fact always kept Gladstone on the side of the angels, to perceive that his religious faith deeply informed his private and political actions. Whether Gladstone was always true to the tenets of his faith is a question separate from speculation on the motivation and character of his thought.

For Gladstone, conscience obviously meant a sharp sense of right and wrong, a Christian standard by which actions in private and political life were to be governed. Conscience was, according to the journal of the young Gladstone (3 December 1833), "the Christian secret"—"we have only to ascertain among many acts offering themselves to us, which is most agreeable to conscience and to the law of God as by the answer to the question all the rest are set aside." That simple, if comfortable, view soon suffered the rude shock imposed by the complexities of the political world. The maturing Gladstone was quick to discern that it was not possible to know with any sureness what God thought about free trade, democracy, social policy, or foreign affairs. Yet this was no reason to surrender the political sphere to secular or utilitarian standards of conduct. Gladstone was determined to link conscience to public actions, rather than allow his ardent Anglicanism to become a kind of private mysticism. He worked indeed from the fundamental belief that "all action (not 75% as M. Arnold says) is moral." His three-volume edition of the *Works* of the eighteenth-century divine, Bishop Butler, begins with the declaration that "All duty . . . is to be regarded from a religious point of view, and all human life is charged with duty" (1896).

Gladstone's view of public life, and his understanding of the greater events in the historical existence of the state, also drew upon the ancient Christian doctrine of Providence in a manner so important, yet so personal, that it poses the deepest problem of analysis. "Belief in God surely implies much more than that He is superhuman and imperceptible," as Gladstone wrote in the *Edinburgh Review* of March 1877: "Over and above what He is Himself, He is conceived of as standing in certain relation to us; as carrying on a moral government of the world. He is held to prescribe and favour what is right; to forbid and regard with displeasure what is wrong; and to dispose the course of events in such a way that, in general and upon the whole, there is a tendency of virtue to bring satisfaction and happiness, and of vice to entail the reverse of these, even when appearances and external advantages might not convey such an indication."

Gladstone accordingly saw the "laws of this moral government" extending intimately into both public and private life. He believed indeed that even at a complex social level the tides of man are Providentially shaped. He held, for example, that the moral failures of nations and their rulers—wars, aggression, despotism—were intimately related to God's redemptive lessons for mankind. Further, great cataclysmic events and tragedies, such as the Irish famine, were also dependent upon the Providential will. "Here is a calamity most legibly Divine," as he wrote privately to Manning in 1847 of the suffering in Ireland; "there is a total absence of such second causes as might tempt us to explain it away. . . . How can the handwriting be made clear against us if it is not clear now?"[17] Acceptance of the Doctrine of Providence did not, however, imply mere quiescence in the face of such events: rather it called for a spiritual response in the nation. In the case of Ireland, Gladstone advocated mortification in England, coupled with remedial policy for Ireland.

In fine, if history did indeed reveal "the steady march and coming of the Lord's kingdom," as Gladstone held, then it was the function of Christianity in the nation, working through the conscience of the individual citizens, to bring the life of the state "into conformity with the blessed Pattern given us." In times past this had proceeded through the invocation works of the moral leaders of the community. That was still to apply, but in the modern state moral progress could also proceed through the state itself—the great collective expression of national ethical sensibilities. "There has been a great shaking in our times; and many have done no more than substitute a new set of mere opinions for the old," as the mature Gladstone reflected on the great transformation of British society under the impact of industrialism. "But the foundation of the Lord standeth sure; He will find instruments for His work, in His time, and happy are we if we are among them."

By the close of his extended career in high office, Gladstone inclined to see a natural moral harmony between Providential will and the progress of the age. The nineteenth century had, in overall perspective, marked an advance toward "the moral government of the world." The era of *laissez-faire* liberalism was a tribute not merely to the Utilitarian idea of progress but also to the divine idea. The age had been "predominantly a history of emancipation—that is enabling man to do his work of emancipation, political, economical, social, moral, intellectual."

The doctrine also, not so surprisingly, found Gladstone absolutely accepting that the events of his own life and that of his family were simply in the gift of Providence. Some of the most poignant passages in his extraordinary journal relate to this, particularly with respect to his wife, to his children, to suffering, and to death. He struggled with Christian obedience. He also found in prayer and the Scriptures what he read to be inspiration for public action in the name of Christian values applied to the complexities of the world. His public life was avowedly dependent upon his Christianity. The result was an enormously powerful force of eager will.

An early decision in his life led him to record in his journal a strong sense of "Divine purpose pointing to the path I have chosen, though it is not a thing to be noised abroad." Over fifty years later he could document his post-Midlothian triumph in not dissimilar idiom: "Looking calmly on this course of experience, I do believe that the Almighty has employed me for His purpose in a manner larger and more special than before, and has strengthened me and led me on accordingly." In the midst of the debate on Irish home rule—that veritable serbonian bog of political entanglement which ensnared politicians then and historians now

—Gladstone could record simply and tantalizingly: "What we have all to look at is the accomplishment of God's work in the world by those whom He seems to choose as instruments." This ultimately private view of events can never of course be proved—or disproved—as an explanation of motivation. It has simply to be "allowed for."

The importance of Christian dogma and practice in Gladstone's statesmanship is not beyond some degree of measure. It gave character and style to his politics, as well as his political ideas; and, even more immediately, it deeply shaped what is now termed his "personality formation." It certainly lay at the source of his indominatable will and his rather closed method of developing his inimitable political interventions and missions. A titanic struggle with self, with original sin, and attempts to divine and hold true to Christian criteria of action, can now be seen to have formed the inner history of the famed outer career. "Few people take easily to a plan of self-improvement," Patrick White has written in his great novel *Voss*. "Some discover early their perfection cannot stand the insult. Others find their intellectual pleasures lie in theory not the practice. Only a few stubborn ones will blunder on, painfully out of the luxuriant world of their pretensions into the desert of mortification and reward." There was to be much intense mortification in Gladstone's own struggles with sin, justification, and salvation; and the forty-one folio volumes of his life's journal are soaked in it. But there was also indeed reward. Christian practice subjected his intense and volatile emotions, as well as his high sexuality, to massive if not quite complete control. It was the basis of his formidable powers for concentrated work. It harnessed great wellings of sentiment and passion for creative, controlled use. It most probably provided him with such personally precious gifts as moral courage, magnanimity, and confidence. In short, Christian practice and conscience gave Gladstone key qualities of character; and it indicated, in ways only he fully understood, what he perceived to be a general sense of purpose in an age of immense change. Gladstone was acutely aware that "politics are like a labyrinth," filled with "ironic intricacies" (memorandum, 19 March 1894). For that very reason he gave unremitting attention to the great problem of relating isolated events, fractured pieces of knowledge, and the generally distracting swirl of party-political conflict and strategy at Westminster to the larger, discernible patterns of historical change, together with their ultimate meaning for moral progress in the state. He increasingly admired Daniel O'Connell for the Liberator's centrality of purpose in the buffeting of public life: "his boomerang always came back."[18]

Gladstone's private and public life found its focus in his driving

Christian concern to account for life to God: this is the major feature of his journal and probably its rationale. He was possessed of a passion to "redeem the time"—St. Paul's famous injunction to Christians. He advocated a strict routine of tightly disciplined life to his son Willy, in 1854, as a means to making the best accountable use of every hour in the day: "this division of time itself goes far towards securing its proper use, and giving to our life that constancy and earnestness of purpose without which it can neither be pleasing to God nor honourable in the eyes of men."[19] Gladstone's own method of redeeming the time took such personal forms as prayer and fasting coupled with Anglican ritual, charity, and missionary work. He also, most significantly, came to redeem the time through public service and administration. His journal carefully records the hours spent in public work as time morally expended. This became so much a feature of his evolving career in the Peel administration that despite his rigorous sabbatarianism—he counted himself an inveterate "twicer" at church on Sunday—cabinet meetings on the Lord's Day became acceptable forms of service in a God-given world.

Interpreting the mysteries of Providence in public life, through faith and conscience, was of course not only awesomely complicated but fraught with the all too real dangers of confusing personal will and ego with the Divine Plan. Gladstone himself was not entirely blind to this fact, as some of his more self-rebuking entries in the journal indicate. He knew he could judge individuals and strategies quite wrongly; he worried very greatly over ego and ambition; above all he feared "the subtle powers of self-deception" (memorandum 16 July 1892). Late in life he also recorded at some length (7 November 1894), what he took to be his grossest errors in public life, dividing them into "general misdirections of policy" and "what may be called errors of occasion."

Contemporaries were also not reticent to point out his failings to Gladstone.[20] For example: Bagehot spoke for those who doubted in 1860 Gladstone's claim to essential consistency, in political positions, in his shift from the Tory to the Liberal party; Labouchere wittily articulated that sense of irritation which Gladstone's moral earnestness provoked, in remarking that he did not mind an ace up Mr. G.'s sleeve, but he did object to the claim that Providence had put it there; and Salisbury, most trenchantly of all, as a devout fellow Anglican who yet had graver reservations about the mystery of immediately interpreting Providential will, questioned the inspirational source of Gladstone's major initiatives in the public scene. "What could his motive . . . have been?" he asked in the *Quarterly Review* (July 1866) of Gladstone's apparently sudden enthusiasm for franchise reform. Setting aside as facile the notion that it derived merely from simple "sincere conviction"—"It is difficult to use such a phrase in reference to Mr. Gladstone's mind"—Salisbury drew attention to Gladstone's often overbearingly eager will:

> His ambition has guided him in recent years as completely as it ever guided any statesman of the century; and yet there is not even a shade of untruth in the claim made for him by his friends that he is wholly guided by his convictions. The process of self-deceit goes on in his mind without the faintest self-consciousness or self-suspicion. . . . We should be forced to conclude that the conscience which activates him, though a very active organ, is, like some diseases, intermittent in its activity; and that its energy at the time of the paroxysms is fully made up by a simple torpidity during the intervals that come between . . . if we believe that Mr. Gladstone's mind is constructed upon any ordinary plan. The only mode of reconciling his sincerity with the facts, is to assume that the process by which the mind is made to accept the most advantageous or most convenient belief, is with him automatic and unconscious.

Salisbury could pen so brilliantly acerbic a view of Gladstonian politics simply because at their core *was* this extraordinary complex symbiotic relationship between ethical principles and acute sense of the opportune, between the moral imperative of conscience and the hard Parliamentary realities of power pragmatically wielded with such zeal.

The possibilities for endless scholarly debate exist in this matter. The intricacy of the Gladstonian mind, and its expression in public life, certainly require an analytic approach which is equally complex in probing the many layers—of ideas, ideals and impulses—out of which his politics grew. "When all the detail has been accummulated, we must prepare for a picture that is not at first glance a simple one," as Dom David Knowles once cautioned in a celebrated discussion of this very matter in his *The Historian and Character* (17 November 1954); whether a man as subtle as a Gladstone is at any time being true to his faith, to himself, and to his friends and colleagues, we "can only hope to know, if ever, from the fullest indications of a biographer."

We still await a definitive life of Gladstone. But we can surely speculate on how he attempted to conceptualize the means to moral progress through public action in the state. Clearly, he did not propose to erect yet another abstract edifice of ethical idealism. That he surrendered with the last edition of *State and Church*. Rather, through a painful and tardy process of mental adjustments—at age 35 (in 1846) he could still admit to seeing politics as essentially an abstract function devoid of "the elements of flesh and blood which counts for so much"—he developed moral stances which attempted to reflect both the imperatives of conscience and the rigors of political realities. In the view of the editor of the

Gladstone Diaries, who has provided the most incisive explanation yet of the evolution of Gladstonian political idealism, the young politician abandoned the abstract bias of *State and Church,* if not its ethical goals, and now worked increasingly to "arrive at a series of practical positions which would further national moral progress."[21]

If we accept that trenchant view of Gladstone's gradual intellectual metamorphosis—from moral idealist to moral pragmatist—then Christian conscience was obviously no infallible guide to the development of detailed policy and legislative statute, nor indeed to the creation of a systematized set of beliefs retrospectively dubbed "Liberalism." The politics of the mature Gladstone are much better seen—to adapt a Gandhian image—as practical experiments in truth. Rather than expressing a rigid political ideology, Gladstonian politics represented instead a series of evolving strategies, policies, postures, enthusiasms, missions, and tactical forays, which formed the pragmatic expression of intensely held ethical yearnings and basic, sometimes commonplace, presumptions about the *laissez-faire* state. Gladstonian liberalism was, in so many ways, more a method than an ideology; if it was to be defined in any precise sense it was best considered in the light of what it excluded.[22] Its major characteristic was its capacity to express changing and specific meanings for unchanging moral verities; and in that regard was not unlike Newman's view of "development" in Christian thought and faith. Gladstone's politics thus found him constantly boxing the compass of conscience as he tried to map practical paths to moral progress in the public life of the state. In his extraordinarily complex life-journey in high politics, he saw his Christianity as offering what Bishop Butler had referred to as "moral insight" in dealing with the business of this world. Gladstone shared with Newman, too, the deep if mysterious notion that "Faith is knowledge."[23] Here was a critical point of departure for the moral traveller and high-minded man of ambition.

Politics also, of course, reflected the stimulus and constraints of the contemporary public environment. Each major issue raised was to be given a close contextual assessment, which involved the dynamics of party-political life, before being translated into legislative or diplomatic form—quite apart from being theologically tested. The ultimate result was a strikingly personal brand of politics, which fitted ill under the banner of Liberal or Conservative. It is not uninstructive that the mature Gladstone appears as a "Liberal-conservative" until 1870 in Dod's Parliamentary handbook. For at the heart of his deepest view of the political process was probably the tension which existed between these polar points in his own intellectual makeup. He himself constantly stressed the conservationist aims of his reforming public actions, whether domestic or international. But his method of accomplishing these stabilising ends often involved strikingly new, and sometimes radical policies and postures. Conservation would only truly work, as he frequently indicated, if it was based on essentially moral social and political bulwarks. It was "justice", however complex, which made for stability in an age not only of improvement but of highly de-stabilizing change. In his determination to offer a personal set of answers to the problems of reconciling the old and new world, the organic and industrial society, he came to act in a manner which defies neat ideological tags. Gladstone was essentially Gladstone. Party became the vehicle for his zealous will, his capacity for administrative work, his cabinet aspirations, and his version of conscience politics.

This is manifestly revealed when the general style and content of Gladstonian politics is considered. His method of developing moral political insight on the greater issues of state was strikingly and essentially personal: it ranged from instructing himself in the political economists, the writings of political philosophers such as Burke, and the works of the great historians, to a fascination with the ideal form of the state discussed in such classical authors as Aristotle and Homer. He also drew much from the literary legacy of the patriarchs of the church: St. Augustine, above all, offered a remarkably practical thesis for the moral pragmatist on crucial questions of human rights and the exercise of power, within and between states, in his concern to expose the "lust for domination" in mankind.[24] Gladstone's foreign policy ideas thus owed much to the great African. Within the domestic environment, Gladstone's mind was early shaped by the major Anglican theologians as well as the Cranmer Prayer Book. His abiding fascination with variants on the theme of the confessional Christian state most directly reflected that tradition of writings which went back to Hooker.

Christian dogma and idealism also intruded on his capacity for intellectual growth, and may indeed have been the critical catalyst in its dynamic character. "The Christian is particularly called to carry his thinking outside that framework which a nation or a political party or a social system or an accepted regime or a mundane ideology provides," Herbert Butterfield has asserted in his noted essay on *Christianity, Diplomacy and War* (1953). Gladstone's openness to new ideas, and the creative feature in the growth of his thought—an organic process which never really reached stasis—reflected such a capacity constantly to rethink the critical questions of his times. This did not mean, as a consequence, any orthodox move steadily to the left (or to the right) in the political spectrum: the fundamentals of social theory, political economy, and moral individualism which he had developed early in life tethered Gladstone too tightly. But it could mean dramatic initiatives in state policy—Irish disestablishment, Bulgarian agitation, Irish home rule—as he moved to deal with an intractable or inflammatory problem at source in his pursuit of moral order in the world. In effect, it also meant that he radiated a sense of optimal possibility, itself a reflection of his determination to test all major issues against his conception of moral justice in society.

A strong, almost overwhelming sense of evangelical conscience, also provided a powerful moral framework within which Gladstone could draw together what were not always harmonious political positions and policies. Christian moralism here acted as the ethical compound which might hold together, in artificial suspension as it were, the constantly adjusting Gladstonian response to specific issues of policy. His immensely powerful, vivid, and elaborate rhetoric increasingly assisted this function. His oratory, with its unashamed scriptural imagery and metaphor, became the vehicle by which a moral exegesis could be placed on a range of distinct administrative, diplomatic, and commercial activities on the part of the nation. As one eminent late-Victorian writer acutely observed, Gladstone had the extraordinary capacity to spiritualize material things.

This was to be of critical importance in Gladstone's emergence as a mass politician. He was among the first political figures to have his personality, or at least a version of it, projected to a mass audience. Accordingly, what he was came to count for almost as much as what he did. He was seen to be earnest even in an age of earnestness. John Keble could even refer to the young Gladstone as "Pusey in a blue coat." [25] Gladstone did not give up smiling or take to wearing a hairshirt, as Pusey had once done; but the analogy was not inapposite in other respects. Earnestness and moral solemnity, a solicitous concern for the dignity of the individual elector, and the high tone of his conscience politics—it was these elements which first made Gladstone into "the People's William"—not the ringing and ineffectually qualified views on the franchise question. "What Gladstone was offering was emotional subsistence level," as our authority on the formation of the Liberal party has observed; "commitment, the possibility of participation, antagonism, struggle, eventual victory, a sense of power and domination—to people normally entirely subject to circumstances and to other people. The permanent issue behind Midlothian and Reform and Home Rule was what kind of people should have power, in whose name, and in accordance with whose ideas. Gladstone offered the psychic satisfaction of ruling to the ruled. . . . Gladstone offered this for what it was, and the people accepted it for what it was—a question of self-determination and of the union of hearts: not of bread. Nobody deluded anybody."[26]

The twentieth-century eye, looking through largely secular and post-Freudian lenses, almost invariably focuses attention on Gladstone's piety and puritanism as exemplars—either frightening or amusing—of a peculiarly Victorian frame of mind. And we all now know that the Gladstone bag contained the Gladstone whip. A society more nearly Christian—at least in common ideals, imagery, language, thought, and ritual—could find considerable identity with a man who made no secret of either his Christian idealism or his solemn Augustinian view of life as duty, a man who invited his audience to share this personal philosophy in confronting the world. Through his participation in the major issues of state, domestic and foreign, Gladstone accordingly managed to convey to an avid and avowedly moral mass constituency in the nation—which cut across class and region in a unique manner—what he took to be the true reality and solemnity of life. And he did so in language which congregation and chapel would instantly recognize. The world, in this vision, was "merely a large room into which it has pleased God to place us"; public as much as private life was to reflect "the deep meaning, the enduring effects, especially upon ourselves of all we think and do; the immense opportunities which God opens for us; the unbounded riches of that field . . . that all must traverse, but that few will cultivate at all, and that only the choicest saints of God cultivate so that it yields them an hundredfold."[27] In short, the Christian culture and conscience of Victorian Britain provided Gladstone with a mass audience which enabled him to become—in Professor Vincent's phrase—a "folk myth."

Gladstone was ever acutely aware of the gulf between church and state as symbols of the divine and mortal. "What a contrast between the voices of melody in the sanctuary today," he noted in his journal on Sunday, 27 June 1841, during a vigorous election campaign, "and the voice of contention in the market place without its wall tomorrow: the voices of the Church and the world in their outward form." But just as he was not naturally ascetic, so he was not naturally an intellectual or spiritual recluse, no matter how intense his awareness of sin or his concern for personal salvation. "I felt as if one side of me, which lies towards the world, were like ice," his journal reads in the year of *State and Church*; but significantly he added, "this is a dangerous and carnal state: indifference to the world is not love of God." Gladstone was too well versed in Wilberforce's famed tract, *A Practical View . . . of Christianity* (1797), to believe that good works could ever earn salvation: justification came by faith alone. But faith in Gladstone's case presumed—in Milton's

phrase—an active virtue. In Gladstone's complex and manifold struggles, not for faith but for "worldly holiness" there was to be the kernel
and source of a driving public career.[28]

Gladstone as Peelite: Morality as High-Minded Pragmatism

A highly developed sense of Christian conscience, and a fierce concern for the moral imperative in the use of time, was hardly to turn Gladstone into a saintly figure. Machiavelli once suggested that a man "who
wishes to make a profession of goodness in everything must of necessity
come to grief among so many who are not good." Gladstone did not
come to grief as a politician: he was not really an unworldy figure; nor was
he a utopian. Nor, again, did he work politics merely through the abstraction of principle. As Cowling has rightly observed, "the language of principle is not the only language in which political ideas can be expressed."[29]
Gladstone was constantly concerned to devise specific, practical applica-
tions of Christian dogma and moral concerns. Political principle was
also to be adduced from the cumulative impact of high-minded pragmatism, and then expressed through the parliamentary process.

Gladstone's hagiographers have done him a great disservice in pre-
senting far too simplistic a portrait of "the good Mr. Gladstone." He was
as tough-minded and subtle as a Thomas More; his greatness as an individual and statesman lay in his concern to express truth, as he saw it, by
taking it into the center of the political arena. Here lay power for its implementation, and here also lay great fallibility in action itself. Gladstone
came to perceive his brand of ethical politics as developing out of the lib-
erating functions of government, where he was accordingly drawn into
all the inevitable problems for the individual conscience in high politics—
compromise, tact, strategy, party loyalty, cabinet solidarity, and the
temptations of personal ambition. The overall result was that Gladstone's public life hardly bore on questions of "saintliness."[30]

Moreover, the traditional dichotomy between the idealist and the
pragmatist is also particularly misleading when applied to a man like
Gladstone. What made him so powerful, and so complex, was his unique
blend of Augustinian moral gravitas and practical politics. Gladstone
had become Burke's best pupil in seeing an ultimate connection between
ideals and political context, between ethical ideas and their time of fruition. Gladstonian politics increasingly came to reflect the noted Burkeian
dictum that "circumstances, which some gentlemen pass for nothing,
give in reality to every political principle, its distinguishing and discrimi-

nating effect." The best analogy in establishing the character of Gladstone's politics is thus the law. Gladstone approached the constitution,
liberty, and reform as does a powerful jurist: liberty best survived in the
thickets of the statutes of the state; justice is given its finest expression in
the famed idiom of "natural law with a varying content."[31]

Detailed recent studies of the mature Gladstone working the institutions of the state have together also revealed this particular genius for
combining ethical urges with tough, tactical, and partisan maneuver. Indeed, as John Morley observed more than seventy years ago, "Hard as he
strove for a broad basis in general theory and high abstract ideal, yet always aiming at practical ends, he kept in sight the opportune."[32] Gladstone himself thought, in political terms, that if "Providence has endowed
me with anything which can be called a striking gift" it had been revealed
at "certain political junctures" in the form of "what may be termed appreciation of the general situation and its results." In short:

> To make good the idea, this must not be considered as the mere acceptance
> of public opinion, founded upon discernment that it has risen to a certain
> height needful for a given work, like a tide. It is an insight into the facts of
> particular eras, and their relations one to another, which generates in the
> mind a conviction that the materials exist for forming a public opinion, and
> for directing it to a particular end. [Unfinished autobiographical note,
> 1890s]

Of course there were occasions, notably over the Bulgars in 1876, when
opinion was already aroused before Gladstone moved to harness its
power, raised it to new heights of fervor, while offering himself as its
leader. But more frequently, the major initiatives in his politics developed from conjunctions involving his own sense of ethical values, political timing, and the ever-shifting tides of public opinion. "You cannot
. . . judge in the abstract what law ought or ought not to be passed at a
given time in a country like this," he stated to a Midlothian audience.
"You must have regard to the ripeness and the unripeness of public opinion, and favourable and unfavourable conjuncture of circumstances."

This stress on efficacy, as well as morality, gave peculiar distinction
to Gladstone's statesmanship. It also ensured that Gladstone measured
all potential political action by the gauge of its likely success. Gladstone
was not a relativist; his sense of principle and moral imperative was too
strong for that. But he *was* a tactical pragmatist. If he lost causes it was
only after he had initially assured himself that they were potentially win-
nable. His formulation of policy on electoral reform and on Irish Home
Rule was infused with the intelligence provided by his political antennae.

And his preference not to take up certain causes for which he in fact had an emotive and moral sympathy—such as the anti-vaccination campaign, or the fate of Russian Jews under the tsar's regime—further reflected on this sense of the tactical and the pragmatic in his thought.[33]

Gladstone once supplied readers of *The Times* (21 July 1863) with this general rule: "No Government ought to commit itself in any cause except where it is righteous, and . . . no cause is really righteous with reference to its being taken up by Governments, unless the objects that are contemplated are practicable and attainable."

It was during his political apprenticeship under Peel during the 1840s that Gladstone first appears to have arrived at this blend of the ethical, pragmatic, and opportune. He later readily admitted to learning from Peel the vital lesson that "the great art of Government was to work by such instruments as the world supplies, controuling and overruling their humours." With obvious fascination the maturing Gladstone observed how Peel conducted a high-minded stewardship of government—an administration which Gladstone increasingly believed *had* furthered national moral progress—through rigorously pragmatic means. In his journal he keenly noted how Peel's power derived not from principled theory, but from "the manifest and peculiar adaptation in Peel's mind to this age in which he lives, and its exigencies."

Peel's conduct of government provided Gladstone with practical experience of a kind of politics midway between utopian idealism and pursuit merely of partisan advantage. "What occurs to me in these discussions," he duly noted in his journal in 1844 after a series of heated cabinets over factory legislation, "is that Ministers are not in fact men of mere expediency as they are sometimes thought and called—that they act upon a strong, rigid and jealous sense of honour, and they are perpetually dwelling on principle as apart from expediency." The result was to make Gladstone as much of a Peelite as an Anglican in his approach to moral progress. "Abstract principles, urged without stint or mercy, provoke the counter-assertion of abstract principles in return," he could subsequently lecture a clerical correspondent; "The effect, in my opinion, of persistence in this course will, and must be, long adjournment of practical benefit."[34]

An increasingly important parliamentary role reinforced the lessons learned in cabinet. As Gladstone vividly reflected: Parliamentary debate subjected ideas to tough scrutiny, thereby "demanding the entire strength of a man and all his faculties," not unlike "a swimmer swimming for his life." It had also "a further advantage" if the MPs' "occupation be not mere debate but debate ending in work. For in this way, whether the work be legislative or administrative, it is continually tested by results, and he is enabled to strip away his extravagant anticipations, his fallacious conception, to perceive his mistakes, and to reduce his estimates to the reality" (9 November 1894).

Involvement in the day-to-day workings of a major administration had forced a lower focus on the intense Gladstonian concern for conscience and politics. It also indicated how he might apply his ethical yearnings and moral enthusiasms to the mundane and dense intricacies of government. The "government" he had in mind was not, of course, a utilitarian and intrusive state, but rather government as the liberator of individuals, the adjuster and reformer of institutions, the interlocuter between interest groups, the remover of commercial restraints, the vigilant guardian against fiscal profligacy and rising taxes, above all the agent of edification, the representative of responsible and moral opinion, the reconciler of the old and new social dynamics in the nation.

The Peelite experience of government began the integration of Gladstonian idealism with the great economic, commercial, and fiscal changes which formed the basis of the new industrial, *laissez-faire* state. Capitalism and conscience, political economy and the Scriptures were closely examined with both an ethical and practical eye for contradictions and then found to be in harmony: "The principle of the accumulation of stock or capital arises out of the division of labour. But the division of labour economises labour and multiplies its power. It seems therefore to be a beneficial and laudable use of the faculties which God has given us—and one that honours God" (memorandum, 31 January 1846). Here was the basis of the position which Gladstone adopted on a range of major domestic issues in the years ahead: poverty, unemployment, social reconstruction. Christianity had subsumed capital. Faith in the largely benign progress of liberal capitalism did not, however, mean moral complacency in dealing with the human consequences of industrialism. Gladstone could still reflect on the "thorough rottenness" of the cash-nexus bond in industrial societies, a "system which gathers together huge masses of population having no other tie to the classes above than that of employment."[35] But this was where the moral work of government entered, offering justice and edification through domestic reform and international peace for the free-trading state. Despite his later proclivity to conduct politics by "missions," the hallmark of Gladstone's politics in the 1850s and 1860s, when he secured his status as a leading cabinet-rank politician, and likely national leader, was a capacity to see public policy as a whole. As he clearly intimated to the editor of a leading quarterly journal in 1856, he stood firmly for "the policy of peace abroad, of economy, of financial equillibrium, of steady resistance to abuses, and the promotion of practical improvement at home, with a disinclination to questions of reform gratuitously raised." In fact: Peel in moral dress.

Gladstone's budgets of the 1850s occupied a special place in not merely completing the Peelite revolution in tariffs, and the routing of protection, but in setting out the general Gladstonian view of moral progress through cabinet and administrative leadership.[36] The major reforms in taxation and tariffs which he indeed advocated on 18 April 1853 accordingly embodied an attempt to unite economic individualism and personal freedom, economic growth and national social harmony, under the broad banner of laissez faire. "While we have sought to do justice, by the changes we propose in taxation, to intelligence and skill, as compared with property—while we have sought to do justice to the great labouring community of England by further extending them relief from indirect taxation, we have not been guided by any desire to put one class against another." Rather,

> by declining to draw any invidious distinction between class and class, by adopting it to ourselves as a sacred aim to diffuse and distribute . . . with equal and impartial hand . . . we have the consolation of believing that . . . we contribute not only to develop the national resources of the country, but to knit the heart of the various classes of this great nation yet more than heretofore to the Throne and to those institutions under which it is their happiness to live.

The creative moral role of laissez faire was to be even more marked in the budget of 18 July 1859 and the Anglo-French Commercial Treaty of 1860. Domestic fiscal reform was coupled with free trading internationalism, highlighted by the signing of the Cobden-Chevalier commercial treaty. Reform of the tariff, remission in personal income tax, removal of paper duties for the press, and the Anglo-French agreement were recommended by Gladstone to the nation"not only on moral and social, and political, but also . . . on fiscal and economical grounds." Liberal capitalism, resting on the potential of laissez faire at home and in overseas trade was to produce moral *and* material progress. The House of Commons was duly informed on 10 February 1860—when Gladstone introduced the Anglo-French Treaty—that

> By pursuing such a course as this it will be in your power to scatter blessings among the people, and blessings which are among the soundest and most wholesome of all the blessings at your disposal, because in legislation of this kind you are not forging mechanical helps for men, nor endeavouring to do that for them which they ought to do for themselves; but you are enlarging

the means without narrowing their freedom, you are giving value to their labour, you are appealing to their sense of responsibility, and you are not im-
pairing their sense of honourable self-dependence.

The new political economy was contrasted with the mercantalist era, and
was recommended as representing "the altered spirit and circumstances
of our times." Emancipation was to be the hallmark of legislation: "laws
which do not sap in any respect the foundations of duty or of manhood,
but which strike away the shackles from the arm of industry, which give
new incentive and new reward to toil, and which win more and more for
the Throne and for the institutions of the country the gratitude, the confidence, and the love of an united people."

A critical factor in the evolution of Gladstonian liberalism was accordingly to be a deep concern for institutional reform: the state must be
representative of responsible opinion, the new source of power, progress,
and legitimacy in government. This did not imply a levelling process toward social equality: "England is a great lover of liberty; but of equality
she has never been so much enamoured." Gladstone relied upon the capacity of the individual in a modern, yet Christian state, to provide the
creative moral power to solve the Condition of England Question. "It is
the individual mind, the individual conscience; it is the individual character, on which mainly human happiness or human misery depends."

Moral progress in the nation accordingly existed in the harmony
between the public conscience and the public institutions. And here
Gladstone had in mind not alone the central institutions of state at Westminster, but that myriad of smaller, local institutions of government in
the boroughs, counties, and parishes—the institutions most closely in
touch with popular moral sensibilities in the nation at large. "I am
friendly to local government. I am friendly to local privileges and power.
I desire, I may say I almost intensely desire, to see Parliament relieved of
some portion of its duties." Local government was moreover favored by
Gladstone as a means of political education for the emerging classes
within the new industrial state. He depicted local government as being
the critical agent "at the root of all our national aptitudes" for it taught
"the art of government in various and limited, but effective forms . . . to
those persons who have an opening towards public life." He accordingly
made a political principle out of an efficacious practice: "I am much attached to decentralising doctrines."[37]

In similar vein, Gladstone insisted naturally that the great problems
of modern societies could only be solved by the quickened moral opinion
in the nation itself, and not by the programme politics of an intervention-

ist state. "Those who propose to you [such] schemes . . . are quacks," he told the working men of Blackheath in his noted two-hour defense of Liberalism, in the cold rain of October 1871. "They are misled and beguiled by a spurious philanthropy . . . to delude you with phantasms, and to offer you glowing fruit which, when you attempt to taste it, will prove to be but ashes in your mouth." The great problems which he presumed his mass audience to have in mind were the problems of drink, the altered role of women in society—"how, without tampering with the cardinal laws that determine providentially their position in the world, how are we to remove the serious social inequalities under which I, for one, hold they labour?"—as well as the status of labor itself, economic disparity among the classes, and class friction. In each case it was most tempting to see the answer in some form of central state intervention. But this was a chimera, an only partial solution to the underlying moral issues involved. "Depend upon it, I do but speak the serious and solemn truth when I say that, within the political questions that are found upon the surface, lie deeper and more searching questions that enter into the breast'. Accordingly, the ultimate solution to such problems in society must reside in 'the conscience and mind of every man."

The domestic prescriptions for moral progress found corollaries in Gladstone's international politics. Foreign affairs generally reflected the development of his mature political ideas in two ways. First, European politics of revolution and nationalism in the mid-nineteenth century held up an external mirror in which Gladstone could review his own political theory. It was 1848, in France and Austria and Prussia, which reinforced evolving domestic notions about reform, revolution, and social order. It was Italy, and the famed *Letters to Lord Aberdeen,* which revealed his growing concern for the nationality of peoples and cultures, the likely consequences if it became a thwarted force, and the need to use such "natural" forces as the very means to ordered freedom, stability, and progress under law in the European states.[38]

Apart from acting as a constitutional laboratory for his domestic political ideas, international events in Europe and overseas also pressed Gladstone to develop ethical responses to the major foreign and imperial questions facing the British state in the half-century after the 1830s. The steps by which he established his mature version of a principled external policy were more spasmodic and less continuous than "the action of home causes," as he himself put it. Yet his connection with foreign and colonial affairs was extensive, and it began early through the Gladstone family. His father was deeply involved in overseas trade, was a leading West Indian sugar-estate absentee landlord and slave owner, and had close connections with the Canningite Tories: before William had declared for national self-determination in the celebrated Italian question, he had already celebrated the triumph of Greek nationalism in the conservative home of John Gladstone. Further, the sequence of major international problems which marked each decade from the young Gladstone's entry into the parliamentary arena in the 1830s—ranging from China policy and the opium trade, the revolutions in Europe of the 1840s, Italian, Crimean, and Ionian questions in the next decade, extending on to the Schleswig-Holstein and central European crises in the 1860s consequent upon the rise of Prussia to great power status, coupled with increasingly uneasy relations with the United States of America, and climaxing in the Balkan embroglios in the Near East in the 1870s—all forced him to bring his earnest Christian mentality to bear on the ethics of power in international politics and, in particular, on the role of Britain in the world. As an empire state, but also as a free-trading economy, Britain and her role abroad also moved the maturing Gladstone to devise practical views on the meaning of the colonial settlement connections, the problems of British frontier advances in the tropics through the "imperialism of free trade," and the character of administrative policy in the Indian Raj.

In foreign affairs generally, even more than in his domestic statecraft, Gladstone's development consisted essentially of a response to specific issues as they arose in mid-century. Yet ultimately the mature statesman did possess a most definite set of views which together expressed what was ultimately seen as a distinctly Gladstonian view of international relations. It was not so much a theory as a set of strong presumptions, informed by ethical principle, and held together by a chain of moral conceptions, about power and interstate relations. At the level of cabinet politics first, and later as a key element of his mass conscience politics, he intervened on foreign policy issues to the extent that Gladstonian liberalism became as much associated with international as with domestic politics in the Victorian state.

In both his domestic and international thought, Gladstone was concerned with reconciling power and moral opinion, politics and conscience. He responded to the great international problems of the mid-nineteenth century in typical manner. First, he developed a clear view of the function of foreign policy in the life of the British state: "the great duty of a Government, especially in foreign affairs, is to soothe and tranqualize the minds of the people, not to set up false phantoms of glory which are to delude them into calamity, not to flatter their infirmities by leading them to believe that they are better than the rest of the world and so to encourage the baleful spirit to domination; but to proceed upon a principle that recognises the sisterhood and equality of nations, the absolute equality of public right among them; above all, to endeavour to produce and maintain a temper so calm and so deliberate in the public opinion of the country, that none shall be able to disturb it." That was the ethical ideal which did justice to Gladstone's contemporary mentors on foreign policy—Canning, Peel, Aberdeen, and not least Cobden—but which clearly separated him from the spirit of Palmerston and Disraeli. Yet the ideal had to match reality. It was sometimes necessary to rouse moral opinion and harness it as a power behind ethically justified forms of selective intervention abroad, or as a means of reshaping foreign policy after a Palmerston or a Disraeli had been overzealously active. To do so created a further need to legitimize power by reference to the conscience of the nation. Selective intervention required, and rested on, moral sanction. "I may do," Gladstone explained to Lord Bryce, "as a private man, acts which motives of generosity and liberality suggest, and yet not be entitled to do similar acts as a Minister . . . because I am not sure that I am within the authority given me. If I wish to go further I ought to consult Parliament and obtain its authority."[39] Power, in a most specific sense, then, had to derive from "the genius of the nation," a moral source for activism but also of restraint.

Power exercised in international politics had also to meet the test of "international opinion." Intervention abroad had to serve the public law of Europe and not merely British interests. Gladstone came therefore to invest great moral significance in the concert of Europe as the ethical international means of sanctioning the exercise of British power: action would be on behalf of such internationalist concepts as public law, human rights, and the proper conduct of diplomacy, and not merely the moral urges or even selfishness of a single nation state alone.[40] Seeing Europe as essentially a Christian community of states—Gladstone often spoke of the European "moral union" of nations—he also came to place the greatest importance on "the principle of the equality of nations," acting in and through the concert for peace, "because without recognizing that principle there is no such thing as public right, and without public international right there is no instrument available for settling the transactions of mankind except material force." At the very "basis and root of a Christian civilization" was, yet again, the concept of equality before the law. And, as in his domestic liberalism, Gladstone did indeed increasingly believe that international politics had entered upon a morally progressive age in which conscience could not only be applied to foreign policy, but in which ethical norms of interstate conduct were gaining a general acceptance. Citing cases where nationality had, for example, been accepted as a principle of international right, Gladstone commented to Granville in 1870 that "These acts may be said to form a series. They are no longer mere isolated precedents. They go near to constitute one of those European usages which, when sufficiently ascertained, become the basis of public international law, and they appear, moreover, to be founded on natural equity."[41]

Just as domestic liberalism was to secure the individual in dignity and security under laws derived from morally representative institutions, so Liberal foreign policy was to secure the states of Europe in the independent enjoyment of their national cultures. "Modern times have established a sisterhood of nations, equal, independent; each of them built up under the legitimate defence which public law affords to every nation, living within its own borders, and seeking to perform their own affairs." Europe was now an aggegate of nation states, none of whom aimed at "universal dominion"; and there was a gradual, general acceptance in international politics of "the sound and sacred principle that Christendom is formed of a band of nations who are united to one another in bonds of right." When Bismarck claimed Alsace and Lorraine for the new German state after the Franco-Prussian war, Gladstone accordingly wished to oppose his actions not because they altered the European balance of power, but rather because they offended against "questions of public right."[42]

Such a moral, high, and generally optimistic conceptual view of international politics and the international order of states was perhaps bound to suffer rather cruelly in the age of blood and iron after 1870. As Medlicott well suggested some years ago, where Bismarck was to see power as essentially residing in organized authority, Gladstone had come to fix power in mass moral opinion. A cabinet memorandum of October 1862 aptly illustrates that interpretation: Gladstone argued powerfully in support of "the enthronement of this idea of Public Right" in international politics so that it might operate in "a manner more or less analogous to nations in which public opinion acts upon the institutions in a well-ordered country." It was a view he was to hold right through the test of high government and international diplomacy, though he was aware of its shortcomings: "In moral forces, and in their growing effect upon European politics, I have a great faith," he once commented to Granville, in the context of the drama of European power re-alignments in the early 1870s, "possibly on that very account, I am free to confess, sometimes a misleading one."[43]

Empire and imperialism were examined by Gladstone from the same point of view. India and the crown colonies were relatively clear-cut problems for the Liberal statesman. They were responsibilities inherited from the past, at variance with free trade ideals, but which moral duty required to be handled with humane guardianship until the native societies under British rule and tutelage could, at some rather distant future date, be emancipated to enjoy their own national independence. The British settlement colonies of empire in North America, Southern Africa, and Australasia required different treatment. Gradually Gladstone came to accept colonial responsible government, and its attendant element of colonial self-defense, as a recognition of local nationality in these overseas British polities, and as a prime means of teaching local self-government. But in its overall thrust responsible government was not directed toward a disintegration of the settlement empire. The British settlers were still "Britishers" overseas, and very much part of a world-wide British family. The Roman spirit of *imperium* was to be decried; but the Greek ideal, of mutually responsible polities, constituted into an empire of close familial asssociation, was to be pressed forward. This was mainly to be accomplished through bills of colonial government passed through the mother Parliament, which would distinguish imperial and local power. Thus responsible government really meant local home rule within the British liberal empire; and home rule in a fashion both earlier and more devolutionary than was ultimately suggested for Ireland. Devolution did not, however, imply decolonization. Local colonial nationality would be encouraged, on the presumption that—in Gladstone's own idiom— England could not stamp its culture on a new society overseas in the manner of a seal in wax. Such local diversity, in the character of the British as a world society, would be welcomed as a dynamic and positive growth of the culture. The goal was a constantly evolving and adjusting empire of family association, not an abandonment of the British settlement empire. The moral principle for colonial policy was clear: free settlers must have free institutions of government. Yet the manner in which power was devolved, from motherland to new society, was complex: an ethical colonial policy in practice took into account questions of scale, economic or strategic vulnerability, social structure, race relations, and the political maturity of the colony concerned.[44]

The New Imperialism of the late nineteenth century, focused on the massive European scramble for Africa and its partition, along with other tropical regions of the globe, naturally found no sympathy at all with Gladstone. The New Imperialism threatened to ruin his budgets. It was filled with that baneful spirit of domination which he believed to be at the core of an immoral state policy. It also meant acting aggressively, in competition against fellow Christian states, so destroying the growth of

public law, encouraging military and naval spending, and generally sub-
verting the spirit of internationalism which was at the basis of peace and
prosperity for European societies. In short: imperialism was the road to
domestic ruination and international anarchy. Conscience also predis-
posed Gladstone against frontier advances overseas. Such territorial expansion as did take place during his important second administration
(1880–85)—not least the laying of the famous "egg" of a potential North
African empire in Egypt, after the British bombardment of Alexandria
and the occupation of the interior which followed—found him anxiously,
though forlornly, trying to reconcile defense of urgent British interests
on the Mediterranean-Indian axis and international public law in the face
of hostile colleagues and rival great powers.[45] The Sudan disaster at
Khartum soon symbolized the utter failure of such compromise policies
within the battleground of his own government: the "GOM" (Grand Old
Man, used after 1882) became now the "MOG" (murderer of Gordon) in
1885. For many critics of Gladstone's principled foreign policy, Gordon
became the martyr who paid the price of weakness inherent in the Liberal
internationalism which the GOM, or MOG, favored.

Anglicanism and Peelism had together, then, in company with Cob-
denism, made Gladstone into an extraordinarily formidable public figure. Stanley detected the future prime minister as early as 1844. *State and
Church* seemed a long way back in time. Yet Gladstone had never actually
thrown away the blue coat of his early Christian piety and idealism—no
matter how "liberal" his supporters claimed him to be. Instead, he had
progressively stitched a whole series of separate and practical patches onto
the original, transforming it into a more workaday garment. The design
of the original was never obliterated entirely however, a reminder of his
abiding fascination with conscience in the national life of the state and
empire.

*A Practical Example: State, Church, and the Conscience of the Nation,
1838–68*

Financial economy, retrenchment, laissez faire, and franchise
reform, as well as the readjustment of institutions to society, were all intended to serve moral progress in Gladstonian statecraft. Colonial self-
government and self-defense were to perform the same function for the
settlement empire. And far from wishing to act as "agent of negation" in
foreign policy—Lord Salisbury's famous jibe—Gladstone saw increasing
opportunity for selective moral action in international politics. As

Checkland has therefore incisively suggested, though the mature Gladstone had "been obliged to abandon the idea that the State had a soul, it was still to have a conscience, especially in foreign policy."[46] But it was still not clear where Gladstone had in fact come to locate the conscience of the state. If a union of church and state was clearly impossible, some major intellectual adjustment must surely have taken place to allow Gladstone to speak so boldly of politics as potentially the expression of the public conscience.

Expressed in simplest terms, what Gladstone had done was move conscience out of doors. The state could not be trusted to adjudicate on religious truth; pluralism and the rather secular condition of Parliament had destroyed any hope of a confessional state. Therefore, conscience must reside in the church and the Christian people of England at large. This transference of conscience in politics from state to nation also interestingly paralleled the formal shift in Gladstonian allegiance from toryism to liberalism. Politics was still to reflect a collective conscience, provided that representative government and representative institutions could express the moral sensibilities and values of society.

Gladstone's revised view of the moral basis of the polity required a leap of faith. His early ideal in politics had rested on the authority of an established church within the state. His mature progressive ideal, associated with his liberalism, vested the conscience of the nation in the Christian citizens—even if he conceived of cabinet government as being executive administration by a selfless governing class. The Christian idealist of the 1830s had presumed that moral progress lay in ethical authority emanating from above; the emerging Christian statesman of mid-century saw ethical advances reflecting the liberty of the mass of individual consciences in the nation. "Early education, civil or religious," as he later reflected (memorandum 12 July 1892), "had never taught me, and Oxford had rather tended to hide from me, the great fact that liberty is a great and precious gift of God, and that human excellence cannot grow up in a nation without it."

The evolving public character of Gladstone's public Anglicanism accordingly offers us a fascinating illustration of this reshaping and growth in his political thought. In particular, his changing views on church, state, and conscience well suggest how, in the critical years 1838–68, he transformed his view on the moral source of government, while yet holding powerfully to his ethical perception of the politics of the state. Where Gladstone had in 1838 attempted to establish conscience in the constitution, he was in 1868 to suggest that conscience could only be developed in society through a revived, visible church—working in association with the Nonconformist religious agencies—to provide a moral constituency in the nation out of which the politics of edification and progress could be developed. And where in 1838 he had presumed an antithesis between liberal reformism and the survival of a Christian conscience in the public life of the State, by 1868 he was acutely aware of the possibilities of drawing moral power out of the respectable individuals who composed the broad mass of Victorian society.

The connecting element between 1838 and 1868, and the factor which gave intellectual continuity to Gladstone's political thought, was his abiding concern for the state as a moral agency for ethical progress. He had never doubted, as he wrote in 1868, that the fundamental issue was "not in the existence of a conscience in the State so much as in the extent of its range." He had relinquished his impractical and simplistic thesis of a church-state union as the means to that moral progress in the nation. But he had never accepted the equally simple view that the secular and moral functions of the state could be neatly isolated from each other: he was adamant in questioning whether it was in fact possible "to cut out, as it were, with a pair of scissors, the patterns of policy, which shall solve for all time and place, the great historical problem of the relation of civil power to religion." Indeed, the author of *State and Church* was to offer this emphatic codicil to his earlier treatise when he came to write *A Chapter of Autobiography* in 1868:

> It seems to me that in every function of life, and in every combination with his fellow creatures, for whatever purpose, the duties of man are limited only by his powers. It is easy to separate, and in the case of a Gas Company or a Chess Club, the primary end for which it exists, from everything extraneous to that end. It is not so easy in the case of the State or the family. If the primary end of the State is to protect life and property, so the primary end of the family is to propogate the race. But around these ends there cluster, in both cases, a group of moral purposes, varied indeed with varying circumstances, but yet inhering in the relation, and not external to it or merely incidental to it. The action of man in the State is moral, as truly as truly as it is in the individual sphere.

It was this view of conscience in politics which acted as the intellectual and psychological guide-rope to which Gladstone could hold securely as he climbed away from the abstract treatise of his youth.

In fact, within the sequence of the four revised editions of his first book, 1838–41, there can already be detected this crucial shift in his thought, on which Gladstone himself later laid stress. "My doctrine was that the State was a person with a conscience. The Catholic Church founded by our Lord was what the State ought to establish and establish alone," he noted in a private reflection on 11 September 1897, "but I made accommodation to meet existing cases which went beyond this line. These accommodations were largely unfolded anew in the fourth edition of the book . . . after Macaulay's slashing article." It is also interesting to take note of Gladstone's response to William Palmer's *Treatise on the Church of Christ* which he read most carefully in these years when he was absorbed with writing and rewriting *State and Church*. Palmer's book "took hold upon me: and gave me at once the clear, definite and strong conception of the Church which . . . has proved for me entirely adequate to every emergency and saved me from all vacillation." *But,* "I did not however love the extreme rigour of the book in its treatment of non-episcopalian communions."

It was in this context that Gladstone wrote *Church Principles Considered in their Results* (1840)—a most "sanguine guide to Anglicanism," as he later said—and also prepared the last edition of *State and Church* (1841). He now made the critical admission that some societies, and notably the pluralistic societies of the New World in North America and the British settlement colonies in the Southern Hemisphere, might well express their religious nationality, and accordingly the moral personality of the state, through a variety of religious forms. In other words, he was beginning to perceive that, in the making of new societies overseas, pilgrims and settlers alike looked to the creation of a new order in government, but not necessarily devoid of moral function. Conscience could still apparently exist in the public life of a polity without an established religion.

Gladstone was not as yet fully ready to bring home this view to the domestic British scene. But, within the next few decades, a series of political and social changes acted as critical agents forcing further the adjustment in his thought. Ireland moved him repeatedly to think again about the principle of establishment in relation to the religious nationality of the mass of Irish people. And in England, the voices of Nonconformity became ever louder: Chapel often now drowned church on a Sunday in the new urban regions.

Engagement in executive government from 1840 to 1846 assured the progress of his thought, and supplied him with both revised method for moral progress and revised perception of the relationship of church, state, and conscience. Within the first two years of taking office under Peel, Gladstone could draft a private memorandum on "Politics" which in fact drew together new pragmatism and old idealism. "It may be difficult to determine the point of declension at which institutions, in themselves wholesome, must be surrendered: but there is such a point," he now wrote; "the practical issue will in most cases . . . decide it." The meaning for the church-state nexus was clear: "When the Church is divorced from the State, they cannot be reunited by any agency of Catholic principles in Parliament." What, then, was the answer? "When the Catholic Truth is so far lost or relaxed in the hearts of the people as to allow of their surrendering the Union between the Church and the State, the command of God is not, re-unite the Church and State, but 'become faithful members and children of the Catholic Church, then the Church and State will re-unite themselves.'" This development in his thought was only tentative. But it is discernable and vital: "The people must recover their moral health *as individuals* (in a polity where they exercise a main control) before they can enjoy its consequences as a combination."

The language may not have been plain, but the consequences were clear. In the 1840s Gladstone was coming to advocate a new and pragmatic means by which he could draw church and society together—a fundamental matter if Christian values were to inform popular opinion in the nation, and act as conscience to the state. As a Peelite, his method of action was not to rely on a narrowly ideological base, but was rather to consist of a variety of practical Christian works, each of which was intended to contribute to the growth of the Church, and to the moralizing of the public culture of the nation. As a Tractarian he also wished to strive for a great revival of the spirit of the church, going beyond mere physical creation of the famed "Peelite parishes" provided by the church commissioners. In short: "no endowments will procure, will win back for the Church, that intelligent and cordial reverence which as respects great masses of the people she has lost, unless they see she has the mission of reforming the heart and life by an administration of Divine ordinances, conformed to the unalterable distinctions between right and wrong, between truth and untruth."[47]

Gladstone's idealism had not slackened one bit after *State and Church*. He could still, for example, become passionately involved in contemporary religious controversies, struggles over Oxford poetry professorships, attempts to establish a Protestant bishopric in Jerusalem, as well as putting himself forward as a potential British envoy to the Vatican.[48] And, in later years, this Anglican idealism could still surface in his intemperate assault on "Vaticanism" in the 1870s: his last outburst in favor of England as a "Protestant confessional State." But his idealism was now largely to be tempered by a hardening perception of what was possible in the public life of the State. In its curious way, his convoluted behavior over the Maynooth issue in 1845 was a signal of this change. He was still reluctant to accept state funding of a non-Anglican, indeed a Roman Catholic institution of education such as the college at Maynooth, on the old grounds that such an action was "a further declension in the religious character of the State in these realms," as well as being an "acknowledgement of the R.C. priesthood as instructors of the Irish people." But there were also overriding and practical reasons which made support for Peel's policy of giving financial support to the college at Maynooth essential.[49]

By his actions over the Maynooth grant Gladstone had at last publicly surrendered the ideal of an established conscience for the state. The cabinet records, and his journal, also show that, two years previous to Maynooth, he had already begun that critical step in the wake of Graham's abortive factory act of 1843. This bill had incorporated the Gladstonian ideal of State support for Anglican education. But militant Dissent had rallied, and the cabinet had given consideration to modifying the bill, so that its Anglican tone might be diluted in the education clauses. Gladstone was appalled: "spoke strongly against limited exposition of the Scriptures: i.e., exposition restrained to what are supposed to be general principles. I likewise questioned the wisdom of merely reading the Scriptures without exposition." His intense Anglicanism moved him to see all education as properly denominational (a view he never really renounced).

His pragmatism, however, pressed him to accept state support for non-Anglican institutions, even if he still shivered at the unwelcome logical consequences of such a policy.[50] In December 1843, in the aftermath of the factory bill debates, the British and Foreign School Society gained equal status with the church's National Society in the eyes of the state, and Gladstone accordingly recorded in his journal this "great though unavoidable step downwards" in English religious nationality. More joyously, in the same year he supported legislation which would remove disabilities affecting Dissenting chapels, a move which he later took to be an important one in his own development toward acceptance of full religious liberty in his politics. Indeed, as the author of *A Chapter of Autobiography* in 1868 he was inclined to be more generous in assessing the import of these enforced moves away from his early establishment view of conscience in the state. Where in the 1840s these steps toward accepting religious liberty under the constitution had seemed drastic and unwelcome concessions to reality, by the 1860s they appeared to indicate a new spirit in society which was both progressive and Christian: "It was really a quickened, and not a deadened conscience in the country, which insisted on enlarging the circle of State support, even while it tended to restrain the range of political interference in religion. The condition of our poor, of our criminals, of our military and naval services, and the backward state of popular education, forced on us a group of questions, before the moral pressure of which the old rules properly gave way."

Still it was Gladstone, though the most ardent Anglican in Peel's cabinet, who argued, on the basis of his new found principle, against moves to provide direct state support for church-building in England and Wales as a response to the Nonconformist expansion. The proposal—"I am thankful to say"—soon collapsed. Thus Gladstone recorded a great shift in his thought on the moral sources of politics. He was reluctantly coming to accept the sociological realities of Christian denominational pluralism in the nation.

To summarize: after 1845 the maturing Gladstone would no longer rely on the state to support the church; nor see the church as official conscience to the state. Instead, he would approach the whole question of church, society, and conscience as he approached the complexities of government itself: he would apply his urgent sense of moral imperative through a range of pragmatic strategies, in a kind of super tractarianism of individual moral action, as he joined with those working for the Christianizing of England. Before the shocking findings of the religious census of 1851—when half England failed to go to worship on Easter Sunday—Gladstone already listed nearly ten major religious projects as the main priorities of his life, outside administrative work in the state. He became an active and life-long member of nearly every important Anglican voluntary organization. Through involvement in a Tractarian prayer and "life-support" group, The Engagement, he became involved in his major charity work of prostitute rescue. He wrote and spoke extensively on religious topics, especially as they bore on Anglicanism and education. And, in his capacity as advising first minister to the sovereign after 1868, he took the very closest interest in the senior clerical appointments which fell vacant while he was premier: the archbishopric of Canterbury, seventeen bishoprics, and assorted deaneries. D. L. Edwards has aptly termed these most carefully chosen appointments as "Gladstone preaching by proxy," and, in the case of the bishop of St. Asaph, proxy-preaching in Welsh—Gladstone giving Wales its first native-speaking bishop in 150 years, in support of both revived Anglicanism and a belief in serving local nationality.[51]

Some of these roles drew Gladstone into heated controversy. His vehement opposition to the Ecclesiatical Titles Bill of 1851, an attempt by the state to defend Anglican prerogatives and British Protestantism against ultramontane Roman Catholicism, revealed his independence of stance and the growing conflict, as many churchmen saw it, between his own firm Anglicanism and his commitment to religious liberty. But more controversial than these single episodes was the evolution of Gladstone's underlying viewpoint. He wished to defend the ancient and venerable Christian institutions of the state not by Erastianism, but by sensitive adjustment of their roles and prerogatives within the larger society of Britain. This determination to bring new realities to old institutions, and to reconcile new ideas with old principles, gave him great institutional and political power. It also cast him in the role of a dynamic controversialist, who apparently cared naught for precedent in politics: issues were to be judged in the light of both principle *and* realities. "On the subject of change, my conscience is sound," he wrote to a clerical critic on the subject of university reform. "Not that I can say or wish I am in every point and particular what I was in 1847 [when elected MP for Oxford]: to say that would be to plead guilty to having learned in five busy years absolutely nothing. But as to principles, civil, religious or mixed, I feel conscious that I am what I was, as to everything of ground and substance."[52]

Controversy also began to surround his evolving view of the general church-state relationship. The "hinge and hub" of his position here was, as he put it, "to maintain the State Alliance, subject to the higher obligation not to endanger Faith"; "Faith without State alliance is better than State Alliance without Faith."[53] Speaking on the Ecclesiastical Titles Bill, he declared his conversion to the principle that "we cannot change the profound and resistless tendencies of the age towards religious liberty," and the corollary, that the church must reflect in its national role this deep current in the broader society. He also warned those so-called friends of the church who wished to make no adjustment in the role of the church in society, or who thought that Anglicanism could be saved by the state in the face of "papal aggression," that their confidence was unfounded and unworthy. As he wrote on a different occasion, "If . . . you are determined to fight in the name of religion against natural right and justice, you will not only set your teeth upon a file, but vitally hurt that which you dream of upholding."[54] After an old friend had, in May 1851, preached the opening sermon at the Episcopalian Glenalmond College in Scotland, Gladstone noted bluntly in his journal: "Wordsworth was on his respectable but impracticable ground of the old Church and State system."

Gladstone's own response to the "respectable but impracticable" thesis of church and state was to search out ways of adjusting the old civil status of the national church to the changing face of English society. In practical terms, this meant reform, sometimes by isolating the "fit subject matter for concession"—not concession as a deliberate step toward disestablishment, but concession to protect the church in its national moral role. "It is sometimes necessary in politics to make surrender of what, if not surrendered, will be wrested from us," Gladstone wrote to his son on Easter Sunday 1865:

> And it is very wise, when a necessity of this kind is approaching, to anticipate it while it is yet a good way off; for then concession begets gratitude, and often brings a return. The *kind* of concession which is really mischievous is just that which is made under terror and extreme pressure: and, unhappily, this has been the kind of concession which for near 200 years it has been the fashion of those who call (and who really think) themselves "friends of the Church" (a strange phrase) to make. Early and provident fear, says Mr. Burke, (whom you cannot read too much or too attentively) is the mother of security.[55]

It was of course this very view which soon got Gladstone into such trouble with his Oxford electors. "Gladstone . . . moving in the turmoil of politics claims for himself to see political expediencies or necessities," Wordsworth wrote to Hope-Scott in some anxiety over Gladstone's position on the admission of Jews to Parliament in 1847, "which I cannot admit of . . . living in another atmosphere and subject to experiences, as I think, of another kind." Much pressure was put on Gladstone in this very case to stand by the ideals of his *State and Church*. But Gladstone's conviction did not waver—"voted with a very clear conscience, *for* the Jews in 234:173." Interestingly, because of his awareness of English religious nationality expressed in Anglicanism, he was sympathetic to the argument that the presence of Jews at Westminster meant "again divesting ourselves of some part of our religious nationality." And he agreed that the resultant question "of the secularization of the State must in my opinion be considered in connection with the organization of the Church." But he saw the alignment of the church to the true nature of society as a vital necessity. He was sure that this particular reform, or concession, was wise.[56]

Not all were so sure. Jeers of "Gladstone and the Jew Bill" greeted him when he received an honorary degree from his old university in July 1848. To those bigoted voices, and others who were uneasy about the ultimate moral results of applying a sociological test to the institutions of the state, he offered this reply:

> I agree . . . it is a decided *note* of retrogression in the matter of that text, "the kingdoms of the world are become the kingdoms of the Lord and of His Christ" [Revelation 11:15]; but there is *a* point at which it becomes not politic only, but obligatory, to let down the theory of civil institutions—namely, when the discrepancy between them and their actual operation has

become a hopeless falsehood and a mischievous and virulent imposture. It was time, I think, to unveil realities.[57]

The step from his courageous vote of 1847 to 1883, when he advocated admission to Parliament of a celebrated non-believer, was accordingly not large.[58] Gladstone had reluctantly come to accept the secularization of the state at Westminster as a way of protecting the church and true religion from Erastianism, though not as something he welcomed in itself.[59]

The combination in Gladstone of the strict denominationalist and the political realist had turned him away from the easy accommodating pretense of a Christian state. A "secret memorandum" exactly captured the complexity, yet also the practicality, of his evolving position:

> The State will adhere longer . . . to religion in a vague than in a defined form: but I, for one, am not favourable to tearing up the seamless garment of the Christian faith in order to patch the ragged cloak of the State.
>
> Keep religion alive, and you secure at least to the individual man his refuge. Ask therefore on any occasion not what best maintains the religious repute of the State but what is least menacing to the integrity of Catholic belief and the Catholic Church. [19 June 1845].

From that vigorous idealism can well be projected his later position on such crucial matters as state education in the 1870s. Ideally he would prefer Anglican instruction, next denominational teaching, least of all an undenominational Christian curriculum determined by the state.

In a vital sense, then, Gladstone indeed came to believe that conscience must now be vested in Anglicanism and the Christian faithful generally in England. "I can now look for less than you look for at the hands of the State," as he plainly admitted to a close clerical friend; "I feel that the very brightest hopes are necessarily treasured up for us in the religious energies of the Church, unless we ourselves shall destroy them."[60] That last disaster was always possible: Gladstone suffered agonies for this very reason when so many of the luminaries of the Oxford Movement declared their apostasies between 1848 and 1851. He was also distressed by the implications of the Gorham Judgement (1850), the Ecclesiastical Titles Bill (1851), and the Public Worship Act (1874), events which he took to be tragic self-inflicted wounds on the part of the Church—Anglicanism destroying itself in the face of Erastianism and the challenge of organized Dissent. He himself had completely rejected—as he set out in his 1851 article on the "Functions of the Laymen in the Church"—the "servile doctrine" that religion could not survive without the state. Instead, he advocated a policy on church which mirrored that generally on conscience: "As the Church grows out of doors she will be felt more indoors." Accordingly, "the Church must descend into the ranks of the people and find her strength there, and build up from that level."

As one highly practical step toward that end he gave vigorous support to the revival of convocation as a means of drawing laymen more closely into the corporate life of the church, reflecting his growing view of Anglicanism as a communion of the faithful.[61] This was not an argument for completely democratizing the church, just as, by extension, it was not a principle of unqualified democracy in the state. But it did involve commitment to a self-governing church; and thus it can again be seen how the hopes of progressive reformers might be vested in a man who had begun to perceive the future security of the church, religion, and the national conscience in the respectable mass of Christians at large. This hope was reinforced by his ability to declare that he refused to be bound by abstract principles in public life, which "I may some years hence be forced to abandon" in the face of new realities. As to church and state directly, he accordingly assumed that "recent changes have made resistless an argument, a practical argument . . . that it is now impossible to regulate the connection between Church and State in this country by reference to an abstract principle." He still held "as firmly as ever, that the connection between church and state is worth maintaining," but he declined to defend the status quo forever. "I cannot pledge myself to uphold, under all circumstances, all the civil and proprietary claims of the Church."[62]

His churchmanship had simply begun to reflect his growing political pragmatism. He would loyally defend the established order. But he would also advocate parting "earlier, and more freely and cordially, than heretofore with such privileges here and there, as may be more obnoxious than really valuable" to the church. Gladstone had in mind a considerable list of such items which might serve "the special work of the age . . . to clear the relations between Church and State," as he once expressed it to Bishop Wilberforce: primarily "Church Rates and National Education," but also the law of marriage and divorce, clergy relief, the court of appeal, clergy discipline, and the prickly question of the oaths still required of Roman Catholics and Dissenters in taking up state service. Each of these matters represented "a separate knot as yet untied." In untying them the church would be making itself safe from Erastianism— "the State, when it is strong and masterful, cares nothing as a State about . . . limits"—while securing its national moral role among the people: "I

am convinced that the only hope of making it possible for her to dis-
charge her high office as Stewardess of Divine Truth is to deal tenderly
and gently with all the points at which her external privileges *grate* upon
the feelings and interests of that unhappily large portion of the community who have almost ceased in any sense to care for her.[63]

It was church rates which, of all the issues here involved, perhaps
best symbolized this policy. Under the bold, radically appealing slogan
of "Give up gold to save faith," Gladstone in fact moved very cautiously,
if surely, to advocate a progressive reform of the ancient tithe system,
first in the cities, then in the counties, too.[64] As in other areas of his political churchmanship, reform had its origins earlier than his Liberal connection of 1859. Since the last years of the previous decade he had
favored forms of adjustment, never complete abolition, of compulsory
church rates, partly to appease aggrieved Nonconformists, and equally
to protect the denominational character of the vestry. He planned to accomplish this by introducing the general principle of voluntary payment
of church rates under law. Between 1865 and 1868 he accordingly worked
at Westminster, with the Nonconformist Liberation Society in eager association, to abolish the compulsory character of church rates and replace it with what he took to be a moderate compromise scheme—but
which, rather ironically as it transpired, was given a more sweeping and
radical effect by amendments in the House of Lords.

Outside the politics of Westminster, Gladstone also tried to remove
those "grating" and "sore points" between church and chapel. He accepted the invitation of Newman Hall, to have discussions with moderate
Nonconformity—discussions which in fact extended over several years—
toward a better understanding between Churchmen and Dissenters. This
classic Gladstonian version of traditional Anglican toleration was soon
to draw in a diverse range of other "sore points": notably the opening of
church burial grounds to Dissenters and the reform of the oaths question
for civil servants. In each case Gladstone's aim was a mixture of Anglican concern to protect the church against militant Dissent—"Acts like
these weaken the invading army"[65]—and moral desire, to see the institutions of the state reflect the ethical norms of society.

Nonconformists now began to claim at least half of Gladstone, and
some Anglicans began to renounce more than half of him. He personally
held neither viewpoint. He was not trying to embrace the principle of voluntaryism, nor was he conceding any fundamental church principles. He
had some hard words to say to those Anglicans who took church-rate
reform to be a weakening of the national position of the church. The real
enemy of the church was, in Gladstone's view, neither the Liberation

Society—which he treated with much respect in communications—nor the Secularists, nor even the Roman Catholic Church in England, but the Anglican proponents of "the miserable policy of mere resistence to change, and of tenacious adherence to civil privilege."[66] He saw such an obdurate posture, in the face of societal realities, as simply "a blind and losing game." And indeed he could scarcely countenance the logic of those Anglicans who opposed temporal sacrifices to secure the church in its national religious role—such concessions "should be made as freely as the shipmaster throws cargo overboard to save the lives of the passengers and crew."[67]

A politician who could take a political test to church rates could thus also surely take a social test to the ultimate question of the establishment —as he did in 1868 in the case of Ireland. Gladstone venerated the church as a more than human institution, "founded in, and coincident with, the Divine," as he once remarked to Manning; and he often quoted Moehlr to the effect that the church was in fact "the continuation of the Incarnation." Yet as with all institutions in English society, the Anglican Church should occupy that role in the state which the people saw to be natural and proper. Establishment, as such, was not part of the Divine gift of the Anglican Church: it was a fortunate, historical legacy. Establishments had therefore to rest on the basis of their fitness to the society which they served—a sociological rather than theological premise: "It is . . . by a practical rather than theoretic test that our Establishments of religion should be tried." And in making that test, an establishment could only be defended if it measured up to an acceptable standard of national service: "an Establishment able to appeal to the active zeal of the greater portion of the people, and to respect the scruples of almost the whole, whose children dwell chiefly on her actual living work and service, and whose adversaries . . . are in the main content to believe that there will be a future for them and their opinions."[68]

These were generous standards. They were a close reflection of his mature belief that an age of representative government meant an age of representative institutions. The conscience of the nation, resting now in society at large, required religious liberty as an integral part of the moral progress of the polity. Establishments could expect to face a time of challenge, not least from the acceptance "of the principle of popular self-government as the basis of political institutions . . . [and] the disintegration of Christendom from one into many communions." Establishments maintained against the will and conscience of the nation could thus become "no longer the temple but the mere cenotaph of a great idea."[69]

Gladstone was given strong support in this view by the working example of the church in the colonies of settlement. Social structure had there made establishment impossible, with surprisingly happy results: "a remarkable, indeed a wonderful spectacle, likely not only to adorn the Church of England, but also greatly to strengthen her for the work she has to perform."[70] The devoted colonial bishops excited Gladstone's missionary impulse, and he came to eulogize them as "men who have succeeded the Apostles not less in character than in commission."[71] To those Anglicans overseas who turned to the author of *State and Church* and complained of the church's standing in the colonies without an imperial support, he had scant words of comfort. As early as 1838 he had pressed on the Bishop of Nova Scotia—who had hope for an ally in "maintaining with a high hand the perpetuity of the British connection"—the view that ideals must square with realities; and here the realities of colonial social structure, and the impossibility of an Anglican establishment, simply meant that the future of religion in the colony lay in the hands of the colonists: "the issue of the contest must mainly and ultimately depend upon yourselves than upon us." Where other Anglicans were to worry deeply over the fate of the church in the colonial context—as was revealed in the hotly debated opening of the Upper Canada Clergy Reserves, to endow a variety of local denominations—Gladstone turned a necessity into a moral virtue, and saw the best hopes of the church in colonial freedom. As "a member of the Church of England, and I hope not indifferent to her welfare," he could think of no more "bitter and pernicious gift" than mixing up attempts to secure church privileges with "resistance to the rights and privileges of your fellow subjects in a distant land."[72] His several colonial church bills accordingly reflected this attempt to free the Anglican communion abroad so as to serve its local societies, rather than to act as agent of the imperial connection.[73]

Gladstone's mind responded positively to big, creative ideas; and the history of the colonial church clearly excited his interest in the challenges of voluntaryism. Ultimately, he believed this colonial church policy, of "spiritual compensations for temporal concessions," had been directly responsible for "recognising and securing the action of the Church as a religious body" in the settlement empire, and that this had yielded a great spiritual harvest for the Anglican communion generally. In short, what he described as "the emancipation, so to call it, of the Church in the Colonies," had provided him with historical and intellectual material upon which he could draw in working further adjustments in church-state relations at home.

1868 and Disestablishment: The Morality of Representative Institutions

Irish church disestablishment together with Gladstone's vindication of his action offered in *A Chapter of Autobiography,* published in November 1868, epitomized his evolving thought on state, church, and conscience. In 1838 he had made out a high establishment theory of conscience. In 1868 he struck down an establishment in the name of conscience—"the Church of Ireland must be maintained for the benefit of the whole of the people of Ireland, and must be maintained as the truth, or it cannot be maintained at all." In *State and Church* Gladstone had conceded that the church in Ireland could only be upheld as a missionary agency of the true religion, and even before Maynooth he had his doubts about the validity of that argument. But he determined to give the Irish church "its day of grace" to accomplish its missionary purpose—"my mind recoiled . . . from the idea of worrying the Irish Church to death." But by 1865 the day of grace had come and gone; and he admitted frankly to his friend Phillimore, "I am not loyal to it as an Establishment." After three decades of "exceptionally favourable trial" he saw its existence as an establishment "as no more favourable to religion . . . than it is to civil justice and to the contentment and loyalty of Ireland."[74]

If Gladstone was to be loyal to his own sense of conscience and the conscience of the nation, he could not indeed "construct out of rags and tatters, shreds and patches, a new and different case" for maintaining the Irish establishment "on the grounds of favour, or, as it is termed, justice to the Protestants." Simply because of his devout Anglicanism, and because he now believed so strongly in the moral efficacy of representative institutions, the Irish church must feel the Gladstonian legislative axe of disestablishment—which it did in late 1868, to the distress of some English Anglicans and to the abject dismay of many Irish Episcopalians. Bishop Deny's wife wrote a suitable hymn to greet the new era and the New Year, to be sung in Derry Cathedral:

> Look down, Lord of Heaven, on our desolation!
>   Fallen, fallen, fallen is our country's crown,
>   Dimly dawns the New Year on a churchless nation . . .[75]

British Nonconformity, on the other hand, was elated. Gladstone had fulfilled many high hopes and appeared to hold out promise of yet more. Newman Hall had already sent Gladstone the answer, in verse, from the world of chapel to that of the Irish cathedral:

Can mere ambition safely steer the State
   to port long shunned with fear and factious hate?
We need a Captain, able, brave and sincere,
   Trusted, admired, beloved, by whom is sent
His own heart onward to the haven dear.
   Gladstone! on thee a nation's eyes are bent.[76]

Irish disestablishment was to reveal the power of Gladstone as a Christian statesman. For it excellently suggested his capacity to combine conscience and the sense of the politically opportune. As in the case of Irish home rule twenty years later, it had all the complex hallmarks of his version of conscience politics. He came to the decision believing that what he proposed was morally right in serving "justice" in Ireland and true religion, but also that, as a political initiative, it well reflected a general concern among Liberals, not least those who were Nonconformists, many of whom held views in advance of Gladstone over the confiscation of Irish Church wealth; that such a policy would be electorally advantageous to the Liberal party, not least in Ireland itself, where the tide had begun to shift in their favour since 1865; and that it was indeed practical politics—as ever, Gladstone counted heads before he moved for new legislation. Irish disestablishment was an expression of a long-nurtured tendency in Gladstonian thought, going back to the 1840s, now brought to fruition and implementation by more immediate developments in Ireland and England—Fenianism, Roman Catholic grievances, coupled with infra-Liberal pressure-group struggles, perhaps even attached to political lessons taken from Gladstone's own south-Lancashire constituency where local Protestant and Roman Catholic antagonism offered its own English variant of the enduring "Irish Question."[76]

Disestablishment simply offered an overriding cause which might draw Liberals together, play down their denominational, sectional, and class differences, while stressing their capacity as a progressive movement of opinion, and suggesting the moral potential of responsibly representative government. The policy constituted one of those themes of edification for electors which would call up "right-minded opinion" as a power for an administration headed by Gladstone himself. And, as an issue, it would happily catch Disraeli and many Conservatives in a difficult tactical position: they could hardly hope to trump Gladstone as they had so successfully accomplished over franchise reform in 1867. In short, "1868" had all the vital components to meet Gladstone's concept of "ripeness" in political action. It was certainly politically opportune; it was also in harmony with the "fulness of time." The result, providential or not, was highly efficacious institutional reform, power to the Liberal party, and increasing personal power and popularity for Gladstone himself among a growing constituency of supporters. John Bright had spoken for that morally earnest portion of the national "Gladstone constituency" when he pointed to Liberalism as the party of Christ. It was certainly becoming the party of Gladstone.

Would the Church of England in England be next to feel Gladstone's creative view of conscience politics applied to the ancient establishments? The Liberation Society lived in some hope after the Irish event. Gladstone had then rightly said that he never could "propound the maxim *simpliciter*" that the establishment must be retained in any circumstances. And accordingly, as he wrote privately to a friend in 1874, "I do not feel the dread of disestablishment you may probably entertain," adding, however, "I desire and desire and seek, so long as standing ground remains, to avert, not to precipitate it."[77] He had attempted to make this quite clear in the previous year when he declined to support Miall's motions on English disestablishment, to the cruel disappointment of many Nonconformists: Gladstone tried to explain himself in a great oration which led to many Tory cheers and silence among Liberal backbenchers. "Caesar addressed his troops," the *Nonconformist* commented, "and all Pompey's legions shouted response."[78]

Gladstone's reasoning was complex as ever but, in fact, consistent with his Irish policy. "I cannot promise concurrence in your prayer," he wrote in an open letter to Nonconformists in 1876 on receipt of yet another respectful call for Anglican disestablishment. "In my opinion, the Establishment of England (not of Scotland) represents the religion of a considerable majority of the people, and they do not seem to deserve the change you recommend."[79] Privately, he wrote to the Queen that he was, "with advancing years," ever more "struck with the tenacious vitality of the Church of England," and to Döllinger that the survival of the church as a genuinely national institution was nothing short of Providential— "Death and secession, between them, seem to have removed all our most considerable men; and yet the body has grown; and amidst every kind of scandal, grief and danger." He indeed felt, with Döllinger, as he quoted to the House in 1873, that "no Church is so national, so deeply rooted in the public affection, so bound up with the institutions and manners of the country, and so powerful in its influence on national character" as the Anglican establishment. And he went to some lengths to substantiate this view. In his pamphlet, *"Is the Church of England Worth Preserving?"* written in the context of the Public Worship Act controversy of 1874, he set out his "proof" under the broad banner of the church saved by internal reform and popular affection. "We see a transformed clergy, laity less cold and neglectful, education vigorously pushed forward, human want and sorrow zealously cared for, sin less feebly rebuked, worship restored from frequent scandal and prevailing apathy to uniform decency and frequent reverence, preaching restored to an Evangelical tone and standard, the organisation of the Church extended throughout the Empire."

It is an impression which modern historians of the Church can broadly recognize. The clergy, "a different kind of gentleman," were reformed as pastoral agents, though intellectually their standing declined. The repute of bishops was generally raised. And a new energy appeared to pulse through Anglicanism: more Englishmen, as a proportion of the whole population, worshipped in the church in 1870 than 1830, though they were still too heavily rural in residence; and church building was prodigious, with nearly two thousand new churches constructed 1840–76 and more than seven thousand restored. As an institution, the Church of England was perhaps the most extensive organization in the state, with more than 20,694 clergy and 15,522 churches in 1871. Massive voluntary financial contributions had also given new vitality to Anglican expansion.[80]

Gladstone was inclined to celebrate this history in less muted tones: "this spectacle, as a whole, was like that . . . of a Russian spring: when, after long months of rigid cold, the ice breaks up and is borne away, and the whole earth is covered with a rush of verdure . . . the great heart of England began to beat with the quickened pulsations of a more energetic religious life."[81] The establishment was safe for the moment, provided the church continued to play this truly national role—though in the very long term, disestablishment was a not unlikely possibility. In Gladstone's thought, the conscience of society could only support the official church-state attachment so long as Anglicanism continued to be both truly Catholic in its teachings, and *also* met the sociological test of popular attachment and usefulness.

In his devotion to both Anglicanism and public conscience, Gladstone had, as in so many areas of Victorian public life, deeply affected both the nature and tone of political discussion. His intent had been largely conservative: adjustment of traditional institutions to moral opinion and the reconciliation of an old world to the new. But the result was a heightened sense of public excitement, not of quietude. "Mr. Gladstone's was one of those strong natures which must arouse antagonism in the unavoidable conflicts of public life," as Malcom MacColl wrote in 1899 after a close association going back decades. "It was impossible to be neutral about him."[82] Dean Church had captured Gladstone's impact on the political life of the nation, its values and aspirations, at the very moment when the "People's William" was about to become the sovereign's first minister in 1868, even more pointedly: "There never was a man so genuinely admired for the qualities which deserve admiration— his earnestness, his deep popular sympathies, his unflinching courage; and there never was a man more deeply hated, both for his good points and for the undeniable defects and failings. But they love him much less in the House than they do out of doors. A strong vein of sentiment is the spring of what is noblest about his impulses; but it is a perilous quality too."[83]

Perspective: The Emergence of an Ethangogue?

In 1868, on the publication of Gladstone's *A Chapter of Autobiography,* the *Pall Mall Gazette* had unkindly suggested that the work merely contained this Gladstonian confession: "You may ask how I ever came to write such a silly book as my *Church and State* [sic]. The answer is, I was impressible and carried away with Puseyism, and I have been finding out ever since that it was all a mistake."[84] With larger empathy, it might rather be argued that Gladstone had indeed been educated by experience in the realities of state. Gladstonian thought on the moral sources of power in government had evolved in the thirty hectic and testing years since *State and Church,* an evolution of principle and practice which had taken him from Puseyism to the politics of moral reform and made him into the most striking mass politician of his times.

It was John Morley who first shrewdly argued that "next to faith" the key to Gladstone was "growth." The growth he had in mind was of course not merely an increasing worldliness in party tactics, an awareness of what Gladstone himself referred to in tough-minded psephological articles in the 1870s as "electoral facts." Rather, Morley pointed to the manner in which Gladstone had come to see politics as "connecting itself with the silent changes which are advancing in the very bed and basis of modern society."[85] Gladstone's social theory was conservative, being much more landed even than bourgeois in character. It was also devoid of egalitarianism, as befitted a man who could subscribe without difficulty to Article 38 of Anglican dogma—"Of Christian men's Goods which are not common." But Gladstone's mature political theory was dynamic: "the first responsibility of every Legislature in every age must be to adapt the law and institutions of the country to the wants of the country which it governs." Close involvement in working the institutions of the state had also convinced the mature Gladstone that ideals in politics must live in close harmony with the general movement of ideas in the age: "It is not the duty of a Minister to be forward in inscribing on the Journals of Parliament his own abstract views; or to disturb the existence of a great institution . . . until he conceives the time to be come when he can give practical effect to his opinions." The role of the public man was to act as moral agent for such "opinions"—not slavishly, but by weighing issues with an ethical concern, ready to adjust the old forms and structures in the light of both changing needs and traditional values. Liberalism in Gladstone's hands, meant respect for the inherited fabric of society, but also openness of mind. Politics accordingly developed out of an intimate combination of opinion and conscience. As he wrote in 1868:

> If it is the office of law and institutions to reflect the wants and wishes of the country . . . then, as the nation passes from a stationary into a progressive period, it will justly require that the changes in its own conditions and views should be represented in the professions and actions of its leading men. For they exist for its own sake, not for theirs. It remains indeed their business, now and forever, to take honour and duty for their guides, and not the mere demand or purpose of the passing hour; but mere honour and duty themselves require their loyal servant to take account of the state of the facts in which he is to work, and, while ever labouring to elevate the standard of opinion and action around him, to remember that it is his business not to construct, with self-chosen materials, an Utopia or a Republic of Plato, but to conduct the affairs of a living and working community of men, who have self-government recognised as in the last resort the moving spring of their political life, and of the institutions which are its outward vesture.[86]

Gladstone's theory of political action largely rested in this passage. And that view was only possible because of the great adjustment which had taken place in Gladstone's thought on the conscience of the state since 1838. Gone was the establishment theory of the ethical polity, to be replaced by a perception of conscience which located it in the broad mass of respectable Victorian society. Christianity might still be "under strain," he commented vividly in 1867, but it was "like a good ship in the roaring sea as it leaps from wave to wave." The crisis in moral order, which had so deeply concerned him in youth, had called out "the high and noble emotions of a devoted service," resulting in the "blessed outcome" of what he believed to be an increasingly moral and Christian nation at large.

Throughout his emergence as a mature politician Gladstone was emphatic that if the state had lost its claim to a conscience, then the nation was still possessed of such a Christian conscience, which required expression in its public life. He readily admitted that "what may be called the dogmatic allegiance of the State to religion had been greatly relaxed." But by 1868 he was adamant in asserting that "conscousness of moral duty has been not less notably quickened and enhanced" in the life of the state. Indeed, in the largest and most important sense,

> we are still a Christian people. Christianity has wrought itself into the public life. . . . Precious truths, and laws of relative right and the brotherhood of man, such as the wisdom of heathenism scarcely dreamed of and could never firmly grasp, the Gospel has made to be part of our common inheritance, common as the sunlight that warms us, and as the air we breathe. Sharp though our divisions in belief may be, they have not cut so deep as to prevent, or as imperceptibly to impair, the recognition of these great outlines and fences of moral action.[87]

This belief was to be the very source of his political vision. He declared he was never a "sanguine believer in progress." But neither the warnings of Jevons about the exhaustion of national resources nor Arnold's view of the triumph of philistinism nor Tennyson's gloomy view of England in the Jubilee Year of 1887—a nation divided by power, wealth, and false human values—could shake Gladstone's fundamental optimism. He gloried in the material progress and the individualism of the citizen which others took to be the very enemies of a moral community in industrial society; Gladstone saw these advances as "absolute and without discount." He also attached strong moral significance to the march of society in Victorian England:

> the sum of the matter seems to be that upon the whole . . . we who have lived, fifty, sixty, seventy years back, and are now living, have lived into a gentler time; that the public conscience has grown more tender, as indeed was very needful; and that, in practice, at sight of evils formerly regarded with indifference or even connivance, it now not only winces but rebels: that upon the whole, the race has been reaping and not scattering; earning and not wasting.[88]

Gladstone also placed a distinctly positive interpretation on the general progress of religion in the century, playing down schism and theological division, and celebrating the fact that by the 1890s more than 450 million Christians throughout the world could be counted as sharing common cardinal beliefs. "I bow my head in amazement before this mighty moral miracle," he wrote in his study, "The place of Heresy and Schism in the Modern Christian Church." He indeed detected a "marvellous concurrence from the heart of discord." British religious advances became a variant therefore of this universal moral phenomenon. The progress of Christianity at home reflected the Anglican revival, but it also drew upon the growth of Nonconformity, especially in the great industrial cities of the North. His earlier antipathy to the varieties of Nonconformity—which had not the least denied him his establishment ideal—mellowed as he came to accept the principle of full religious liberty and as he grew to respect the earnestness, the dignity, and the self-reliance of Dissenters.

Gladstone had read the religious census of 1851 with "astonishment"; it was not the scale of heathenism which struck him so forcibly as the spread of chapel. By the 1860s he was enjoying increasing contact with the leaders of moderate Dissent. He was ultimately (1894) to pronounce on the "noblest triumphs" of the voluntary churches in the Christianizing of urban England, regions where Anglicanism had not always been successful: "we cannot dare to curse what God seems in many ways to have blessed and honoured, in electing to perform duties neglected by others, and in emboldening it to take a forward part . . . on behalf of the broadest interests of Christianity." Many had been called; all had been chosen for the civilizing, Christianizing mission.

Gladstone's yearnings for the unity of Christendom found ultimate expression in his European ecumenism, and much more immediate fulfillment in his growing empathy toward the works of Nonconformity. Yet again the evangelical child was father to the moral man. Gladstone several times recollected in the 1890s "a precious saying which was spoken to me . . . in 1828 by Mrs. Milnes Gaskell. . . . It sank into my mind and had a gradual and silent but lasting influence over me. She said that assuredly the real question was whether a soul was 'united by faith and love to Christ': this was the essence and decided the matter. I remember when she said it, how new it seemed to me. Doubtless it took some time for its full apprehension: but I did not in any way repel it." The practical consequence for his dogmatic beliefs, as Gladstone bluntly put it, was that "Nonconformists and Presbyterians . . . I always let off pretty easily."

Newman had early, and prophetically, argued that Gladstone's "great object is the religionising of the *State*." By the heyday of his power as a public figure Gladstone believed that this was sufficiently advanced to see the democratic process as moral in its potential, and to identify a conscience in society which might speak with an ethical voice on the greater issues of state. Thus despite his great intellectual journey he could still in 1868 subscribe to the *ideal* of 1838: politics as an expression of "a national conscience." He could take politics to the people because they were largely a Christian people, and not a society of pagans.

Here was a critical basis of Gladstonian power. His apparent "moral incandescence" (Lecky's phrase) acted as a beacon of possibility, promise, and hope to an increasing mass electorate—even though Gladstone offered little that was materially advantageous in electoral terms. In return, it was essential for Gladstonian politics that he himself believe that there did indeed exist a "moral nation" of earnestly respectable electors to which he could appeal, from which he might draw power, and through which the state might be said to have found again its collective conscience. Not only did his Christian moralism and optimism draw him into an increasing closeness with a mass electorate, but it appears to have satisfied a deep psychological need in Gladstone himself. Without a belief in a conscience at large in society—later expressed in his talk of the moral nobility of the masses, and the fall from grace of much of the aristocracy and plutocracy—it is hard to see how he could have aligned himself with the "movement of the public mind" as he termed it; or have made his famous 1864 declaration on the moral boundaries of the franchise qualification; or even accepted the secret ballot of 1872. And it is inconceivable that the greater political missions—for Bulgars and Irish and against Beaconsfieldism and jingoism—could have been launched. He left politics temporarily in 1875 not least because he felt he had lost touch with the temper of his moral constituency; he returned, with alacrity, when it excited him again over Bulgarian atrocities and the great mass meetings in the North—"I went into the country and had mentally postponed all further action . . . when I learned from the announcement of a popular meeting to be held . . . that the game was afoot and the question yet alive" (11 July 1894, autobiographical memorandum).

After faith and growth, method. Sir Charles Dilke was later to remark that once Gladstone sat for a large industrial constituency, and was accordingly separated from his Oxford electors, then his democratic tendencies could no longer be contained. In fact, it could be argued that Gladstone had already adjusted his thought on representative and progressive government before his political translation to South Lancashire in 1865 and his famous "unmuzzling."

The process by which Gladstone came to discover what Meredith described as "the God in the conscience of the multitudes" was notably extended, if broken.[89] Before South Lancashire there were Gladstone's northern tours in 1863-64: the importance of "response" and "re-response" at public meetings and assemblies, in shaping Gladstonian mass politics, cannot be underestimated. And before that experience there was the great Newcastle meeting of 1862; Gladstone's profound impression of the fortutude of Lancashire cotton workers in the crisis precipitated by the American Civil War; and the evolving image he appears to have developed of the artisan class taking advantage of his post office savings scheme, developing their cooperative movements, and avidly reading the new popular press now reduced in price, partly as a result of his paper duties abolition bill. Even further back in time there was his speech of 1853 unveiling Peel's statue outside the Royal Infirmary in Manchester, when he was much struck by working class respectability, and his address to a coal-whippers meeting at Shadwell in May 1851 at which he so admired the artisan speakers ("These men were a delight to see and hear"). Among the "chief heads of legislative work" which he drew up in January 1896 Gladstone interestingly included: "Coal Whippers Act [1843]. Small but of much interest and consequence." His journal contains many passing references to the steady worthiness of working men, going back as far as November 1833, when he paid a three-hour visit to the tenants of his brother Tom, and in whom he found "much industry, cheerfulness and content" as well as a goodly "fear of God."

From these particular experiences Gladstone gradually developed his mature view of the moral potential of skilled labor. He believed that he had detected another of the great morally progressive forces at work in the age: "a steady movement of the labouring classes . . . onwards and upwards," as he declared in his celebrated Reform Bill speech (27 April 1866). He readily conceded that "like all great processes" it was "unobservable in detail," but it was still as "solid and undeniable" as it was "resistless in its essential character." The history of mid-Victorian labor accordingly created in his mind an unanswerable moral case for an expanding political nation: "I cannot see what argument could be found for some wise and temperate experiment of the extension of civil rights among such people, if the experience of the past four years does not sufficiently afford it."

Underneath that declaration lay a dynamic moral view of politics and the constitution. It was upon a Peelite base that he built his progressive concept of politics: the state was to be "the organ of the deliberate and ascertained will of the community, expressed through legal channels." That practical yet principled position had dramatically important implications. Politicians were to be high stewards of the nation's interests. They were to draw knowledge and power from moral opinion in society itself. The statesman's role was also now to include that of "the public orator"; political theory was "inextricably mixed up with practice. It is cast in the mould offered to him by the mind of his hearers." Indeed, the moral orator-statesman worked essentially with the "sympathy and concurrence of his time," which thus became "joint part of his work." In short: "he cannot follow nor frame ideals; his choice is, to be what the age will have him, what it requires in order to be moved by him, or else not to be at all."

Gladstonian politics, accordingly and progressively, gave witness to the "transfer of political power from groups and limited classes to the community" and to "the constant seething of the public mind, in fermentation upon the vast mass of moral and social, as well as merely political interests" in the nation.[90] His method of representing opinion, as an orator-politician, was not of course to become an orthodox radical—no matter what the Court and many of the ruling classes suspected of him. Rather, Gladstone's desire was to recognize the emergence of mass moral opinion in society, and then to harness it—through the "consultation" of mass meetings, where he spoke as much *with* his audience as to it, and where he might also invoke its voice or stir its conscience—as the power behind great national causes which overruled class or sectarian or regional interests, a posture which elevated the individual at the very moment that it assailed the wrong-doer.

Government was to be in the name of the conscience of the people; it was also to be government by an executive drawn from the best representatives of the selfless governing class, of Whiggery and its allies—men who owed their loyalty to duty, not economic interest groups. In the curious combination of Christian moral opinion in society at large and high-minded elitist government, Gladstone saw the best hopes of a moral polity. Even after the Bulgarian and Irish home rule initiatives Gladstone could still remark, to John Morley, on his belief in the continuing value of the hereditary principle in a mixed constitution.

Whether Gladstone was ever the Liberal his supporters made him out to be was, accordingly, a moot question. His development since the 1830s had been palpable; but it had also been peculiar—more lateral than obviously progressive. He had expanded the range and base of his constitutional ideas, to take into account a larger political and moral nation; and his language had indeed increasingly come to reflect the ethical sensibilities of that broadening moral constituency in the state. Within the party alone, as Gladstone admitted, Nonconformity was the very backbone of liberalism. But he had not broadened his social theory. Applied to the Condition of England Question, Gladstonian liberalism meant primarily institutional reform and individual liberty under law, faith in the personal conscience of the voter, together with the regenerative power of capitalism and free-trading internationalism. It did not countenance social reconstruction directly through the state. With advancing years, Gladstonian liberalism found its natural focus in the causes most congenial to

Gladstone himself: reform of national institutions, support for nationality and local cultures, defense of human rights, and an ethical foreign
policy. These became moral goals in themselves. Yet their primacy and
advancement was necessarily at the price of a more radical "new liberalism," as the Newcastle Programme of 1892, with its part Gladstonian
priorities—beginning with Irish home rule—clearly indicated.[91]
   Given this reality in the practice of liberalism, coupled with the absence of egalitarian impulses in the Gladstonian temper, it is often suggested that he had no deep appreciation of the Victorian working man
and his social conditions. In fact, because of his own work of moral redemption in the London, and the very considerable charity work of
Catherine, his wife—to take but two ways in which his life extended beyond that of the comfortable middle classes—Gladstone was all too
aware of the social conditions on the back streets of urban England; not
least, as he once wrote movingly of the blackening grime which covered
body and soul among the children of the poor. It was perhaps as one response to this struggle for survival and self-respect among the laboring
classes, that Gladstone came so strongly to admire the self-improved
working man, and ultimately even came to overestimate the moral potential of the respectable artisan as a member of Gladstone's "nation" of
ethical Liberals.[92] Looking past the bread-and-butter economic realities
which were increasingly to motivate the late-Victorian voter-worker,
Gladstone reached out to them as fellow Christians who shared his myth-
ology of conscience politics, with its moral priorities in national regeneration and progress. And because, in Kitson Clark's words, great sections
of British society recognized "in the ring of his voice, in his choice of
words, in the sanctions to which he appealed, the same spirit as that
which possessed them," and responded accordingly, Gladstone's later
politics took on the definite tone of moral radicalism.[93]
   It was the radicalism of the Evangelical conscience, however, and
certainly not that of the Christian socialist or even the social gospeler.
Gladstone launched the great Bulgarian agitation in thunderous tones
and idioms not inappropriate to an Evangelical sermon. Disraeli's pro-
Turkish policy was wrong, not alone because it was impractical and dam-
aged true British interests, but because it affronted human rights by
deploying power on the side of immorality. The conscience of the state
was at risk:

> Yes, gentlemen, the disease of an evil conscience is beyond the practice of all
> the physicians of all countries in the world. The penalty may linger; but, if it
> lingers, it only lingers to drive you further into guilt, and to make retribution
> when it comes more severe and more disastrous. It is written in the eternal

laws of the universe of God that sin shall be followed by suffering. An unjust war is a tremendous sin. The question which you have to answer is whether the war is just or unjust. So far as I am able to collect the evidence, it is unjust. . . . If so, we should come under the stroke of the everlasting law that suffering shall follow sin; and the day will arrive . . . when the people of England will discover that national injustice is the surest road to national downfall.

Gladstone's out-of-doors liberalism had taken on the style of a religious crusade: the Midlothian campaigns were conducted as "festivals of freedom" and an "interchange of sentiment"—his own proud assertions —in the face of growing open hostility from the upper and educated ranks of society. The Queen spoke bitterly of his "royal progress" among the cheering crowds of Midlothian, and she admittted to her secretary that she "would sooner abdicate than have anything to do with that half-mad firebrand who will ruin everything and be a *Dictator*." More quietly, though not less severely, Salisbury wondered if the aging Gladstone was entirely sane. The fact that Gladstonian liberalism now appeared to propagate a kind of moral class warfare, which became an open fact when the bitter Irish home rule debate entered the public domain after April 1886 and brought from the GOM a denunciation of the ethics of the hostile ruling classes, meant that the monied middle strata of society—led by the professions—deserted the party in alarming proportions. Gladstone may well have seen to the heart of the Irish question; but it was still an open issue whether, in the manner of his politics, he was not now subordinating his original Peelite grasp of the pragmatic as the highest ethical justification for government action, in favor of a growing zeal to couch public issues in moral absolutes. Equally tellingly, as J. A. Hobson, among younger and distinctly more left-wing Liberals, were beginning to ask in the 1880s and 1890s: had the great Gladstone of mid-century, who had done so much to make the party a vehicle for mass opinion, not become the "great spoiler" in the evolution of the party's potentially positive response to the social and economic needs of labor?[94]

Rhetoric itself certainly grew even more important in developing the style, and perhaps even the content, of Gladstone's radical-sounding conscience politics. Marx has left us with a most memorable if critical commentary upon it. Trying to describe the character of a Gladstone speech to his German readers he recalled Dicken's Circumlocution Office in *Little Dorrit,* and epitomized it as *Um-die-Sache-herumsschreibungs-burostil.* In fact, the mixture of high moral assertions and complex pragmatic qualifications which characterized the later speeches well reflected the changing features of Gladstonian politics. Most obviously, rhetoric was intended to stir and move audiences, to educate and elevate at one and the same moment. And for that function more than a dry recital of facts was needed. But the complexity of his speech also reflected a desire to allow himself freedom of development at a time when changing public opinion made rigid consistency impossible. As J. H. Grainger put it, he "needed those ambiguities to preserve his own inner freedom of action." Complexity and qualification were also important to a man acutely concerned with idealism and truth in his utterances but whose politics were formed around pragmatic ideas of "ripeness" and the "opportune" in forwarding issues. Rhetoric also allowed him to attempt a constant synthesis of changing opinion in society by relating it to enduring Christian moral values. For some, accordingly, Gladstone was and always will remain "the old spellbinder up to his tricks again"; for others, the very "syntactical devices which enabled him to bear the consequences of his own oratory were testimonies to his own high responsibility."[95]

Placing Gladstone in historical perspective may ultimately prove more difficult than exposing the complexities of his statesmanship. Even the publication of his massive private journal will not bring any finality to understanding this extraordinary man. As he once wrote of Stonehenge, "It is a noble and awful relic, telling much and telling too that it conceals more." However, on another occasion, Gladstone provided an assessment of Daniel O'Connell which may serve as a pointer to the nature of his own politics: "It is . . . a misnomer to call him a demagogue. If I may coin a word for the occasion, he was an *ethnagogue*. He was not the leader of the plebs or the populous against the optimates; he was the leader of a nation."[96]

The pluralistic character of British society prevented Gladstone from being that kind of "ethnagogue"—much as the author of *State and Church* might have wished it. But Gladstone was ultimately the leader of a historically particular "nation": the morally earnest and solicitously concerned Victorians. He was never to solve the problems of the state-church nexus, though he brought an attentive sensitivity to its constant pragmatic adjustment. But his thought had found a conscience in the larger society of the nation, around and through which his politics could develop. At the same time, he did much to infuse Christian concepts of morality and conscience into both the public conduct and the political culture of Victorian England; and he provided a model for many colonial politicians in the overseas settlement empire. He also attempted, as few major political figures have ever done or even claimed, to bring the ethical insights of private conscience to bear upon the inner works of government, to strive for national moral progress through the minutiae of legislation and diplomacy, and not merely through cant moral invocations.

This view of Gladstone is supported by a valuable assessment made in the year of his death by Norman Hapgood. Writing in the July 1898 edition of the *Contemporary Review,* he depicted Gladstone as essentially a man of action; a moral pragmatist in politics; a political actor who lived in a constant state of "energetic tension"; and a phenomenal personality who created his own fields of force and dynamics of change, as he worked his way through all the great issues of the century, intent on advancing Christian morality in the state. Gladstone's method in so doing was focused around his capacity to place moral frames of reference on the disparate processes of state, and thus to gather about him a vast if inchoate aggregate of supporters, from all classes and sections of British life, who could provide the power for this "civilizing mission" within the nation. They looked to him not merely for the prosperity of the laissez-faire state, but because he offered a vision of public life in the nation which appeared to transcend the *embourgeoisement* of society, with all its mannered and monied values; Victorians triumphing over Victorianism in the cause of Christian civilization.

Whether Gladstone became more "old fox" than "old lion" in his half century of endeavor was not easily decided: "Men of his sort are as genuine as their parts are varied. The lion and the fox lived on equal terms within him. On a few things he may have broken faith even with parts of himself, compelled by a higher necessity of escaping rapidly: but, when we consider the length and breadth of his career, one of its most surprising elements is the ease with which he grouped it under a few cardinal maxims. It was in perfect honesty that when one tool didn't work he took another. The great thing was to do the work." Gladstone's talent was accordingly of a very particular kind: "the power to absorb abstract tendencies, political and economic theories, and execute them in practice—a genius for figures, work and popular influence." And practical politics involved *both* ideals and tactics: "Opportunism with him meant, not that he would go anywhere with the tide, but that, his course being towards righteousness, subsidiary opinions were made to fit the moment." Gladstone's style in this labor was often irritatingly aloof, tortured in method, and heavy with moralizing sentiment. Yet: "it is probable that for posterity his portrait will take its tone from his moral genius." Hapgood concluded,

> His eager will became the servant of the threats and promises of democracy. His long experience and manifold gifts gave him highest place in her service. A man so able and so earnest, to alter a sentence of his own, is never wholly

wrong. In pursuit of one truth he may trample upon others; in his crusade against one error another may gain root; but the man of action has to choose, and Mr. Gladstone lifted for his standard the reconciliation of democracy with the preservation of spiritual light. . . . This fight he waged with such endurance and such valour that thousands who had confided in nobody brightened at the name of Gladstone. They were the poor and the commonplace, into whose lives he had forced confidence and hope. The fewer and more critical thousands, whose eyes discern in this great monument of our age flaws of common human clay, will yet decide . . . that with the dazzling abilities and the splendid fighting courage there was an ardent and true moral ideal, without which one man can hardly have done so much to quicken millions, receiving his messages in vapour and pouring them back in a flood which left the spiritual life of his age purer and more abundant.

The overall result of Gladstone's statesmanship was indeed complex and not easily placed on a balance sheet. In domestic policy, there was great individual liberation and institutional reform, combined with fiscal adjustments, which encapsulated real moral advances. Yet fundamental social and urban problems remained, which tight Gladstonian budgets were unlikely to remedy. In foreign policy, moral standards were determinedly proclaimed for the conduct of a great power, and an imperial power; and within the cabinet, Gladstone often fought for those ideals against colleagues who doubted the soundness of his principled activism in safeguarding the national interest. But the gap between moral ideals and actual external policies in his administrations was sufficiently wide to prompt the question whether there was ever a truly Gladstonian style in the overall working of British foreign policy after 1868. In his churchmanship he had attempted to reflect much more than personal devotional piety. Gladstone took up a version of what Henry Chadwick has recently described as the church's function in a utilitarian and modern world: "to humanize the government's educational and welfare schemes; to instil respect for legality, while reminding an omnipotent Parliament that a moral and just purpose is indispensable to (and a restraint upon) authority; above all, to urge that civilization requires humane culture and is not mere increase in the general standard of physical comfort and prosperity.[97] And in that great quest there had been undoubted gains in the Gladstonian years. But whether orthodox religion truly established a moral revolution in England, as Gladstone himself wished to believe, was more doubtful. Lastly, within the European political tradition, Gladstone had tirelessly set out the conception of a liberal-democratic state, rooted in Christian morality and the conscience of the individual citizen, which still possesses the attraction of an ideal form—not least, in fact, to the 1970s when political corruption and insensitive bureaucratic conduct in social-democratic polities have become flagrantly real. However, the critical conclusion of Vidler, examining *State and Church* more than thirty years ago, is also still relevant in evaluating Gladstonian political ideas: "If he had understood that the strength of *laissez faire* England depended on favouring circumstances, that in the nature of the case would pass away, he would have been less optimistic and less moralistic. He would have left a larger heritage of political wisdom for posterity."[98] The fate of British liberalism is not uninstructive here.

But if the record was indeed mixed in its final accounting, the sheer scale of Gladstone's attempts to draw conscience into the public life of the Victorian state has about it the qualities of a heroic epic.

Notes

1. D. C. Lathbury, ed., *Correspondence on Church and Religion of William Ewart Gladstone,* 2 vols. (1910) I: 69–70; cited hereafter as *Religious Correspondence.* The present essay was drafted before the publication of S. I. T. Machin's excellent study, *Politics and the Churches in Great Britain, 1832–68* (1978), which includes an incisive account of Gladstone's churchmanship.

2. W. E. Gladstone, *Midlothian Speeches* (1879), p. 50; I have used M. R. D. Foot's edition (1971).

3. W. E. Gladstone, *A Chapter of Autobiography* (1868), pp. 104–105.

4. J. Brooke and M. Sorenson, eds., *Gladstone Autobiographica* (1971) I: 231, Appendix 3.

5. M. J. Lynch, "Was Gladstone Tractarian? W. E. Gladstone and the Oxford Movement, 1833–45," *The Journal of Religious History* 8, (4) (Dec. 1975): 364–89. See also David Newsome, *The Parting of Friends: A Study of the Wilberforces and Henry Manning* (1966), p. 318 *passim*; and W. E. Gladstone, "The Evangelical Movement: Its Parentage, Progress and Issue," *British Quarterly Review* (July 1879).

6. Gladstone to Rev. R. Buchanan, 22 June 1838, *Religious Correspondence* I: 44. He had also written a note on conscience and government in April 1837, Addit. MSS. 44727 fos. 28–29.

7. Gladstone to Manning, Sunday 5 April 1835, *Religious Correspondence* I: 25–26.

8. A. S. McGrade and Brian Vickers, eds., *Richard Hooker: Of the Laws of Ecclesiastical Polity* (1975), Bk. VIII, chap. I, para. 7, p. 342.

9. *State and Church* I: 115.

10. *Diaries* II: 38–23, July 1838. Also, *Religious Correspondence* I: 46.

11. Norman, *Church and Society,* p. 104.

12. *Religious Correspondence* I: 71–72.

13. *State and Church* I: 131; and *Diaries* II: 605, 8 June 1839.

14. Gladstone to Manning, 2 April 1837; *Religious Correspondence* I: 29. Kitson Clark, *Churchmen and the Condition of England,* pp. 86–98.

15. Vidler, *Orb and Cross,* p. 153.

16. J. A. La Nauze, *Alfred Deakin* (1965) I: 66.

17. Gladstone to Manning, 9 March, 1847, *Religious Correspondence* II: 275–76.

18. Gladstone, "Daniel O'Connel," *19th Century* (Jan. 1889): 167.

19. Gladstone to son Willy, 22 Oct. 1854, *Religious Correspondance* II: 155.

20. Walter Bagehot, "Mr. Gladstone," *National Review* 2 (July 1860).

21. Colin Matthew, Introduction, *Diaries* III: xli.

22. This paragraph owes much to Oliver MacDonagh and Howard Brasted.

23. W. N. Norton, *Bishop Butler, Moralist and Divine* (1940), pp. 87–96; *Religious Correspondence* II: 164, 192.

24. Kelley, *Transatlantic Persuasion,* esp. pp. 170. 211.

25. Gladstone to Lyttelton 10 Sept. 1847, on "religious nationality," *Religious Correspondence* II: 79–80. I also much thank Colin Matthew for allowing me to read his unpublished paper, "Gladstone's Religious Nationalism," which expertly explores the Vatican controversy of the 1870s. See also, D. M. Schreuder, "Gladstone and Max Müller Debate Nationality and German Unification," *Historical Studies* (forthcoming 1979).

26. J. R. Vincent, *Pollbooks: How Victorians Voted* (1967), p. 45; and also Vincent, *The Formation of the British Liberal Party, 1857–68* Chap. 2.

27. Gladstone to son Willy, 22 Oct. 1854, *Religious Correspondence* II: 154.

28. Vidler, *Essays in Liberality* (1957), Chap. 5.

29. Letter to editor *TLS,* 3 June 1977, p. 630.

30. See Norman Gash interestingly on Wilberforce and "sanctity," *TLS,* 27 May 1977, p. 654.

31. Cited in W. K. Hancock, *Politics in Pitcairn* (1947), p. 48.

32. Morley, *Gladstone* I: 190.

33. I thank Barry Smith for the reference to Gladstone and the anti-vaccination campaign. For Gladstone's refusal to support the cause of Russian Jewry in the 1880s see D. M. Schreuder, "Gladstone as 'Troublemaker': Liberal Foreign Policy and the German Annexation of Alsace-Lorraine," *Journal of British Studies* (Summer 1978).

34. Gladstone to Rev. Baldwin Brown, 29 July 1865, *Religious Correspondence* I: 220.

35. Gladstone to his wife, 18 Aug. 1842, *ibid.,* I: 84.

36. Matthew, Introduction, *Diaries* III and V is superb on the general significance of the budget policy. Also F. W. Hirst, *Gladstone as Financier and Economist* (1931), pp. 50–154.

37. E.g., Gladstone to Granville, 5 Oct. 1885, on "local government" in Agatha Ramm, ed., *The Political Correspondence of Mr. Gladstone and Lord Granville, 1876–86* (1962) II: 403.

38. See D. M. Schreuder, "Gladstone and Italian Unification: The Making of a Liberal?" *English Historical Review* 85 (1969).

39. James Bryce, *International Relations* (1922), p. 203.

40. Carsten Holbraad, *The Concert of Europe* (1970), pp. 165–68.

41. Gladstone cabinet mem., 23 Nov. 1870; addit. MSS. 44759 f. 203.

42. Gladstone to Granville, 25 Sept. 1870, Ramm, *Political Correspondence,* I: 130–31.

43. W. N. Medlicott, *Bismarck, Gladstone and the Concert of Europe* (1956); and Gladstone to Granville, 8 Oct. 1870, in Ramm, *Political Correspondence,* I: 140. See also Kenneth Bourne, *The Foreign Policy of Victorian England, 1830–1902* (1970), esp. pp. 95–96 and 138–45.

44. John Ward, *Colonial Self-Government: The British Experience, 1759–1856* (1976), pp. 80–81, 240–46. Also, Paul Knaplund, *Gladstone and Britain's Imperial Policy* (1927), and D. M. Schreuder, "Locality and Metropolis in the Bitish Empire: A Note on

Some Connections Between the British North America Act (1867) and Gladstone's First Irish 'Home Rule' Bill (1886)," in *Studies in Local History; Essays in Honour of Winifred Maxwell,* edited by T. R. H. Davenport, *et al.* (1976), pp. 48–58.

45. This is best set out in R. Robinson and J. A. Gallagher, with A. Denny, *Africa and the Victorians: The Official Mind of Imperialism* (1961), Chap. 5, "Gladstone's Bondage in Egypt."

46. Checkland, *The Gladstones,* p. 398.

47. *Diaries* III: 190—Easter Sunday, 27 March 1842; and Gladstone to Rev. J. Nicholl, 22 Feb. 1842, *Religious Correspondence* I: 57. For the "Peelite parishes" see G. Best's masterly, *Temporal Pillars: Queen Anne's Bounty, The Ecclesiastical Commissioners, and the Church of England* (1964), pp. 348–460, and Table 7, pp. 547–48.

48. Lynch, "Was Gladstone a Tractarian?" pp. 371–77.

49. G. I. T. Machin, "The Maynooth Grant, the Dissenters and Disestablishment, 1845–47," *English Historical Review* 82 (1967): 61–85.

50. Diaries III: 336–29 Dec. 1843; *Religious Correspondence* I: 60–61 (Gladstone to Wilberforce, 15 March 1844).

51. D. L. Edwards, *Leaders of the Church of England* (1971), pp. 167–68; and K. O. Morgan, *Wales in British Politics, 1868-1922* (1970), pp. 32–33.

52. Gladstone to Rev. C. Marriott, 31 May 1852, *Religious Correspondence* II: 18.

53. Gladstone to Rev. E. Stokes, 17 May 1854, *ibid.* I: 127.

54. Gladstone to Manning, 26 Dec. 1864, *ibid.* II: 36–37.

55. Gladstone to son Willy, Easter 1865, *ibid.* II: 168–69.

56. Gladstone to Lyttelton, 10 Sept. 1847; *ibid.* I: 78–79; and Ursula Henriques, "The Jewish Emancipation Controversy in 19th Century Britain," *Past and Present* 40 (August 1968).

57. Gladstone to Manning, 12 March 1848, *Religious Correspondence* II: 279–80.

58. Walter R. Arnstein, *The Bradlaugh Case: A Study in Late-Victorian Opinion and Politics* (1965), pp. 190–91.

59. Gladstone to Newman, 3 Sept. 1844, T. Kenny, *The Political Thought of John Henry Newman* (1957), p. 125.

60. This view endured: Gladstone to Rev. S. Buss, 13 Sept. 1894, *Religious Correspondence* II: 148; also, G. Best, "The Religious Difficulties in National Education in England, 1800–70," *Cambridge Historical Journal* 12 (1956): 155–73.

61. See *Religious Correspondence* I: 170 (Gladstone to Earl of Shaftsbury, 7 May 1872); and P. J. Welch, "The Revival of an Active Convocation of Canterbury, 1852–55," *Journal of Ecclesiastical History* 10 (1959): 188–97.

62. *Religious Correspondence* II: 7 (Gladstone to Phillimore, 26 Feb. 1847); also Olive Anderson, "The Incidence of Civil Marriage in Victorian England and Wales," *Past and Present* 69 (Nov. 1975): 50–87.

63. Gladstone to son Willy, Easter 1865, *Religious Correspondence* II: 168–73.

64. E.g., Gladstone's letters to his son in the 1860s on Church Rates in ibid.; and the definitive study by Olive Anderson, "Gladstone's Abolition of Compulsory Church Rates: A Minor Political Myth and its Historiographical Career," *Journal of Ecclesiastical History* 25 (1974), esp. 186–87.

65. G. I. T. Machin, "Gladstone and Nonconformity in the 1860s: The Formation of an Alliance," *Historical Journal* 17 (2) (1974): 352 (Gladstone to Wilberforce, 21 March 1863).

66. Gladstone to Phillimore, 26 Feb. 1850, *Religious Correspondence* I: 100.

67. Gladstone to son Willy, Easter 1865, *ibid.*

68. *Chapter of Autobiography,* pp. 150-51.

69. *Ibid.,* p. 149.

70. Gladstone to Miss Burdett-Coutts, 22 April 1866, *Religious Correspondence* I: 147.

71. Gladstone, "Is the Church Worth Preserving?" part 2 of the pamphlet on *"Ritualism"* (1874); *Gleanings* (1879) II: 175.

72. *Hansard* (3) CXXIV, col. 1148.

73. *Autobiographica* I, doc. 67; *Diaries* III, 15 June 1840; and F. D. Schneider: "The Anglican Quest for Authority: Convocation and the Imperial Factor, 1850-70," *Journal of Religious History* 9 (2) (Dec. 1976).

74. Gladstone to Phillimore, 13 Feb. 1865, *Religious Correspondence* I: 153-54. Also E. R. Norman, *The Catholic Church and Ireland in the Age of Rebellion* (1965).

75. P. M. H. Bell, *Disestablishment in Ireland and Wales* (1969), p. 158; and Machin, "Gladstone and Nonconformity," p. 35, citing Newman Hall to Gladstone, 16 May 1867.

76. See E. R. Norman, *Anti-Catholicism in Victorian England* (1968); and J. C. Lowe, "The Tory Triumph of 1868 in Blackburn and in Lancashire," *Historical Journal* 16 (1973): 733-48.

77. *Religious Correspondence* I: 121-25.

78. *The Nonconformist* (21 May 1873), quoted W. H. Mackintosh, *Disestablishment and Liberation: The Movement for the Separation of the Anglican Church from State Control* (1972), p. 248. See also N. J. Richards, "British Nonconformity and the Liberal Party, 1868-1906," *Journal of Religious History* 9 (1977): esp. 388-99.

79. Gladstone to *Nonconformist,* 22 March 1876.

80. See Brian Heeney, *A Different Kind of Gentleman: Parish Clergy as Professional Men in Early and Mid-Victorian England* (Conference on British Studies, 1976); D. M. Thomson, "The 1851 Religious Census—Problems and Possibilities," *Victorian Studies* 11 (1967-68): 87-97.

81. *Chapter of Autobiography,* pp. 140-41.

82. M. MacColl, "Mr. Gladstone as a Theologian," in *The Life of W. E. Gladstone,* edited by W. Reid (1899), Chap. 5, pp. 245-73.

83. Dean Church, 1868 in Morley, *Gladstone* II: 175.

84. *Pall Mall Gazette* (24 Nov. 1868), in Bell, *Disestablishment in Ireland and Wales,* p. 77. See also S. M. Ingham, "The Disestablishment Movement in England, 1868-74," *Journal of Religious History* 3 (1964).

85. *Chapter of Autobiography,* p. 98; and *19th Century* 21 (Nov. 1878), for "Electoral Facts."

86. *Chapter of Autobiography,* pp. 101-102.

87. *Chapter of Autobiography,* p. 150; also *Gleanings* (1879) II: 103: "Our conception of the law of nature itself is, in the main, formed by Christian traditions, habits and ideas," and *Midlothian Speeches,* p. 245.

88. Gladstone, "Locksley Hall and the Jubilee," *19th Century* (Jan. 1867): 17; and *Personal Papers of Lord Rendel* (1935), p. 95.

89. Hammond, *Gladstone and the Irish Nation,* p. 549.

90. *Chapter of Autobiography,* pp. 102-103.

91. Hamer, *Liberal Politics in the age of Gladstone and Rosebery,* pp. 71-76.

92. R. T. Shannon, *The Crisis of Imperialism* (1974), p. 71.

93. G. Kitson Clark, Introduction to R. T. Shannon, *Gladstone and the Bulgarian Agitation, 1876* (1963).

94. J. A. Hobson, *Confessions of an Economic Heretic* (1938), pp. 18-19.

95. J. H. Grainger, *Character and Style in English Politics* (1969), pp. 94-101; Marx is quoted by Hugh Lloyd Jones, reviewing S. S. Prawer, *Karl Marx and World Literature* (1977), in *TLS,* 4 Feb. 1977, p. 119.

96. Gladstone, "Daniel O'Connell," *19th Century* (Jan. 1889): 152.

97. TLS, 16 Dec. 1977, p. 1481.

98. Vidler, *Orb and Cross,* p. 153.

THE NONCONFORMIST CONSCIENCE
Richard J. Helmstadter

IN THE NINETEENTH AND EARLY TWENTIETH CENTURIES religious Nonconformity played a prominent role in English public life. During that time religion was a generally more important feature of the social and political landscape than it became after the first World War, and those Protestants who dissented from the Church of England constituted an important interest group. Congregationalists, Baptists, Methodists, Presbyterians, Quakers, Unitarians, and members of a host of minor sects differed from each other in many respects, but they shared social situations, social values, and political goals sufficiently that they were conscious of forming a distinctive community within English society. As Matthew Arnold vigorously pointed out in *Culture and Anarchy,* Nonconformists also shared a tendency to emphasize rigid codes of personal behavior. They were the heirs of the Puritans, and their views of life were suffused with considerations of conscience. It is not surprising that the term "Nonconformist conscience" came to be used as the name for Nonconformist opinion on public affairs.

The term, "Nonconformist conscience," did not, however, come into common use until the last decade of the nineteenth century, and it identified a configuration of views peculiar to that time. Nonconformity was then in the midst of a critical period in its history. It still enjoyed considerable strength, but it was beset with deep-seated confusion from which it never recovered. Earlier in the century the Nonconformist community possessed a relatively cohesive culture and a clear political orientation. It is the argument of this chapter that Nonconformist culture began to disintegrate in the late nineteenth century, and that the "Nonconformist conscience," when compared with the synthesis achieved earlier, sheds some light on the nature of that collapse.

On the surface there were few signs of weakness in the Nonconformist community toward the end of the nineteenth century. The only clear and readily visible evidence of declining vitality was the fact that Nonconformists constituted a smaller proportion of the whole population of England than they had in the middle of the century. At the time of the religious census in 1851, Nonconformists had accounted for about half the church-going public. There was never another national, official census of church attendance, but numerous local inquiries suggest that, at the turn of the century, rather more than half of those who normally attended church on Sunday were Nonconformists. Neither Nonconformity nor the Church of England, however, managed to increase their numbers sufficiently to keep pace with the growth of the population as a whole in the second half of the nineteenth century. On the political front, moreover, advancing democracy provides an additional reason for the decline in relative size and importance of the Nonconformist portion of the electorate. Reinforced by Victorian social convention, church-going was a normal and expected feature of upper and middle-class life. This was emphatically not the case among the working classes, the majority of whom had little or no connection with any church. Therefore the Reform Acts of 1867 and 1884, by extending the franchise further among the working classes, increased the number of voters who lived outside the range of the pulpit, and, presumably, beyond the reach of the religious press.

Nonetheless, Nonconformity toward the end of the century could still hope to wield considerable political power. With the exception of the Wesleyan Methodists, the large denominations, the Congregationalists, the Baptists, and the various schismatical Methodist bodies, were traditionally supporters of the Liberal party. From the middle of the century, the Wesleyans had been moving in a leftward direction, and by the 1890s they too, for the most part, had joined the Liberal camp. When they spoke with a united voice, Nonconformists were able to make their influence clearly felt in the Liberal party, and, when opinion among them was aroused and organized, they were able to have some impact on national affairs.

The machinery for organizing Nonconformist opinion, moreover, became much stronger and more efficient in the last two decades of the century. In most of the denominations central organization was improved, and the movement for reunion among the Wesleyans and the other Methodist groups was growing. The desirability of more cooperation among the denominations was clearly perceived in the 1880s, and in a number of towns free church councils were created to coordinate Nonconformist activity. This movement produced several national free church congresses in the 1890s, and eventually, in 1896, the National

Council of Evangelical Free Churches was established. By 1901 the National Council had gone some way toward establishing machinery for unity among the free churches. Almost every eminent free church leader supported the movement, and seven hundred local councils and thirty-six district federations helped organize the rank and file.

Developments in religious journalism also helped to make more possible the organization of Nonconformist opinion in the twenty-five or thirty years before the war. Throughout the century there was an enormous number of religious magazines and newspapers, and a great many ordinary secular newspapers adopted an editorial position which actively supported either the Church of England or Nonconformity. Some of those periodicals and newspapers were ably conducted, of high quality and great influence. One thinks of the *Eclectic Review,* the *British Quarterly Review,* and, on a less exalted literary level, the *Methodist Magazine.* Among newspapers, the *Leeds Mercury* under the Baines family from the beginning of the century, the *Patriot* under Josiah Conder in the thirties and forties, and the *Nonconformist* vigorously edited by Edward Miall from its foundation in 1841 until his death in 1881, were outstanding leaders of Nonconformist opinion. In the 1800s, Nonconformist journalism was able to draw on the techniques that were being developed to encourage massive increases in circulation for secular newspapers. At the height of its influence in the 1870s, the *Nonconformist,* a paper produced in the old-fashioned, staid, high-toned style, did not achieve a circulation above 15,000. In the early 1880s, the *Christian World,* more brightly written, less rigorously political, more chatty and with features for the ladies, edged toward a circulation of 150,000. Two newspapers which emerged in the eighties quickly became recognized as authoritative voices within the Nonconformist community. With their very large readership, they helped shape Nonconformist views on public affairs more effectively than had previously been possible. The *Methodist Times* was founded in 1885 by Hugh Price Hughes, and edited by him in order to propagate the generally progressive views which constituted what he called the Forward Movement. The *British Weekly* was established in 1886 as the successor to the *British Quarterly Review.* That canny man of letters, William Robertson Nicoll, edited it until his death in 1923. He made it the preeminent newspaper of Nonconformity. Less adventurous than Hughes, and more concerned with the economic implications of a large circulation, Nicoll succeeded in making the *British Weekly* the principal voice of moderate free church opinion.

Nonconformists had traditionally put great stress on conscience. They were, notoriously, men easily roused to militant defense of those principles which they considered rooted in conscience. Their great struggle, indeed, had been for freedom to worship as they pleased, for freedom of conscience. John Stuart Mill accorded religious Dissenters an honored place in the story of the progress of liberty. John Morley echoed a widely held view when he said of Nonconformity in 1873: "Its creeds may be narrow, its spirit contentious, its discipline unscriptural, its ritual bleak, its votaries plebeian. . . . Dissent is not picturesque, but it possesses a heroic political record."[1] Ironically, the late Victorian improvement in the organization of Nonconformity, and the appearance in general usage of the expression "Nonconformist conscience," occurred when the heroic days of politics and conscience were over for religious dissenters. Their leaders at the turn of the century seemed frequently concerned with problems too petty to warrant the energy and grand language expended on them, and the Nonconformist conscience seemed too often to draw on what was narrow rather than on what was heroic in the Nonconformist tradition.

The term "Nonconformist conscience" was first used, as far as I can discover, in the correspondence columns of *The Times* in late November, 1890. Parnell, the leader of the Irish Party, had been named a correspondent in a divorce action brought by Captain O'Shea against his wife. No defense was offered, and when the judgment was handed down on 17 November, it touched off a wave of scandalized indignation in England that eventually drove Parnell from public life. *The Times,* inspired with its own grievance against Parnell, played a leading role in rousing public opinion to righteousness, as did a number of other newspapers. But the most unbridled denunciations of Parnell, from the beginning until the end, came from Nonconformist ministers, especially, perhaps, from Hugh Price Hughes the militant Methodist who liked to compare himself with Savonarola. On 19 November in the *Pall Mall Gazette,* John Clifford, the most eminent among a new wave of progressive Baptists, put the Nonconformist position on Parnell clearly and carefully: "He must go. British politicians are not what they were. Men legally convicted of immorality will not be permitted to lead in the legislature." Hughes was less restrained. "Parnell must go," he told his family. "If necessary everything must go. What are parties and causes compared to an issue like this—the establishing of Christ's kingdom?"[2] And on the Sunday after the judgment, Hughes pressed on his congregation at St. James's Hall the rather strained argument that to permit Parnell to remain leader of the Irish Party would be "to sacrifice our religion."[3] More to the point, Hughes urged Gladstone to consider that, unless he got rid of Parnell, he might be sacrificing the support of Nonconformist voters, for "there is no subject on which the Free Churches of the country feel so deeply as on social purity."[4] On 28 November "A Wesleyan Minister," possibly Hughes himself, demanded in a letter to *The Times* "unconditional abdication" from Parnell: "Nothing less will satisfy the Nonconformist conscience now." Thus the term emerged, and over the next twenty-five years it was frequently heard.

The Parnell affair helps to illuminate the nature of the Nonconformist conscience. It is true that the Nonconformist community in the late nineteenth and early twentieth centuries was corporately concerned with a wide range of political and social issues. The central organizations of the various denominations, and the National Free Church Council, felt increasing pressure during this period to speak out on problems of poverty and the slums, on the significance of socialism, on war in general and the Boer War in particular, on old age pensions, the place of the Lords in the constitution, and other important questions of the age. The more influential newspapers and the leading ministers encouraged the community to take up all these concerns and more. But special emphasis was concentrated on a narrow set of problems that related personal sin and social or political behavior. Parnell's scandal is a case in point. Along with improper sex, gambling and drink made up a trio of sins that the Nonconformist conscience found peculiarly irritating—a trio that Nonconformist leaders tried, sometimes successfully, to raise to the level of important public issues. "The three deadly enemies of England" were identified by Hugh Price Hughes in the *Methodist Times* (6 June 1895) as "drink, impurity and gambling."

Was the Nonconformist conscience rooted in a coherent view or philosophy of society and politics? Clearly the answer must be negative. While there was a definite drift among Nonconformist ministers in the generation before the war toward greater sympathy with the problems of the poor, there was no distinctively Nonconformist solution to the problem of poverty and, indeed, no consensus within the free church community as to what should be done. There was clearly an increasing disposition on the part of many Nonconformists to encourage the state to play a more active role in maintaining social welfare, but there was no consensus on specific measures. Paradoxically, at a time when the community and its organs of opinion were better organized than ever before, a systematically organized Nonconformist vision of the state and the means of social progress did not exist. There was a striking unity of free church opinion on "the deadly enemies of England," but this agreement on the evils of sex, gambling and drink represented an unstable amalgam of half-rejected tradition and current fashion. The Nonconformist conscience did not bring about a consensus of distinctive free church opinion on more important issues.

There is a parallel here, of course, between the Nonconformist conscience and the so-called New Liberalism of the same period. Nor is the parallel merely a matter of accident. Perhaps those who claimed that Nonconformity was the backbone of the Liberal party claimed too much, but there can be no doubt that the Liberals, at least from the beginning of Gladstone's leadership in the mid 1860s, owed a great deal to the organized support of Nonconformity. Near the end of the nineteenth century a number of leading Liberals lost confidence in what one might call the Gladstonian synthesis which dominated the party in the previous generation. This happened at the same time that a number of leading Nonconformists were rejecting the coherent mid-Victorian synthesis which had prevailed among religious Dissenters. Both the leaders of the Liberal party and the leaders of Nonconformity were responding to similar problems, and neither the politicians nor the religious chieftains succeeded in reshaping their traditions sufficiently to meet adequately the demands of the twentieth century. Both groups of leaders treated their traditions with profound ambivalence. Both rejected much that was considered fundamentally important by their predecessors. Neither group succeeded in creating a satisfactory new synthesis.

    In sharp contrast to the weakness and tendency toward triviality of the Nonconformist conscience at the turn of the century, was the synthesis Dissenters achieved in the early and middle portions of Victoria's reign. For fifty years, from the 1830s to the 1880s, Nonconformists shared a comparatively well-integrated and coherent view of society, social progress, the state, and conscience. During this period, before the creation of the National Free Church Council and before the appearance of dissenting newspapers with circulations as large as that of the *British Weekly*, Nonconformists did not possess the organizational machinery that became available a little later on, but their community was probably more solidly united by widely held social and religious attitudes that interlocked and therefore reinforced each other. Central to these interrelated attitudes and ideas was the theology of evangelicalism.

    By the middle of the 1830s all the Dissenting denominations had felt the force of the great Evangelical revival of the eighteenth century. Even that intellectual elite among the Nonconformists, the Unitarians, had felt the emotional attraction of religion of the heart, but the Unitarians never fully entered the Evangelical fold. As their social position declined in the later nineteenth century, Unitarians found themselves increasingly on the fringe of the Dissenting world, or beyond. The National Council of Evangelical Free Churches did not admit Unitarians. All the larger denominations, however, and a considerable portion of the Church of England, warmly embraced the central tenets of Evangelical truth by the 1830s. Evangelical theology was by no means as systematic and logically precise as the theology of Calvinism or the medieval schoolmen. Nor was it as intellectually demanding. But evangelicalism did contain a sufficient number of interrelated and widely shared theological positions that it is possible to describe it systematically.

Evangelicals all placed primary emphasis on the salvation of individual souls. In this, as in all its essentials, evangelicalism reflected the theological position developed in Wesleyan Methodism in the second half of the eighteenth century. Emphasis on individual salvation was a part of the Arminian theology advocated by John Wesley, but such emphasis was familiar among the Calvinists too. It was easily accepted within those Evangelical denominations such as the Congregationalists and Particular Baptists whose theological traditions were Calvinist. In the sixteenth and seventeenth centuries Calvinists had placed much more emphasis on the community of the saved, the visible and corporate elite that constituted their churches. Evangelicals did not stress the select community of the saved because, following the Arminian position and rejecting the Calvinist, they avoided the question of predestination and preached that all men might be saved. That Christ died to save all men was universally believed among evangelicals, and this more than anything else distinguished them from Calvinists. Nevertheless, confusingly and illogically, most Congregationalists and Particular Baptists, reluctant to admit a clear break with their theological past, continued to call themselves Calvinist as late as the 1880s. While most accepted the label "modified Calvinist," some insisted on being called "strict" or even "hyper-Calvinist" while preaching the possibility of salvation for all. Salvation, for most Evangelicals, meant going to heaven after death. Those poor souls who were not saved were thought to suffer never-ending pain in hell. More sophisticated versions of salvation were available, but they were exceptions to the general rule.

A standardized version of the process of salvation was accepted throughout the Evangelical community. It was preached from countless pulpits; it was taught in the denominational seminaries where ministers were trained; it was published in manuals intended to help sinners along their own roads to glory. John Angell James, the Congregationalist pastor of Carrs Lane Chapel in Birmingham, published the most successful of the manuals in 1834. The angel James, as he was sometimes called, designed *The Anxious Inquirer After Salvation* for those who asked, "with some degree of anxiety, what shall I do to be saved?" He took his readers step by step through the process which culminated in conversion, that religious experience which Evangelicals frequently confounded with salvation and confidently regarded as the most important step preliminary to permanent residence in heaven. *The Anxious Inquirer* subsequently appeared in many further editions and was very widely distributed by the nondenominational Religious Tract Society. "Millions in heaven are already saved," James assured his readers, "and myriads more are on the road to salvation. God is still willing, and Christ is still as able to save you as he was them."[5] That was the central Evangelical message.

In keeping with their very strong tendency to treat men as individuals rather than as members of a larger corporation such as the church or the state, Evangelicals accorded to each individual a heavy weight of responsibility for his own salvation. This belief in the ability of individual men to shape their own destinies ran directly counter to the older Calvinist belief in divine predestination. Almost certainly, the Evangelical commitment to the idea of freedom of choice and the significance of individuals reflects the dramatic opening of new ranges of opportunity for individuals in England during the time of the Industrial Revolution. "You are invited" proclaimed the *Anxious Inquirer.* "If you neglect the invitation . . . you will find at last that you were lost, not in consequence of any purpose of God determining you to be lost, but in consequence of your own unbelief."[6]

Each individual's active responsibility for the ultimate destiny of his soul began with the awakening of his conscience. The conscience was, indeed, fundamentally important in the Evangelical scheme of salvation, and conscience pervaded the Evangelical view of the world. Conscience, for Evangelicals, was the principal guide to action. Conscience was essential to salvation, and the key to individual improvement and social progress. Without conscience, all would be lost. Every man's concern for salvation began with his conscience, with his awareness of sin in general and recognition of his own sinful condition in particular. Once aware of the depth of his own depravity and frightened, perhaps terrorized, by the prospect of eternal damnation, the sinner was ripe for reformation. Thus did conscience, or awareness of sin, lie at the base of his subsequent pilgrimage of grace.

The next step on the road to conversion for the sinful Evangelical was recognition that he could not overcome his sinfulness entirely by his own efforts. Striving to increase anxiety at this stage, James admonished his anxious inquirers: "You have not only sin enough in yourselves to deserve the bottomless pit, and to sink you to it unless it be pardoned; but sin enough, if it could be divided and distributed to others, to doom multitudes to perdition."[7] At this point the sinner was caught in painful tension between his own responsibility and his apparent helplessness. Resolution lay in the Evangelical view of the Atonement.

Aided by the Holy Spirit, the successful inquirer learned to accept as if it were part of his own experience that Christ died on the cross to cleanse every man of sin, to take upon Himself the guilt of every man so that every man might be saved. He who truly believed in Christ and His atoning sacrifice was thereby enabled to cast himself on His mercy and rise above the intolerable burden of his sinful humanity. The feeling that this had really happened, the feeling that one had accepted Christ and the Atonement in a way that was profoundly vital and meaningful, the feeling that Christ had at that very moment welcomed oneself into a new and better life, all this is what evangelicals called conversion. Conversion was an experience, not an intellectual conviction. Evangelical theology was rooted more in feeling and practical experience than in thought. Central to the experience of conversion was a starkly simple theological version of the Atonement. The Atonement was, therefore, the central theological doctrine of evangelicalism. That is why Evangelicals could advertise their orthodoxy by claiming loyalty to "Christ and Him crucified," a phrase with implications commonly understood throughout the evangelical world.

Until late in the nineteenth century, in order to become a fully joined, communicating member of most evangelical Nonconformist chapels, an applicant was required to testify that he had experienced conversion. Because conversion was a formal requirement, the testimonies of many must have been mere formalities. Applicants of good character, or good reputation at least, were never turned down. Nevertheless, the sense of having been born anew was clearly real for some, and the insistent emphasis upon conversion in Victorian chapel life, along with the increased status enjoyed by the converted in the chapel community, encouraged most Nonconformists to treat conversion very seriously. Certainly the rhetoric in which the experience was discussed—and it was discussed frequently—helped to reinforce the view that an individual's personal relationship with God was much more important than corporate worship. Also the idea that each individual was master of his fate was strengthened by the Evangelical preacher's perpetual plea to the unconverted to decide for Christ before death made decision impossible.

Underlying the simple evangelical interpretation of the Atonement was a simple view of the Bible. Almost all Evangelical Nonconformists, until Biblical scholarship and Biblical Criticism began to make headway among them in the 1880s, considered that the Bible was God's revelation written down by men acting under the direct guidance of divine inspiration. They accepted the Bible as true in a straightforward literal sense, and they made frequent reference to proof texts to support their central message about sin, salvation, and the Atonement. When the nature of Biblical inspiration began to be questioned in the late nineteenth century, and when evangelical Nonconformists felt the force of scholarly criticism which called into question the authority of the Bible as a repository of true statements, Evangelical theology began to crumble.

Evangelical Nonconformity produced no great scholars in the nineteenth century. The general drift of evangelicalism, which stressed feeling and experience more than systematic thinking, was toward practical rather than intellectual concerns. The Dissenting Academies which had been progressive centers of learning in the eighteenth century became, for the most part, seminaries for training ministers in the nineteenth. Ministers, moreover, concentrated on expository preaching aimed at encouraging conversions rather than on communal worship or on systematically raising the level of religious knowledge among their congregations. The thrust of evangelicalism toward the practical tended to de-emphasize the distinction between the ministry and the laity; and, in spite of the great attention given to the fate of the soul after death, the Evangelical orientation toward usefulness tended to encourage activity in this world. In practical philanthropy and practical politics Victorian Nonconformists were very active indeed, and in both spheres they developed policies and ideas that stressed the conscience and were in harmony with their theology of individualism.

The basic political posture of nineteenth-century Nonconformity derived from the traditional struggle of Dissenters for liberty of conscience, for greater freedom to decide for themselves in matters of worship and ultimate truth. After the Glorious Revolution of 1688, which resulted in toleration for Protestant Dissent, the political attention of Dissenters centered on achieving relief from the civil disabilities which their Nonconformity still entailed.

Heading the list of Dissenters' grievances were the Test and Corporation Acts. The Test Act (1673) made it illegal for any persons not receiving communion in the Church of England to hold office under the Crown, and the Corporation Act (1661) did the same for offices in municipal corporations. Conscientious Dissenters were thereby barred from many public offices, and Dissenters held up the Test and Corporation Acts as the principal symbols of their inferior status as citizens of the realm. Wealthy Dissenters in the City of London created an association, the Dissenting Deputies, in 1732 to press for repeal of the Test and Corporation Acts.

The Deputies soon became a sophisticated pressure group, working behind the scenes to protect the interests of Dissenters. In the late eighteenth century the Deputies helped organize a campaign for repeal that came close to success, and, finally, with the dissipation of the conservative reaction associated with the wars with France, the Deputies played a major role in pressing liberal Whigs to force through repeal in 1828. The Deputies, who continue to exist, have never abandoned the political style they developed in the eighteenth century. Consequently, when the techniques of pressure politics changed soon after 1828, the Deputies lost their role as the principal political voice of Nonconformity. More thrusting and vigorously optimistic leaders, including a number of newly powerful men from the self-confident industrial towns in the Midlands and the North, attracted Nonconformists toward associations designed to organize public opinion and exert pressure on Parliament from without.

Repeal of the Test and Corporation Acts was an event of high symbolic significance, for it conferred constitutional confirmation upon the movement toward religious pluralism in English society. But repeal was not the end of the Dissenters' battle for liberty. After repeal, Nonconformists continued to call for increased toleration and soon began to demand full equality with the Church of England. Their continued failure to achieve equality, along with their more successful but very long and drawn out struggle against legally imposed religious discrimination, encouraged Victorian Nonconformists to distrust the state. That the state should intervene as little as possible with the lives of its citizens was an axiom among Nonconformists. Furthermore, because they tended to confound conscience and religion and because they adamantly opposed any formal or legal connection between religion and the state, many Victorian Nonconformists assumed that there should be no connection between conscience and the state.

For a few years after repeal of the Test and Corporation Acts, Nonconformists hoped they had entered a new era in which the burden of discrimination under which they lived would be lifted. Their expectations were further raised by the passing of the Reform Act of 1832, but by the end of that decade they had achieved less than they had hoped for. A conservative reaction was making further progress difficult. Immediately following repeal of the Test and Corporation Acts, Nonconformists turned their attention to what they considered legal discrimination in five areas: church rates, marriages, civil registration of births and deaths, the ancient universities, and burials. They fought for reform in all five areas during the 1830s.

Church rates were taxes levied at the local parish level for the up-keep and repair of the parish church building. Anglicans and non-Anglicans alike were liable for these taxes which were based on the assumption, clearly false by the 1830s, that all the ratepayers would be worshippers in the Church of England. Nonconformists naturally found church rates oppressive, and in the 1830s they began to mount a campaign against the rates. In some parishes some Nonconformists refused to pay the church rates on the ground that conscience prevented their paying for support of a church whose association with the state they deplored. Some of those who refused to pay the church rate had their household goods seized and sold, and some went to prison. The battle against church rates was fought hard for more than thirty years. Beginning in the later fifties, the Liberation Society (see below) began to coordinate the thousands of local skirmishes and to carry the campaign into Parliament. The struggle, in which the language of conscience was freely employed, did not end until Gladstone secured statutory abolition of compulsory church rates in 1868.

The marriage question was more quickly settled by legislation passed in 1837. Before then Dissenters could not be married in their own chapels by their own ministers, but only in the Established Church by Anglican priests. The settlement of 1837 was not entirely satisfactory for it left lingering minor irritants, but the basic problem was solved. The Whig government dealt with the question by instituting civil marriage. Marriages could now be performed by the civil registrar of births, deaths, and marriages, or by Nonconformist ministers in chapels licensed for marriages so long as the civil registrar was present.

Civil registration of births, deaths, and marriages was itself introduced in 1837 to improve record keeping, and it incidentally met another Nonconformist complaint. Before 1837, the only official record of births, deaths, and marriages was the parish register, kept by the priest in each of the nearly 15,000 parishes. The record of births, moreover, was a record of baptism only, presumed in those days of precarious infant lives to have taken place soon after birth. Nonconformists, therefore, were compelled to have their children baptized in an Anglican ceremony by the parish priest if they wished to be able to establish a legally valid record of their birth dates. Civil registration resolved this difficulty entirely. It was, moreover, one more step toward further separation of the functions of the Church and the state, a step in the direction that Nonconformists approved.

Nonconformists were effectively excluded from taking degrees at the two ancient universities by the requirement of submission to the thirty-nine articles, the doctrinal code of the Church of England. At Oxford submission was required upon matriculation, at Cambridge upon taking a degree. Wealthy Nonconformists were, therefore, able to send their sons to Cambridge, where if they were conscientious about their Nonconformity they were unable to receive degrees. Oxford and Cambridge further irritated Dissenters by opposing in the early 1830s the granting of a charter to the new London University. London received its charter in 1837. Oxford ceased to require submission to the thirty-nine articles upon matriculation after the mid-1850s. But Nonconformists had to await Gladstone's first administration before, in 1871, they obtained full access to the degrees and most of the fellowships at Oxford and Cambridge.

Burials proved a much more difficult and troubling issue than marriages, perhaps because the solution to the problem involved interfering with the control of the Church of England over its own property. The burial question added heat to the Nonconformist contention that the property of the Established Church was in fact the property of the nation at large, that it ought to be removed from the control of the Church and devoted to national and nondenominational uses. In the nineteenth century most urban Dissenting chapels, and the poorer rural chapels, had no ground in which to bury their dead. They were compelled to use the churchyards of the Established Church, where they might meet with several sorts of trouble. The parish priest might simply refuse permission to use his churchyard; he might dictate what should appear on the tombstone and disallow the title "Reverend" for a departed Nonconformist minister; he would almost certainly deny Nonconformist ministers permission to conduct services in his churchyard. Not until the Burials Act of 1880 did Nonconformists win significant rights of entry into parochial churchyards. The Burials Act opened the churchyards to any Christian and orderly form of service, and the major Nonconformist complaint was answered. In the meantime, however, the creation of public cemeteries in densely populated areas helped make burials, next to church rates, the most acutely distressing and widespread Nonconformist grievance in the mid-Victorian period. The legislation of 1855 creating public cemeteries provided that each cemetery be divided into ground consecrated by an Anglican bishop and intended for Anglican burials, and unconsecrated ground intended for the rest. Endless trouble ensued, about the lower social status of unconsecrated ground, or about the character of the wall dividing the two areas. Nonconformists favored inconspicuous walls; the notorious Bishop Phillpotts of Exeter insisted on solid masonry at least three feet high; Dissenters, quite rightly, interpreted this as insulting. Time, and diminished antagonism between Dissent and the Established Church, gradually resolved these difficulties. They were never of great consequence, perhaps, but they distressed many families at times of personal grief and made the conflict between Church and Dissent seem deeply meaningful to a great many ordinary people.

Nonconformists, then, distrusted the state in the early and mid-Victorian periods because it dealt so slowly with their grievances. The state took more than fifty years to do what they hoped, just after the great reforms of 1828 and 1832, would be done in less than five. Furthermore, the state created new grievances as it moved into new, and religiously sensitive, areas of national life. Chief among these new areas was primary education for the poor. Among churchmen and Dissenters both in the 1830s there were many who recognized that a substantial amount of public money would be required every year in order to support an adequate number of primary schools for the great majority of English children who were unable to pay the cost of their education. At this time character building and improved morality were considered important goals in primary education. The state, indeed, was pressed to support education in order to create a more moral and therefore more peaceable, less potentially rebellious, citizenry. Partly as a consequence of the stress on morality in education, religion and education were closely intertwined.

Both churchmen and Nonconformists, therefore, watched closely lest the state act in a way which would give an advantage to their ecclesiastical rivals. Governments proceeded cautiously, anxious not to become the victims of sectarian feuding. The state began to give annual grants for primary education in 1833, distributing the money through two educational societies, the National Society for Educating the Poor in the Principles of the Established Church, and the dissenting British and Foreign School Society. All went fairly smoothly for ten years. The basis of a department of education was established at the national level in 1839, a system of school inspectors was created, and the parliamentary grants grew larger each year.

Suddenly, in 1843, there exploded a major controversy which had a significant impact on the general Nonconformist view of the state. In that year the home secretary, Sir James Graham, introduced a bill for the better regulation of labor in factories. The bill contained clauses setting up a system of primary schools associated with the factories and effectively under the control of the Church of England priests in whose parishes the schools would be located. Nonconformists reacted violently to these educational clauses. Even the Wesleyan Methodists, the most conservative of the denominations and the least active politically, joined their more militant fellow Nonconformists in denouncing the clauses. Petitions and demonstrations helped organize the anger of the Nonconformist community, and the government hastily withdrew the clauses that were attracting the clamor. At no other time over the course of the century did the Nonconformist community act with such unity and such determination. As time went by, Nonconformists looked back with nostalgia on the events of 1843. They drew from their victory the assurance that they could prevent the state from enlarging the sphere of the Established Church if they kept a jealous eye on all the activities of the state. Their predilection to distrust the state, to think of the state as a dangerous potential obstacle to social progress, was confirmed and heightened by the educational clauses of Sir James Graham's factory bill.

As a direct result of the controversy of 1843, Edward Baines the younger, editor of the powerful *Leeds Mercury* and a prominent Congregationalist, mounted an attack on all state intervention in the realm of education. He convinced Congregationalists to set up a system of voluntary schools which refused all assistance from the state. For many years he campaigned for what he called the Voluntary Principle, a version of *laissez faire* with religion and education at its heart, couched in the language of political liberty. He insisted that Nonconformists, rejecting state support for religion in the name of liberty, must logically also reject state support for religious education. And he broadened his opposition to state interference to include most areas of life: "Governmental interference often retards advancement and shackles freedom. In support of my views, I appeal to the free press, the free literature, the free science, and the free education of England, in opposition to countries where all these things are taken under the care of Government."[8]

Strict voluntaryism in education proved impossible; it was beyond the resources of the voluntaries. Most Nonconformist schools continued to accept state grants after 1843 because they could not raise enough money from other sources. By the late 1860s even Baines recognized that private money would never come forward in amounts large enough to support a comprehensive system of primary education. W. E. Forster's important Education Act of 1870 created a system of nondenominational school boards, funded by local rates, to complement the work of the Anglican and Nonconformist education societies. A new phase of the volatile education controversy had begun.

The passionate vigor of the Nonconformist reaction to Sir James Graham's education clauses in 1843 had an impact well beyond the field of education. The church rate martyrs of the late 1830s had impelled Edward Miall to leave his pastorate of a Leicester Congregational chapel and establish the *Nonconformist* as the leading national organ of militantly radical Dissenters. Nonconformist anger at the educational clauses in 1843 encouraged Miall to organize the Anti-State Church Association in 1844. The association was renamed the Liberation Society on the advice of the more moderate Edward Baines in 1853. From shortly after its foundation until Miall's death in 1881, the Liberation Society was the most important political organization of the Nonconformist community. It took over the role once filled by the more old-fashioned and cautious Dissenting Deputies. It was more stridently militant, and it drew much more support from the industrial provinces. Whereas the Deputies had worked behind the political scenes to influence established political leaders, the Liberation Society appealed to public opinion and tried, with considerable success, to make Nonconformist views heard directly from Nonconformists in the House of Commons. Miall himself sat as MP for Rochdale, 1852–57, and for Bradford, 1869–74. He became a respected figure in political circles, widely recognized as the leading spokesman on political issues for liberal Nonconformity.

Miall and the Liberation Society helped organize the campaign against church rates, against religious discrimination in public cemeteries, against the religious exclusiveness of the ancient universities, and they kept a close eye on legislation in order to prevent new forms of religious inequality from emerging. But the society was committed to the belief that religious equality could not be finally achieved until the Church of England was disestablished and disendowed. Miall was riding the rising tide of democratic sentiment that increasingly threatened the Victorian social hierarchy. He sympathized with the Chartists and supported the Complete Suffrage Movement in the 1840s. He persistently attacked the aristocracy and the social order associated with it. He coupled religious equality with social equality, and he regarded the establishment of the Church of England as an important barrier in the way of general social progress. Not only did the establishment generate legal disabilities against Dissenters that had to be fought one by one, but it also encouraged a climate of snobbery in which Nonconformists suffered. "The upper ten thousand," he wrote, "with very few exceptions regard connection with the authorized ecclesiastical institution of the kingdom as inseparable from their elevated position. Until comparatively recent times, both Houses of Parliament were closed against Nonconformists. To this day, the great national universities are governed with a view to the interests of the State-Church. Is it surprising that, under such conditions, the higher professions gravitate towards it? To belong to the church is to side with respectability; to dissent from it is to cast in your lot with the vulgar. Accordingly, Dissenters, simply as such, are esteemed inferior."⁹

By the late 1850s the Liberation Society had become politically sophisticated. It served as a clearinghouse for information on Dissenters' legal and political concerns. It lobbied for Dissenters' interests in parliament. It sponsored traveling lecturers. Most important of all, perhaps, it began to organize politically aware Nonconformists at the constituency level in order to fight elections. During the decade of the sixties, the Liberation Society controlled what was probably the most effectively organized network of constituency associations in the kingdom. For some time Miall and the society had been moving toward a closer association with established politicians on the left, and as the Liberal Party emerged as a clear-cut successor to the Whigs in the sixties Liberationists tended to put their trust in Liberals. Gladstone, officially a Liberal from 1859, was especially attractive to Nonconformists. His obvious religiosity and his deeply serious moral sense appealed to Dissenters. Gladstone, moreover, was sensitive to Nonconformist fears and ambitions. Aware of Nonconformist power in many constituencies, he was determined at least to appear conciliatory. He introduced the legislation which abolished compulsory church rates, and his first administration disestablished the Church of Ireland, opened the universities more freely to Dissenters, and tried to settle the education question. It is not surprising, then, that Miall's campaign for disestablishment of the Church of England reached its climax during that administration. In both 1871 and 1872 Miall introduced disestablishment motions in the House of Commons, and each time his motions were seriously debated. They were rejected. Never again did disestablishment of the Church of England receive such serious political consideration. Ten years later, at the time of Miall's death, disestablishment had ceased to be an issue that interested politically sophisticated men.

The liberalism of Nonconformity in the mid-Victorian period was much more than a matter of political tactics and the personal attractiveness of Gladstone. The political tradition of Dissent was dominated by the call for liberty, and Dissenters had traditionally relied upon the political friendship of leading Whigs who liked to present their party as a bulwark of civil and religious liberty. Very different, of course, was the political tradition of Wesleyan Methodism. John Wesley himself had been a staunch Tory, concerned more with the preservation of good order than with the progress of liberty. His successor as the dominant figure in the Wesleyan Conference was Jabez Bunting, just as conservative as Wesley and no less willing to impose his will on the denomination. Until his death in 1858 the Wesleyan Methodists officially stood apart from most of the political activity of Dissent. But Wesleyan Methodists represented roughly the same groups in society as did the Congregationalists and the Baptists. It is not surprising, therefore, that over the course of the second half of the nineteenth century, Wesleyans moved into the Liberal camp along with the older Dissenting denominations. In the generation of Baines and Miall, the vision of society prevalent among Nonconformists, their schemes for social reform and their view of what constituted social progress all harmonized with positions taken up by Gladstone and the Liberal party.

Victorian Nonconformity was dominated by families belonging to the urban middle classes. Among the denominations, the Unitarians and the Quakers, both relatively small bodies, probably contained the largest proportion of wealthy families. Unitarians prided themselves on being the best educated and most open minded group among Dissenters. Quakers were probably the most socially exclusive. Congregationalists, New Connexion Methodists, and Wesleyan Methodists came next on a very rough general scale of wealth and social prestige. Baptists, Bible Christians, and other groups of Methodists followed closely behind. Of the major denominations, the least wealthy were the Primitive Methodists, an exception to the general middle-class rule that prevailed among all the other large Nonconformist churches.

It must not be thought that most Nonconformist congregations consisted of eminent merchants and manufacturers, bankers, or professional men. In all the large denominations there were many individual chapels that consisted almost entirely of working-class people. Even in the major urban chapels, such as Carrs Lane in Birmingham or East Parade in Leeds where the Baines family went, the majority of the congregation was drawn from social levels beneath what one usually considers middle class. Skilled artisans, shop keepers, clerks, domestic servants, and unskilled workers undoubtedly made up the majority of Nonconformists. The social mix varied from chapel to chapel, and town to town, but a general pattern seems clear. Most important chapels were dominated by a middle-class elite which provided most of the money and almost all the leadership. The politics of Nonconformity reflected the interests of that elite. The Nonconformist vision of society was essentially a middle-class vision. Writing in 1848, Algernon Wells, secretary of the Congregational Union, considered it a matter for regret that "our churches—everything about them—preaching, buildings, ministers, manners, notions, and practices—all have on them the air and impress of English middle-class life. Our churches," he continued, "have more and more worked themselves into this mould, as time and change have proceeded. They are at this time more exclusively of that class than was the case a century ago."[10] The political and social attitudes of Nonconformists were influenced by class as well as religion, but the influences of class were so much in harmony with those of religion that it is difficult to distinguish the two in the mid-Victorian period.

Early in the nineteenth century progressives of very different sorts, those men who generally approved the social and economic changes which were transforming English life, tended to select certain central features of the old social order as those most worthy of condemnation. They attacked privilege, patronage, and dependency as sources of corruption. They attacked paternalism as an enemy of liberty and manly independence. They attacked the aristocracy as the symbol and embodiment of privilege, patronage and paternalism. Nonconformists joined in this attack, impelled by the general considerations of their social class and encouraged by the individualism of their evangelical theology, by their traditional concern for liberty, and by their powerful commitment to an independent ecclesiology. With the Methodists excepted, the large Nonconformist denominations were made up of independent congregations that were proudly aware of their power to govern themselves. Each chapel financed its own operations, hired and fired its ministers, and established its own rules and regulations. As they became more deeply involved in missionary activity, both overseas and at home, the denominations developed more elaborate institutions for central organization. But the ideal of independence remained strong; perhaps the ideal grew even stronger as the reality faded.

This concern for local self-government fitted in particularly well with the concern for municipal self-government demonstrated by middle-class Nonconformists in the provincial towns. Nonconformists joined enthusiastically in the attack on privilege and corruption in the old order of society by supporting the campaign for parliamentary reform in 1830, 1831, and 1832. Elie Halevy, the great French historian of nineteenth-century England, wrote that immediately after the Reform of 1832, "in every borough, the Nonconformists formed the backbone of the majority. In every constituency they were probably the majority of the Liberal party, and in some places perhaps the majority of the electorate."[11] Yet Halevy could find only eight Nonconformists in the first reformed parliament: five Unitarians, a Quaker, a Congregationalist, and a Methodist. Nonconformity clearly did not include a significant number of men who were sufficiently rich and well established to leave their businesses in other hands and spend a large part of the year in London. But when municipal government was reformed in 1835, Dissenters flooded into town councils throughout the country. Strong at the local level, sparsely represented at the national, Nonconformists and men of their class naturally tended to distrust the central state which was still in aristocratic hands. Naturally, as well, they came to idealize the virtues of decentralized, local government which they could influence or control.

The progressive vision of society which Nonconformists shared with other liberals, a vision in which privilege and patronage were to be replaced with equality and individual independence, was embodied in the movement for free trade. Evangelical stress on individualism and personal responsibility supported the idea of a free market in labor. The idealized localism of provincial businessmen supported the call for an end to state interference in business affairs. Because the Corn Laws benefitted the landowning aristocracy by artificially maintaining the price of grain with tariffs, the campaign against the Corn Laws in the 1830s and 1840s attracted very strong Nonconformist support. Many chapels held anti-Corn Law tea meetings. The Anti-Corn Law League was able in 1841 to organize a meeting of nearly seven hundred Nonconformist ministers to demand repeal of the Corn Laws. After repeal the league organized an essay contest on the effects of free trade and a Baptist minister, Henry Dunckley, won first prize. Nonconformists raised free trade to the level of moral principle, and they saw its introduction as a critical turning point between the old order of society and the new. The Reverend F. A. Cox told his brother ministers in 1841 that, if the free trade movement failed, "despotism was likely to restore the darkness of the middle ages— that society would be on the eve of retrogression, and the bright era of the nineteenth century likely to suffer an eclipse."[12] The *British Quarterly Review,* edited by the Congregationalist historian Robert Vaughan, noted "the parallelism or coincidence of economical truth with practical Christianity"[13] in an article on the free-trade movement. Henry Dunckley wrote boldly that "Free Trade is but a part of the unrestricted development of the national mind; it implies the doing universally what is just."[14] The society of the future, as Nonconformists saw it at the middle of the century, was a middle-class millennium in which the corrupt power of the aristocracy was eliminated, the Church of England was merely another denomination like the rest, and every individual proved his own worth before God and his fellow men.

At this time Nonconformists had a clear view of the meaning of poverty, and there was little disagreement among them on the general question of how the condition of the poor might be improved. They considered poverty the result of two very different causes. Aristocratic oppression was one, and Nonconformists believed that the power of the aristocracy to oppress the poor either directly through taxation, or indirectly through destroying their ambition with paternalistic social arrangements, was rapidly fading away. The other cause of poverty, and the more important one, lay in the individual moral weakness of each poor person. Men were poor because they did not work hard enough, or because they were not thrifty enough, or because they were not independent enough to search out opportunities for self-improvement, or because they drank too much. Charles Haddon Spurgeon, the great Baptist preacher, wrote two series of tracts offering practical advice to the people: *John Ploughman's Talk* (1869) and *John Ploughman's Pictures* (1880). These tracts epitomize the attitudes toward poverty and the condition of the working classes which were widely held by Nonconformists of Spurgeon's generation. Individual self-help is the main theme of the tracts. Sobriety, persistence, work, and the force of independent willpower were pictured as the keys to personal success. "Stick to it and do it," Spurgeon had John Ploughman say. "Set a stout heart to a stiff hill, and the waggon will get to the top of it. There's nothing so hard but a harder thing will get through it; a strong job can be managed by a strong resolution. Have at it and have it. Stick to it and succeed."[15]

Until close to the end of the century, the Nonconformist explanation of poverty was optimistic. Aristocratic power was declining. And Nonconformists were committed to the idea that individuals really could change the course of their own lives so long as they lived in a condition of liberty. Conversion was a central and essential event in the lives of Evangelical Nonconformists. That men and women might be essentially changed, born again into a new way of life, was a principal article of belief among Evangelicals. Conversion from laziness to hard work and conversion from sin to righteousness did not seem far removed from each other, moreover, and evangelicals tended to confound them. The Religious Tract Society, the single greatest force in Evangelical publishing in the Victorian period, issued denunciations of dirt and waste and drink as well as pleas for the unconverted to throw down the burden of original sin and seek repose in Christ. Both social progress and eternal salvation seemed matters which individuals could determine. The choice was theirs. It was the duty of preachers and philanthropists both to make sure that the choice was governed by conscience. "Before you begin a thing," warned Spurgeon, "make sure it is the right thing to do: ask Mr. Conscience about it."[16]

Nonconformist ideas about poverty did not differ a great deal from the prevailing liberal view of the problem during the half century after the New Poor Law was passed in 1834. The more secular and scientific treatment of the poor, however, relied more heavily on pressure than on conversion. The theory behind the New Poor Law was that by making tax-supported welfare arrangements very uncomfortable, only those who absolutely needed such aid would seek it. The Charity Organization Society, founded in 1869, attempted to organize private charity along the same lines so that private generosity did not make unemployment so attractive that men and women would be discouraged from working. While they put much more stress on reformation of character, Nonconformist philanthropists shared with the secular social engineers the assumption that individuals controlled their own social destinies.

Perhaps the most characteristic Nonconformist effort at social reform in the early and mid-Victorian periods was the temperance movement. Drunkenness went out of fashion among the upper and middle classes early in the nineteenth century, and, at the same time, it began to be considered a serious social problem affecting the poor. It was easy to see drink as an obstacle to individual improvement and social progress. Drink inhibited work, destroyed ambition, and ruined health. Drink was a form of waste. Drunkards were dirty. Drink interrupted the orderly rhythm of effort which modern industrial life required. Drink diminished self-control. Drink anesthetized the conscience. It is not surprising that Nonconformists who valued sturdy independence, thrift, self-motivated effort, and success should come to regard drink as a device of the devil. The temperance movement began in the 1830s, and from that time most of the temperance leaders were Nonconformists. Temperance, which gradually came to mean total abstinence for many, became a feature of Victorian chapel life. Temperance societies were organized in many chapels to help provide a wholesome social life for adults, and Bands of Hope were established to set children on the right path. In keeping with the general Nonconformist approach to social reform, the temperance movement did not at first appeal to the state for legislation. Instead, the temperance reformers used the techniques of religious evangelism and appealed to the conscience of individual drinkers. Temperance meetings resembled religious revivals, as speakers, some of them converted drunkards, called upon the unreformed to cast aside their evil ways and enter upon righteous and sober lives.

But progress was disappointingly slow. As time went by, Nonconformists tended to elevate the importance of the drink question. Samuel Morley, an enormously wealthy Congregationalist hosiery manufacturer and an important figure in political and philanthropic circles, said in the early 1860s that "the Temperance cause lay at the root of all social and political progress in the country."[17] Many others must have agreed with Morley, for over the preceding ten years a prohibitionist movement had been developing to complement and support the call for personal reformation. Organized in Manchester in 1853, the United Kingdom Alliance called for law to make the task of conscience easier through legislation that would limit the sale of drink. The policy of the United Kingdom Alliance became, over the next half-century, the central policy of the temperance movement as a whole. Because it appealed to the state rather than the individual conscience, the UKA did not receive the support of the entire Nonconformist community, even at the end of the century. On the whole, however, Nonconformists were much more ready to appeal to the state at the end of the century than at the middle. The evolution of policy within the temperance movement foreshadowed a general shift in the entire range of Nonconformist attitudes toward social reform.

The synthesis of religious, political, and social attitudes which dominated Nonconformity between the early 1830s and the mid-1880s was suffused with individualism. During these fifty years the prevailing emphasis in Nonconformist theology, the dissenting political tradition, the social situation of the Nonconformist elite, dissenting doctrines of church organization, and Nonconformist attitudes toward social reform all complemented and reinforced each other. In all these areas of Nonconformist life, the individual conscience was given a place of high importance. Evangelical Nonconformists rejected the Calvinist doctrine of spiritual predestination just as they rejected theories of social determinism. Each man, they thought, was truly free and master of his fate. Each man could choose to follow Christ and escape eternal damnation. Each man could choose to work hard and escape the poverty and drunken degradation of the slums. Each man ought to shape his life according to the guidance of his conscience. Liberals generally during this period set themselves against aristocratic privilege and state interference in the free working of the economy. Nonconformists attacked the state church as a form of antiquated privilege, they fought for their own civil liberties in the face of legal discrimination, and, on the whole, they set themselves against state interference in the free working of society. Conscience, for them at that time, was properly located in free individuals, not in the community and not in the state.

In the decade of the 1880s the mid-Victorian Nonconformist synthesis began to crumble. No single cause for this can be assigned. Just as the synthesis itself was the product of a number of related intellectual and social factors, its collapse was brought about by changes in a number of areas of Nonconformist life. Major reorientations in theology, important developments in the social situation of Nonconformists, and new approaches to social problems reacted upon each other in such a way that Nonconformity began to lose its cohesive culture. None of these changes was sudden; their destructive effect was felt over the span of at least one, possibly two, generations. Contemporaries recognized in the 1880s that traditional Nonconformity was giving way to something new. On the eve of the first World War there were definite signs of weakness in the Nonconformist community. After the war, Nonconformity was no longer a major force in English public life. Margot Asquith, herself intimately familiar with the parallel decline of liberalism, acidly pronounced its epitaph: "At one time the Nonconformist Conscience was the backbone of the country," she said in 1922, "but the men I know who claim to have it today are maidenly, mulish, and misled."[18]

The progressive democracy and assertive individualism of Evangelical theology had been central to the Nonconformist synthesis. During the last twenty years of the nineteenth century that theology came to seem old-fashioned and outworn among the rising generation of leading Nonconformist ministers. They changed it in several important ways. The new leaders of Nonconformity wished neither to cut their own ties with their religious traditions nor to offend that great majority in their congregations who were suspicious of anything new in their religious lives. Even very advanced men continued, therefore, to proclaim in a general way their loyalty to Evangelical truth. At the same time, they reoriented their theological emphases so radically that they effectively rejected their Evangelical inheritance.

Three powerful currents of change swept through the old Evangelical theological positions, each reflecting a loss of confidence in old truths. Men began to doubt that an all-merciful God would consign a portion of mankind to everlasting pain and torture. Men began to doubt the supreme significance of the cross, and to place more importance on Christ's life than on his atoning death. And the growing respectability of Biblical Criticism encouraged men to doubt the simple Biblical base of the old Evangelical message.

Evangelicalism, over the first three quarters of the nineteenth century, was an essentially optimistic religious mode. Evangelicals believed that progress was possible for both men and nations. They were oriented toward success both in this world and the world to come. The reformed drunkard and the converted sinner were archetypal figures among them.

Sermons and tracts made much of hell and damnation, but always in order to persuade the unconverted to seek salvation while there was still time. The fate of the damned, the misery of the poor, were never matters for dwelling upon in lamentation. Evangelicals were not much interested in failure except as a practical example to encourage those who might succeed. By the 1880s, however, many Nonconformists began to take failure more seriously and to contemplate with sympathy the fate of the damned.

Sympathy for the damned was not altogether a new phenomenon in the 1880s. Frederick Denison Maurice, a liberal Anglican theologian and early Christian Socialist, had been dismissed from his post at King's College, London, in 1853 for daring to deny that eternal damnation really meant everlasting torment. But among Nonconformists concern for the damned themselves became widespread only in the 1880s.

This new fascination with failure is difficult to explain. Perhaps it was associated with anxiety about Britain's prestige as her power and commercial supremacy were clearly challenged in Europe and America. Perhaps it was connected with increasing appreciation for how little progress had been made toward solving the social problems of urban poverty. In any event, a significant number of Nonconformist ministers in the 1880s began to soften their views of damnation, to suggest that their faith in God's mercy prevented their interpreting eternal damnation literally as meaning torture that would go on forever. As early as 1874, R. W. Dale of Birmingham, an eminent Congregationalist and respected theologian, committed himself to the notion that the wicked were annihilated, not everlastingly punished. By the late 1880s, W. R. Nicoll, the astute editor of the *British Weekly,* thought that the increasing rejection of the doctrine of eternal punishment was the most significant development in the theology of contemporary Nonconformity.[19]

Closely associated with the new emphasis on God's mercy toward the unrepentant was the stress on the Fatherhood of God which began to be fashionable in the 1880s. God as a slightly indulgent Father began to replace God the judge who demanded the atonement of Christ and required faith and moral effort on the part of man. The Fatherhood of God became an immensely popular sermon subject, attractive partly because it permitted preachers to speak loosely and enthusiastically about the brotherhood of man. As president of the Congregational Union in 1906, John Henry Jowett complained of the vague effeminate softness of the popular stress on Fatherhood. Four years later in his presidential address to the National Council of Free Churches, Jowett argued that the dominance of the Fatherhood theme in fashionable Nonconformist theology was enfeebling: "a skimmed theology will not produce a more intimate philanthropy."[20]

The Atonement, the central religious doctrine of the old Evangelicalism, was pushed toward the sidelines in the last twenty years of the nineteenth century. The cross lost its supremacy. Christ's death ceased to be considered the most important event in Christian history. Christ's life took its place, and the Incarnation received the attention formerly given to the Atonement. Christ as a model for men, Christ as a teacher of ethics, replaced Christ as the way toward salvation. Just as the humanity of Christ was given greater importance, so was the idea that God dwelt in every man. Divine immanence, the place of Christ in every man, was used to justify pleas for increased benevolence toward those who were failing in life. The old Evangelicalism, a religion of strength, encouraged democracy in the form of equality of opportunity. Incarnationism, a religion of weakness, encouraged democracy in the form of increased welfare for those who were not successful. "Every kindness that you show to the drunkards of the Regent Street slums," said Hugh Price Hughes, "to the harlots of Piccadilly, and to the starving poor everywhere, is a kindness shown to Jesus Christ."[21] Or again: "A harlot is dying in a back slum. You say: 'What is that to me? She suffers for her own sin.' When you spurn that harlot you spurn Christ."[22]

The emphasis on the Incarnation was not a natural development of earlier tendencies in the theology of Evangelical Nonconformity. Nor was Incarnationism peculiarly the property of the free churches. It flourished among Anglicans as well, and its most famous expression was probably a collection of essays, *Lux Mundi* (1889), published by a group of Anglo-Catholics including Charles Gore, the well-known Christian Socialist. The impact of Incarnationism upon Evangelicalism was entirely destructive. Its logical end, to which very few Nonconformists were willing to travel, was the so-called New Theology announced by R. J. Campbell of the Congregationalist Church, the City Temple, in 1907. Campbell argued that man and God were two expressions of divinity, that sin was not so much wickedness as error. Christ's purpose was not to save man from his evil nature, but to show him how to construct God's kingdom on earth. Campbell's humanitarian theology created a public sensation for a time, but it received little official support. Eventually Campbell recanted, left Nonconformity and joined the Established Church. The New Theology, however, epitomized in unacceptably extreme form an important and widely shared tendency in free church religious thought.

The third, and probably least corrosive, force that weakened Evangelical theology in the late nineteenth century was Biblical Criticism. Nonconformists, in common with most other Englishmen, until the last third of the century, held a simple view of the Bible as God's revealed word. They were able comfortably to refer to a number of Biblical passages which they took as proof of the importance of the Atonement and as guarantees of the Evangelical scheme of conversion and salvation. From the middle of the century there were Nonconformist scholars who were aware of the development of Biblical studies in Germany, but not until the 1800s did the generality of educated Nonconformists and their ministers begin to take Biblical Criticism seriously. Even then it was not entirely safe to argue publically that the authors of the Bible were other than inspired scribes who wrote down the words that God dictated to them. Robert Forman Horton, former Oxford don and pastor of Lyndhurst Road Congregational Church in London, conservatively reported the findings of recent Biblical scholarship in *Inspiration and the Bible* (1888). But his rejection of the old idea of verbal inspiration lost him some members at Lyndhurst Road, and he had difficulty finding a publisher among the firms that specialized in Nonconformist works. By the turn of the century, however, Biblical Criticism as a whole was no longer an issue among educated free churchmen. Almost all ministers accepted the validity of using the latest and most scientific techniques of historical and literary analysis in order better to understand the Bible. No sophisticated Nonconformist searched the Bible anymore for texts that would prove Christ died for all men and that all who truly believed in Him would win everlasting peace. Biblical Criticism was, in fact, accepted among free churchmen with very little struggle. There were no great contests to set beside the legal trials and public uproar that accompanied the Anglican battles over Biblical Criticism in the 1860s. The easy progress of Biblical Criticism among Nonconformist ministers at the end of the century was partly due to those Anglican battles having been already fought, partly to the growing number of obviously devout English Biblical scholars, and partly to the fact that Evangelical theology was being abandoned anyway and for other reasons.

No serious, organized efforts were made to stem the tide of fashionable new ideas which swept away the old Evangelical verities. The most perceptive among free churchmen recognized the intellectual weakness and inchoate condition of post-Evangelical theology. R. W. Dale commented as early as 1877 on the general decline of interest in theology and the disappearance of a distinct theological literature in the Nonconformist community.[23] A generation later, on the eve of the first World War, no principle of authority had emerged in free church thought. Dale's successor at Carrs Lane, Birmingham, spoke in 1910 of "the impoverishment of our thought."[24] Yet there was no effectively organized resistance to new currents of thought. Charles Spurgeon, the great Baptist preacher, remained insistently an Evangelical of the old school until the end of his life in 1892. He attempted in 1887 to use his enormous prestige to stop the erosion of old-fashioned truth within his own denomination. But his articles accusing the Baptists of being on the downgrade, sliding into a confused morass of modern thought, did not receive a cooperative response from the leaders of the Baptist Union. Spurgeon, feeling rebuffed, withdrew from the union. The Baptists were the most conservative, old-fashioned denomination among the major free churches. The "downgrade controversy," as it came to be called, demonstrated clearly how widespread was the loss of confidence in the old-style evangelicalism among Nonconformists by the later 1880s.

Insofar as evangelicalism was associated with a distinctive Nonconformist culture, changes in the social aspirations of Nonconformity in the late nineteenth century encouraged leading free churchmen to be open minded toward modifications in their theology. From the 1880s, or a little earlier, Nonconformists began to reject their distinctive culture as provincial and narrow. Their leaders drew them toward assimilation into the mainstream of English society, and they began to grow uneasy about their humble heritage. Wealth and education were the two forces behind the growing anxiety about provincialism. As more Nonconformist families grew more wealthy, they played a greater role in the government of their towns and they sent more members to Parliament. They also, naturally, tended to emulate the manners of their more socially prestigious Anglican neighbors. Peculiarities of chapel culture became embarrassments. Quakers gradually gave up using "thee" and "thou." Nonconformists from wealthy families began reading novels, going to concerts, and finally, in significant numbers in the 1880s, going to the theater. Even ministers began going to the theater in the 1880s, to Spurgeon another sign of the downgrade, and ministers began to write novels as well as read them. The more successful free church ministers by the end of the century modeled their behavior generally on that of the upper middle classes. They delighted in club life; the National Liberal Club was their favorite. Even Spurgeon took his holidays on the Riviera and kept a carriage and pair. And they gloried in golf.

Assimilation was encouraged by education. Nonconformists went to Oxford and Cambridge in increasing numbers after religious tests were abolished in 1871. Wealthy Dissenters sent their sons to the famous public schools or to denominational schools created in the image of Winchester, Rugby or Eton. The Congregationalists even established a theological seminary, Mansfield College, in Oxford in the mid-1880s in order to have an official presence in the heartland of established English culture. At the opening of the college in 1889, A. M. Fairbairn, the first principal, spoke emotionally of the departure of Dissent from the University in the seventeenth century, and the new spirit of assimilation: "Now it is a matter of supreme importance that the old estrangement should cease and the new reconciliation be complete, . . . that our much divided people come to feel a single people once more."[25]

Calls for reunion among the Protestant churches were frequently heard toward the end of the century. The fire had gone out of the disestablishment movement. The Liberation society had difficulty raising money after Miall's death in 1881. After the Burials Act of 1880 opened the churchyards to Nonconformists the Society had no major grievances to fight against. Nonconformists were not prepared to wage a major campaign for disestablishment now that the privileges of the Church of England did not seem as significant or as discriminatory as they once did. During the eighties the Liberation Society ceased to be the effective political arm of Nonconformity. Its place was taken, at the turn of the century, by the National Council of Free Churches. Growing numbers of men and women hostile or indifferent to organized religion caused both churchmen and Nonconformists to discuss the possibility of reunion. The National Free Church Council was itself the product of the need men felt for better organization of Christian forces in an increasingly secular society. Although the possibility was raised, no serious effort was made to merge Nonconformity in the Church of England. But many men called for more cooperation between Anglicans and free churchmen. W. R. Nicoll, with a good journalist's talent for reflecting the temper of his time, told a group of Anglican clergy in 1899 that Nonconformists were puzzled: "They cannot understand why there should be a Nonconformist conscience. They think there should be a Christian conscience, and that there should be an organization of all Christians strong enough to make that conscience prevail in the land."[26]

But assimilation exacted a heavy toll from sensitive and conscientious free churchmen. Ambivalence toward their past was painful. They became restless and uncertain about their identity. They lost the clear and unquestioned sense of purpose from which they fathers and grandfathers had drawn strength. R. F. Horton is a case in point. He had been up at Oxford in the 1870s, and he kept in his study the sixth thwart of the New College boat that he had helped move from the bottom to the top of the river in a single season. Well known as the minister of Lyndhurst

Road Congregational Church, he liked to call himself a nonconforming member of the Church of England. Albert Peel, a distinguished historian of Dissent, wrote that Horton, famous and successful, was in 1900 "the outstanding representative of Nonconformity, one whose status, culture, and ability were everywhere acknowledged and respected."[27] Yet Horton was never sure of his role. He never championed a major cause for long or led an important movement. He spent his talent in a vast amount of ephemeral writing for magazines, in restless traveling and speaking. He wrote fifty-four books, but not one of genuine importance. And he filled his diaries with gloom, despair, and sentimental introspection.

At the time that they were abandoning their old theology and softening their attitudes toward privileged groups in the upper reaches of English society, the leaders of late Victorian Nonconformity changed radically their vision of society and social reform. No longer did they see society as merely a collection of individuals; no longer did they preach the reform of individual character as the principal mode of social reform. They developed a stronger sense of English society as a community with a corporate life, and they turned more and more to the state as the agency best able to bring about social improvement. Hugh Price Hughes, probably the most influential spokesman for the emerging Nonconformist conscience in the late 1880s, made his commitment to an organic view of society entirely clear. He credited T. H. Green and the Positivists with teaching him that no individual can realize his own ideal until his social environment is favorable; they emancipated him from "the selfish individualism and parochialism which have so often disfigured conventional Christian thinkers."[28] He repeated with approval Bishop Westcott's reflection that "We are suffering on all sides from a tyrannical individualism."[29] And he preached numerous variations on the theme that corporate society was divinely sanctioned: "Jesus Christ legislated for *man* —not for individuals only, not for Christian churches only, but for man in all his relations, and in all his circumstances. He legislated for *States.*"[30]

In his stress on the social conscience of the well-to-do and powerful, in his emphasis on the social responsibilities of the state, in his warm sympathy toward the poor and least successful, Hughes was by no means alone. The same general views were preached from all the leading free church pulpits and advocated in the most important Nonconformist journals. Sturdy individualism, highly valued among Nonconformists a short time previously, came to be castigated as a social vice. The mission of Christianity, wrote Silvester Horne, minister of Whitefield's Tabernacle in London and a Member of Parliament after 1910, is "to reconstruct society on the basis of brotherhood, and substitute cooperation for competition, and federalism for selfish individualism."[31] John Clifford, after Spurgeon's death in 1892 the most respected and best-known Baptist minister in London, was for a time an active Fabian socialist. S. E. Keeble, a Methodist minister who worked for Hughes on the *Methodist Times* until the end of the century, became a socialist, and so did R. J. Campbell at the time of the "new theology" uproar.

While most free church ministers did not become socialists in any strict sense, the majority of the leading men certainly did follow the prevailing fashion of humanitarian concern for the poor. In an article commissioned and published by the National Council of Free Churches, J. Scott Lidgett in 1910 summed up the view of social problems that was approved by the leaders of Nonconformity at that time. Lidgett saw slum dwellers as the embodiment of the most important social problem of his age. They were reduced to their state of misery, Lidgett thought, by low wages and unstable employment. Their difficulties could be softened by trades unions, old-age pensions, and housing reforms, but the state ought to approach their problem as an organic whole and aim at "the complete abolition of demoralizing and degrading poverty." Lidgett, a Methodist minister, was not without experience of practical affairs. He had been active in London politics for many years, and from 1908 he was the leader of the Progressive party in the London County Council. He assured his readers in 1910 that the social problem was soluble, but the solution he proposed was strikingly moralistic and without practical point. The answer did not lie in state socialism or any economic doctrine: "The social consciousness must become sovereign in its authority over the national life, subordinating, until it utterly expels, selfish individualism, class jealousies and timid dislike of necessary change."[32] Lidgett did not think that the problem of the slums lay in the unreformed characters of slum dwellers. Therefore he directed his appeal to the conscience of the successful, and ultimately to the conscience of the state.

The shift of emphasis away from individuals toward the conscience of the community was clearly under way in the early 1880s. The London Congregational Union sponsored as investigation into slum life and published its findings in 1883 as *The Bitter Cry of Outcast London.* The report, put into final form by Andrew Mearns, the secretary of the Union and former pastor of a chapel in Chelsea, created a sensation and reached an audience well beyond the boundaries of Nonconformity because it presented a vividly detailed picture of physical misery and moral degeneration in London's east end. *The Bitter Cry* absolved the slum dwellers themselves of responsibility for their plight. It found in the slums some morally upright, hard-working men and women who were locked into miserable poverty by circumstances beyond their control. It argued that the sloth and moral laxity of the majority of the very poor were products of their evil environment, and not the other way around. Samuel Morley, approaching eighty years old and a voice from the past, reacted to *The Bitter Cry* with the comment that most of the misery of London was self-inflicted. But this view was in rapid retreat. The emerging Nonconformist conscience saw in the slums a moral challenge to the community at large.

How was that challenge to be met? On the philanthropic level, Nonconformists accomplished a great deal that was practical and beneficial to the poor. They participated in the settlement movement, establishing outposts of civilization in the slums. These were designed to be both social centers for the poor in the surrounding neighborhoods and places where well-to-do young men might live for a time in the midst of poverty, gathering experience that would help them lead the kingdom toward a better future. Beginning in the early eighties, Nonconformists also built a number of mission halls in the poor districts of large cities. These missions concentrated on social services and recreational facilities; formal religious worship was not stressed. Many city center churches were abandoned by their middle-class congregations who moved to the suburbs at this time, and these buildings were frequently turned into social centers for the poor.

The so-called institutional church had its roots in the eighties. Institutional churches supported in addition to their obviously religious activities a broad array of social clubs, athletic societies, hobby groups, study groups, and welfare services. These philanthropic activities, however, useful as they were, did not come close to satisfying the consciences of those men who felt impelled to attack the social problem at its heart. Silvester Horne, for example, was minister during the Edwardian years at Whitefield's Tabernacle in London, probably the most active institutional church in the kingdom. In 1910 Horne went into Parliament because he thought that fundamental social reform could be achieved only on the political level.

On the political level effective sustained action in support of social reforms proved impossible. On the political level the Nonconformist conscience proved a decidedly inadequate guide. There were two basic reasons for this. In the first place, over the thirty years before the war there was a decided gap between the progressive views of the leading ministers and the attitudes of their more conservative congregations. This was true both in theology and politics. J. D. Jones of Bournemouth, for example, felt that he had to keep from his congregation his advanced position on Biblical Criticism. And R. F. Horton of Lyndhurst Road said "every time I pleaded the cause of the people the wealthy employers and successful professional men charged me with introducing politics into the pulpit."[33] On political issues which united the lower and middle classes—opposition to aristocratic privilege, parliamentary reform, free trade—Nonconformity had been able to take up a clear and strong position. On issues which divided the lower and middle classes—the legal position of trades unions in the nineties, the possibility of a minimum wage —Nonconformity was ineffectual. No matter how strong the drive of their humanitarianism, most Nonconformist ministers could not take the side of labor in a politics of class. The powerful, middle-class members of their congregations would not allow it.

The second reason why the Nonconformist conscience could not support a coherent program of basic social reform was that it provided no principles for determining what that program should be. The theology of Fatherhood and Incarnationism stressed the importance of humanitarian activity, but it provided no political blueprint for establishing the Kingdom of God on this earth. Nothing in their new theology helped late Victorian Nonconformists shape a new political program. This helps to explain why they were driven, like J. Scott Lidgett in 1910, to vague moralism when they described the need for fundamental social change. Their vague theology encouraged vague humanitarianism. A united position on a specific practical question was extremely difficult to achieve. This was true even of major issues toward which Nonconformity had established a traditional posture. War is an example. Dissenters had given support to the peace movement from the middle of the century, and opposition to war was referred to in the 1890s as one of the principles of the Nonconformist conscience. Hugh Price Hughes denounced war with almost as much passion as he spent in attacking prostitution. But the Boer War at the turn of the century split the free church community, and only a small remnant continued to stand up for peace as war fever swept through the nation. Even Hughes supported the war. In public affairs a simple desire to act rightly and benefit mankind is not adequate. A method is required to distinguish right action. Evangelicalism had provided guidelines that worked for a time. But the men who professed to act on the Nonconformist conscience at the end of the century had no clear guide on many issues, and so they swayed uneasily in the breeze of public opinion. The Nonconformist community was unable to take a clear stand on what free churchmen themselves considered the major problems of their time—poverty, slum life, and the relations between capital and labor.

Free church leaders, however, set a high value on united stands. They were most anxious to create a spirit of consensus within the Non-conformist community so that the community might be strengthened through a broad base of voluntary participation in its activities. There-fore they tried to focus the Nonconformist conscience on issues that would unite as many free churchmen as possible. This generation of late Victorians was enchanted by the idea that in a democratic age success could be measured in numbers. They were obsessed with size, and they counted incessantly. How many in the Sunday school? The congrega-tion? The men's meeting? Will a gymnasium attract more young people to church? Or a cycle club? Or a boys' brigade? Or a football team? What is the circulation of this newspaper or that magazine? The *British Weekly,* so that it might start with a bang, included a religious census of London in its first number in 1886. The *Daily News* tried to increase cir-culation with another count of church attendance in London in 1902. A decline in the relative size of the church going public was clearly indi-cated in the surveys, with Nonconformists holding their own a little better than Anglicans. Leading free churchmen saw this decline as a chal-lenge to their ability to hold their community together while they tried to encourage its growth. They were, in consequence, attracted to popular issues which could be easily understood by the unsophisticated masses. "The real Christ," Hugh Price Hughes once remarked, "is the one who, when seen, attracts the crowd everywhere."[34]

The issues that attracted the conscience of the Nonconformist crowd during the twenty-five years before the war were rooted in the Noncon-formist synthesis of the previous period. They were traditional Noncon-formist concerns, and they reflect the inability of late Victorian free churchmen to create a new basis for consensus within their community. In the first place, there were those matters of social reform which in-volved personal sin, a category dominated by that evil trinity—sex, gambling, and drink. Here the conscience lighted the way clearly, and no shadows darkened the path. From early in their pastorates Hughes, John Clifford, Silvester Horne, Robert Horton, and an additional host of ministers of this generation were involved in the campaign against prosti-tution. Several established homes for abandoned girls, several were asso-ciated with Josephine Butler and her drive for social purity, and Hughes and Clifford gave strong support to W. T. Stead when he was in trouble for the sensational adventure he reported in *The Maiden Tribute of*

Modern Babylon. Fierce defenders of the sanctity of the family, Nonconformists staunchly opposed any relaxation in the divorce laws. Gambling, encouraged by the growth of yellow journalism and the development of Association Football, was becoming much more popular among the working classes toward the end of the century, and, like prostitution, it roused the wrath of organized Nonconformity.

But gambling was never considered as important as sex, and Rosebery remained leader of the Liberal party despite the Nonconformist noise about his celebrated activities on the turf. Organized opposition to drink had a long history, and Nonconformity had been the backbone of the temperance movement from its beginning. But not until the last two decades of the century did the temperance movement achieve universal acceptance among Nonconformists. Not until then were ministers expected to set a teetotal example. By that time Nonconformist opinion on drink had hardened into political effectiveness, and it is probably on the drink question that the Nonconformist conscience had its most persistent impact in Parliament.

Drink, intemperate gambling among the working classes, and prostitution were all genuine social problems at the turn of the century. Therefore they appealed to the social conscience of progressive men like John Clifford and Hugh Price Hughes. Because they could be understood in terms of personal morality, these problems appealed to the majority of Nonconformists who traditionally conceived social reform as the reform of individual character. Because Nonconformists could speak out with a fairly unified voice against intemperance, gambling, and illicit sex, these issues came to dominate the Nonconformist conscience. Free churchmen tended to overstress the general social significance of these partly ethical problems. The tendency to exaggeration was natural, especially because Nonconformists had traditionally treated the conscience as something for rousing, not for searching. Nonconformist leaders were men of action rather than discrimination, fighters rather than thinkers. They were most at home with practical problems and they understood practical solutions. What Hugh Price Hughes called "the three deadly enemies of England" had the great practical merit of rousing the Nonconformist conscience. England's more important social problems did not have that advantage.

Among the traditional political concerns of Nonconformity, education remained after 1880 the last major issue that involved the interests of free churchmen as a body. In 1902 the Conservative Government passed an education act that elicited the fury of Dissent. Free churchmen reacted more explosively and with more unity than they had mustered since Sir

James Graham's education proposals of 1843. The Act of 1902 angered
Nonconformists because it made denominational schools, of which the
majority were Anglican with the Roman Catholics next, eligible for direct support from local rates. In the late 1860s Dissenters, with the exception of the Wesleyan Methodists, had given up hope of supporting their
own primary schools and had taken the position that the state should
provide a system of nondenominational schools. An uneasy compromise
was achieved in 1870, when Forster's Education Act established a dual
system: nondenominational board schools financed by local rates, and
denominational schools aided by parliamentary grants. The Act of 1902
seemed a distinctly retrogressive step to most Nonconformists. Drawing
on the tradition of the church rate martyrs of the 1830s, free churchmen,
with John Clifford at the fore, organized a campaign of passive resistance, refusing to pay that portion of the education rate that would go to
support distinctive denominational teaching. The campaign was enormously successful in generating enthusiastic support and a sense of unity
among Nonconformists. The outraged Nonconformist conscience may
well have contributed substantially to the Liberal party's triumph in the
general election of 1906. But the Liberals, in power with a too-
comfortable majority, disappointed their free church supporters. There
were, according to the Nonconformist newspapers, over two hundred
free church MPs in the new Parliament, but less than half of those were
reliable friends of Nonconformity.[35] The Liberal majority was so large
that militant Nonconformists did not have to be kept in a good humor.
After the first years of enthusiasm, the passive resistance movement lost
much of its popular support. The Liberals made a series of only half-
hearted attempts to deal with the education issue. From the Nonconformist point of view, the problem was never satisfactorily solved. The
Education Act of 1902 awakened, for a time, an echo of the once-
powerful political will of Nonconformity. But the echo died away, and as
early as 1906 Lloyd George dared to poke gentle fun at militant Nonconformity. At Clifford's seventieth birthday celebration he said: "When
Dr. Clifford wants a rest cure he sits down, takes up a pen and says
'Whom can I go for?'"[36] In 1922 Clifford received his fifty-seventh sum-
mons for non-payment of the education rate. By then, of course, his protest had lost political meaning. It was Clifford's way of keeping faith
with his past.

     In the late nineteenth century and early in the twentieth, English
Nonconformity began to lose its cultural identity. Its libertarian political
heritage had been developed under a burden of discrimination that was
now so light as to be almost without significance. Its vigorous individual-

ism, coinciding in time with the great days of Gladstonian liberalism, was now rejected by its progressive leaders. Evangelical theology, which had previously reinforced both the political and social ideas of Nonconformity, was now transformed in all but name. Fashionable new emphases on Incarnationism and the Fatherhood of God did not constitute an adequate intellectual base upon which free churchmen might fashion a new view of themselves and their distinctive mission in English society. Free churchmen, in spite of their active press and increasingly efficient central organization, gradually faded into a religiously indifferent social landscape. The Nonconformist conscience, to some at the time an indication of strength, is more accurately viewed as evidence of weakness. Free churchmen were unable to develop a new synthesis of religious, political, and social attitudes. The Nonconformist conscience had no future, but it did, for a time, enable men and women dedicated to the spirit and heritage of Dissent to keep faith with their past.

Notes

1. *Fortnightly Review,* August and September, 1873.

2. Dorothea Price Hughes, *The Life of Hugh Price Hughes,* 4th ed. (1905), p. 348.

3. *Ibid.,* p. 353.

4. *Methodist Times,* 20 November 1890.

5. John Angell James, *The Anxious Inquirer* (1836 edition), p. 5.

6. *Ibid.,* p. 114.

7. *Ibid.,* p. 37.

8. Edward Baines, "On the Progress and Efficiency of Voluntary Education in England," in *Crosby Hall Lectures on Education* (1848), p. 8.

9. Edward Miall, *The Social Influences of the State Church* (1867), pp. 10–11.

10. Algernon Wells, "Thoughts on the Need for Increased Efforts to Promote the Religious Welfare of the Working Classes in England," *Congregational Year Book* (1848), p. 88.

11. Elie Halevy, *The Triumph of Reform* (1950), p. 62.

12. *Report of the Conference of Ministers of Religion on the Corn Laws* (1841), p. 110.

13. *British Quarterly Review* (1845), p. 561.

14. Henry Dunckley, *The Charter of the Nations* (1854), p. 404.

15. Charles Haddon Spurgeon, *John Ploughman's Pictures* (1880), p. 123.

16. *Ibid.,* p. 126.

17. Edwin Hodder, *The Life of Samuel Morley,* 2nd ed. (1887), p. 153.

18. Stephen Koss, *Nonconformity in Modern British Politics* (1975), p. 167.

19. W. B. Glover, *Evangelical Nonconformists and Higher Criticism in the Nineteenth Century* (1954), p. 92.

20. Arthur Porritt, *John Henry Jowett* (1924), pp. 98, 104.

21. Hugh Price Hughes, *Social Christianity* (1889), p. 88.

22. *Ibid.,* p. 61.

23. *Congregationalist* (1877), pp. 3–5.

24. Arthur Porritt, *John Henry Jowett* (1924), p. 105.

25. W. B. Selbie, *The Life of Andrew Martin Fairbairn* (1914), p. 178.

26. W. R. Nicoll, *The Lamp of Sacrifice* (1906), p. 327.

27. Albert Peel and J. A. R. Marriott, *Robert Forman Horton* (1937), p. 15.

28. Hugh Price Hughes, *Essential Christianity* (1894), pp. 32–33.

29. Hugh Price Hughes, *Social Christianity* (1889), p. xii.

30. Hugh Price Hughes, *Philanthropy of God* (1892), p. 51.

31. C. S. Horne, *Pulpit, Platform and Parliament* (1913), p. 3.

32. J. Scott Lidgett, "The Modern Social Problem," in *Christ and Civilization* (1910), edited for the National Council of Free Churches by the Rev. John Brown Paton, Sir Percy Bunting, and the Rev. Alfred Garvie.

33. R. F. Horton, *An Autobiography* (1917), p. 83.

34. Hugh Price Hughes, *Social Christianity* (1889), p. 4.

35. Stephen Koss, *Nonconformity in Modern British Politics* (1975), p. 78.

36. James Marchant, *Dr. John Clifford, C.H.* (1924), p. 196.

THE IMPERIAL CONSCIENCE
John Cell

Just before the first World War the government of India planned its splendid capital at New Delhi, meant to last for a thousand years. Winston Churchill's wartime speeches of 1940 employed the same round number. But the fall of Singapore, just two years later, marked the effective end of British power in Asia. Once apparently so permanent and solid, the British Empire now appears to have been a transitory phase in the leadership of the West, scarcely longer than the earlier ascendancy of the Dutch.

Even at its height the problem of measuring British imperial power with any precision was a problem, and scholars debate it still. Ought the "informal" areas of commercial dominance and "spheres of influence" in Asia, the Middle East, and Latin America to be included? The formal areas that were painted red on maps—the white regions of Canada, Australia, New Zealand, and South Africa; the separate and exceptional empire of India; and the colonies and protectorates of the Pacific, Asia, Africa, and the Caribbean—were complicated enough. Words like *empire* and *possession* imply a static, monolithic, enduring quality quite unlike the confusing reality.[1] Between center and periphery existed a shifting, intricate web of connections, tacit alliances, and mechanisms of collaboration. Without these, even at the height of its power, the British Empire would have been impossible. To invert the famous Jingoist music-hall song of the 1870s, Britain lacked the men, her ships could not go on land, and she was unwilling to spend the money too. In Asia, as an upholder of the China war of the early 1840s reminded his audience in the House of Commons, what they had out there was mainly an "empire of opinion." An unanswered insult here, a small reverse there: once allow *them* to suspect that Britain might not perhaps be invincible, and the whole enterprise might fall apart. Many a "small war" was justified by this truism.

The Pax Britannica needed a lot of policing. One authority lists fifteen wars during the six and one-half decades of Queen Victoria's reign. But this includes only conflicts against countries that were acknowledged at the time to be "organized."[2] Another count, which includes expeditions and engagements undertaken in suppression of rebellions and riots, adds up to seventy-four.[3] Only in 1883 were Her Majesty's military forces completely out of action, and a search of the records of India's Northwest Frontier would presumably fill that gap. Violent "primary" resistance—from the Zulu in Natal, the Ndebele in Rhodesia, the emirates of Northern Nigeria—almost always preceded annexation. Thereafter, once colonial rule had been established, the Indian Army or the Queen's African Rifles were frequently engaged in suppressing "secondary" resistance. And against any particular native group Britain could direct a superior military and naval force that was absolutely overwhelming.

Colonial warfare has never been carried on under any very great restraints, the most obvious reason being that the opponents lack the technology to reply in kind. The appalling statistics of the campaign of 1898 against the Mahdi's Dervishes in the Sudan (an engagement that made the British general Kitchener a national hero) are not untypical, for the Anglo-Egyptian army suffered casualties of 48 killed and 382 wounded, against an estimated 11,000 of the enemy killed, 16,000 wounded, and 4,000 taken prisoner. Charles E. Callwell's standard treatise on the subject, *Small Wars: Their Principles and Practice,* which was first published in 1896 and went into its third edition ten years later, was a compendium of a century's experience of "expeditions against savages and semi-civilized races by disciplined [civilized] soldiers, . . . campaigns undertaken to suppress rebellions and guerilla warfare in all parts of the world." Since "the lower races are impressionable," and because small expeditionary forces had to overcome extremely difficult terrain and supply problems, the basic principle was to take the offensive and keep it, creating a devastating "moral effect." In warfare against savages, "mere victory is not enough. The enemy must not only be beaten. He must be beaten thoroughly. . . . What is wanted is a big casualty list . . .—they must feel what battle against a disciplined army means." Once defeated, irregular forces must be ruthlessly pursued by cavalry. And actions such as the burning of villages and the destruction of crops, "which may shock the humanitarian," were likely to be necessary to make the lesson clear. "The enemy once on the move must be kept on the move." Or, as Sir Garnet Wolseley put it, "when you get niggers on the run, keep them on the run."

The great object in small wars, then, was to increase as much as possible the destructiveness and terror of weapons. Shona guerrilla fighters, along with their women and children, were dynamited out of their caves in the last stages of the Rhodesian rising in 1897. On the ground that the savage mind understands only cruelty and attributes "leniency to timidity," the British sometimes copied methods from their opponents. Thus mutinous native Indian soldiers (called sepoys), as well as those who were unfortunate enough to be "mistaken" for mutineers, were routinely blown from the mouths of big guns in the suppression of the Indian Mutiny in 1857–59. At the Hague peace conference in the late 1890s the British (along with the Americans) resisted the outlawing of the "dumdum" bullet—it got its name from the suburb of Calcutta where it was manufactured—which expanded inside the body instead of merely penetrating, thereby increasing the chances of maiming and infection. Maxim guns were often employed against African villages that were being defended by spears. And in 1933 the British proposed "the complete abolition of all forms of bombing from the air (except for police purposes in certain outlying regions)."

Not that the British waged colonial warfare with unusual cruelty. The French used torture routinely in their wars against the Algerians. Recent motion pictures have presented American viewers with a portrait of the warfare of extermination against the Indians that had been suppressed from their history books. And readers who are old enough to have followed the Vietnam war on their television screens can perhaps recall a parallel or two. Rather, as Callwell observed, it is the very nature of colonial warfare—which is nearly always conducted by small expeditionary forces who must counter superior numbers with technology, organization, and "dash"—to be brutal in the extreme. Defeating the military forces of a more or less organized political unit is the easiest part of the problem: "But campaigns for the subjugation of insurrections, for the repression of lawlessness, or for the pacification of territories conquered or annexed stand on a very different footing. . . . The crushing of a populace in arms and the stamping out of widespread disaffection by military methods, is a harassing form of warfare even in a civilized country with a settled social system; in remote areas peopled by half-civilized races or wholly savage tribes, such campaigns are most difficult to bring to a satisfactory conclusion, and are always most trying to the troops."[4]

The British Empire was not always so violent a process as the foregoing description of colonial warfare implies. Once colonial rule was established, tranquility might prevail for years or even decades. Englishmen overseas usually did not have awesome military power available, and so had to make substantial concessions to native collaborators. In many parts of India and Africa, civil servants went about habitually without weapons. When Joyce Cary's character "Mister Johnson" was sentenced to be hanged for murder—in the end he was shot at his request —neither rope nor hangman was available in the Northern Nigerian outpost where the novel is set. Leonard Woolf wrote books that attacked economic imperialism. Yet the volume of his autobiography that recalls his youth as a civil servant in Ceylon contains no apology or explanation of the apparent contradiction, no hint that he had ever oppressed anybody. As, indeed, he had not.

Nevertheless imperialism was often—and was in essence—an exploitative, discriminatory, destructive, and violent process. It continued, accelerated, and intensified throughout the Victorian period. The white man's energy and power were, for the time being, absolutely irresistible. "The unburnt pot," as the Shona of Rhodesia put it so well, "just handles the world."[5] Two perspectives on imperialism are illuminating, both of them appropriately enough drawn from the Victorian period itself, the first that of Charles Darwin, the second that of Karl Marx.

In the late nineteenth century Social Darwinism affected British attitudes toward "inferior races": it had little enough to do with Darwin's scientific research, and a pernicious, nasty sort of ideology it was. Yet Darwin, after all, was right. The expansion of Europe from the sixteenth century onward *had* greatly intensified the universal competition among the "races" of mankind for control of the world's living space. Contrary to the myths of "virgin land" and "empty frontiers" that have so dominated American history, the entire habitable world had long been populated. European expansion did not initiate the struggle for biological survival, but speeded it up enormously. The impact of epidemic disease upon peoples who had previously lived in isolation was fearful. Within a century after contact, the Amerindian population of South and Central America declined by some 75 percent. Although a ceiling of one million has often been cited by standard works on North American Indians—a figure derived from the circular argument that, since Indians were "savages," the hunter-gatherer economies of the savage stage of evolution could have supported only minimal population densities—there is every reason to believe that a similar decline occurred north of the Rio Grande, which would make the pre-contact level at least eight million.[6] American historians and anthropologists had somehow contrived to bury without trace a demographic catastrophe comparable to the Jewish holocaust of World War II!

Australia, of course, *was* largely an empty continent—as it is still—

but severe depopulation took place there, as well as in New Zealand and the islands of the Pacific. Even the peoples of tropical Africa, who had never been isolated from the world disease pool, may have declined by as much as one-fourth or more during the time of troubles that began with the intensification of long-distance trade before European penetration, that encompassed European colonization and "pacification," and that ended with World War I and the amazingly destructive worldwide influenza epidemic of 1918. Famine became more frequent and more serious in India during the nineteenth century, although her problem was not demographic collapse but the reverse.

This relentless movement, displacement, and relocation of peoples on a global scale became an important fact by the seventeenth century. In the nineteenth it reached its height. Its most obvious facet was the migration of millions of Europeans into North and South America, into South Africa and Australasia, out of European Russia into Siberia: in short, throughout the world's temperate regions except where, as in China and Japan, the indigenous peoples were numerous and strong enough to withstand them. Often the Europeans took with them or they subsequently evolved techniques that enabled the environment to support far larger populations than had been possible in the less advanced economies they had uprooted. But they never took possession of regions that had been wholly unpopulated. "Virgin lands" were invented by propagandists and historians.

European expansion also accelerated the migrations of non-Europeans, usually under conditions of forced labor. Although scholars now think that earlier guesses about the numbers of Africans who were transported in the Atlantic slave trade were wildly inflated, the corrected estimate still stands at 9-11 millions. Not merely unskilled labor, many of them brought with them valuable agricultural and "industrial" skills. Slaves from the Senegambia, for example, were apt to know far more about rice production than their European masters.[7] Until the revolutionary advances in tropical medicine of the late-nineteenth century, Africans were "biologically" superior not only to the Indians (who were being assaulted simultaneously by African parasitic diseases and by bacterial and viral ones from Europe) but to Europeans as well. The movement of millions of orientals—of Chinese coolies and merchants into Southeast Asia and across the Pacific, where they were often joined by East Indians, who also spread into East and South Africa and into the Caribbean after the abolition of slavery—was absolutely essential for the building of such important imperial communications as the Uganda Railway. Asian migration was an integral part of European imperialism; and like the transplanted Africans, it remains as part of the worldwide legacy of empire.

The second important Victorian perspective, that of Marx, is on the magnitude of the energy that was unleashed in the world by the interrelated development of European capitalism and the competitive state system. For Marx this energy proceeded not from ordinary human greed—on which capitalists have no monopoly—but from the absolute necessity, in a fiercely competitive market economy, for the capitalist to extract, accumulate, invest, and expand, all in order to survive. The dynamism of capitalism needed no outside determinant. It was self-generating.

After one has made all the necessary qualifications about the undue emphasis Marx is supposed to have placed upon the "economic factor," his profound insight into the irresistible force of capitalist Europe remains. The "modern world-system" that already existed by the seventeenth century was the arena in which European capitalism developed.[8] The world-economy was even then divided into interlocking zones—center, semi-periphery, periphery—each with its dominant mode of production and appropriate system of labor. This world-system was by no means an economic creation alone. It fed and depended upon the competitive European political framework whose fundamental unit was the state. The power of European capitalism in its agrarian, merchant, industrial, and monopoly phases has been quite fantastic. In the Americas in the 16th and 17th centuries, in 19th-century India or Japan, in Africa in this century, it swept aside pre-capitalist economic patterns that had endured for centuries, decisively reorienting mechanisms of production, distribution, and exchange. As Marx, half in admiration, observed in the *Communist Manifesto,* all that was sacred was profaned, all that was permanent was whisked away.

Together, the Darwinian and Marxian perspectives help to establish what a gigantic, awesome, irresistible force European and hence British imperialism has been. It sent Indians in Peru to work silver mines at above 8,000 feet, with preditably disastrous rates of tubercular infection. It sent Indians of North America thousands of miles into the far north in search of furs, which they laboriously processed and transported for exchange with European traders. In India European demand at first stimulated the domestic cotton industry; then, as cotton manufacturing became the "pace-maker" of the industrial revolution, English competition destroyed it. Within a generation of the diamond and gold discoveries in South Africa in the 1870s and 1880s, African labor had been organized on a scale previously impossible, and the "compound system" had become the characteristic form of labor control throughout the country, as it remains today.

By the end of the Victorian period hardly a people remained on the face of the earth whose social structure, culture, and basic way of life had not been more or less violently disrupted. Anthropologists—and it has often been remarked that only the West has produced a discipline whose business is to record cultures that are becoming extinct—were already becoming aware of the rapid disappearance of their materials. This transformation of primitive and "semi-civilized" peoples at the behest of European "culture contact" may have been inevitable. Some aspects of it were undoubtedly creative. The power of Europe's world-transforming energy was simply not to be denied. Victorian consciences were often troubled by effects, by the behavior of individuals, by the policies of particular governments. But most Victorians, Marx included, took for granted the basic facts of British power.

The Emergence of Conscience

Until the late eighteenth century the British had gone about the business of imperialism remarkably unconstrained by moral scruples. Like the Dutch they lagged behind the Catholic countries—Portugal, Spain, and France—in emphasizing the second part of the famous trilogy, "Gold, God, Glory." Recent scholars have sharply questioned whether the humanitarian factor really made much difference in the early-modern Catholic empires. The conquest of New Spain and its exploitation under the forced-labor system called the *encomienda* were not much affected by the pro-Indian faction at court in Madrid. The supposed ability of the Portuguese Church to make "feudal" slavery in Brazil a more humane institution than the Protestant variety in the West Indies or the American South is contradicted by the demographic facts. Mortality rates were far higher in Brazil. And only in the United States (which received a mere 5 percent of the total trade) did the slave population maintain itself without being constantly replenished.

It is however impossible, until shortly before the French Revolution, to conceive of a British debate on the scale or of the moral intensity of that conducted by Bartolomé de las Casas at the Spanish court against the Aristotelian doctrine of natural slavery. The early English colonial propaganda, as well as the charters of the royal and proprietary colonies, usually had something to say about the duty to convert the heathen. Very little missionary work was attempted. The Society for the Propagation of the Gospel in Foreign Parts, which was founded early in the eighteenth century, devoted its energies to English communities overseas.

Over the course of the eighteenth and early nineteenth centuries, the foundations on which the Victorian imperial conscience would be built were gradually constructed. Centering on two great issues, the abolition of the slave trade and the responsibility of the British Parliament for the East India Company's governance of India, ethical concern became a powerful political force. Its growth did not stop imperialism. Indeed in some ways it added to the acceleration, endurance, and justification of expansion. Certainly, to imagine Victorian imperialism without it is difficult.

The Abolition of the British Slave Trade

The title of David Brion Davis' excellent book, *The Problem of Slavery in Western Culture* (1965), is perhaps a little misleading. During most of the history of the world slavery had been no problem at all. Not the fact of slavery, but expanded ethical sensibilities, which cast slavery in a new light, created the problem. Slavery had been an important and often a dominant mode of production until, as Marx explained in *Das Kapital,* technology and industrial organization developed sufficiently to enable alternative modes of production—first feudal relations based on a peasantry tied to the land; then a free, landless proletariat paid wages— to replace it. Its gradual elimination in medieval Europe depended less upon the condemnation of the Church (whose attitude was in fact ambiguous) than upon the development of more sophisticated agriculture and manufacturing. In the plantation economies of the New World, it swiftly reappeared.

Slavery's rapid resurgence at the periphery of the world-system was a natural thing, a response to a compelling economic need. How else was the work to be done? Europe's population was rising gradually, but there was as yet no demographic explosion. Her technology was quite inadequate to the task of developing the resources of the American continents by any means except forced labor. And it was in the art of managing other people that Europeans most excelled.

European objectives, strategies, and techniques were remarkably similar, and were adapted to the terrains in which they operated. Where Europeans found well-organized political systems (as in India), they traded with them. When those systems broke down, they plundered them and took them over. Where they encountered large but poorly organized populations (as in New Spain), they commandeered labor on a quota system. Where the indigenous inhabitants were few or where they died out (as in Brazil, the Caribbean, and North America), they imported replacements.[9] The fact that Africans are black, a color associated at least in the English language and mind with evil and filth, may have reinforced the system by making it appear all the more natural and appropriate.[10] So may the facts that Africans were undoubtedly heathen and that they often had more open sexual attitudes and practices. But the overriding force was economic. A large, efficient, durable work force was required, and Africans were available.

The systematic cruelty and human degradation of the slave trade—the capture, forced march to the sea, exchange for European manufactures, "tight packing" in the notorious middle passage, display and sale at the market, period of "seasoning," etc.—appear to us to be obviously revolting. To early-modern Europeans, and as a matter of fact to contemporary Africans (who were by no means unsophisticated traders), there was nothing particularly shocking about it. Many businesses had their unpleasant aspects. And (with the vital difference that the migration of Europeans in this period was usually voluntary) many of the conditions of travel in the small, overcrowded ships that plied across the North Atlantic were comparable. In Europe itself, as critics of the abolitionists were fond of pointing out, child labor, poverty, and hunger were common. It was a hard, cruel world.

Why the English should have participated in the slave trade, why they should have come by about 1725 to dominate it, why they should have built their American colonies on the basis of servitude: none of this really requires much explanation. Profits were good—a recent authority on the basis of very careful research and computation has estimated an average annual return of 10 percent[11]—but not unusually high. To presume that profitability must have been astronomical, else so cruel and barbarous a traffic could not have been sustained, is anachronistic. It is to assume that slavery had to be justified by some unusual circumstances.

For centuries, Western thought had sustained and justified the system. The doctrine of Aristotle—that some men are by nature fitted for servitude as others are destined for thought, leisure, and rule, the interests of master and slave being nicely balanced and complementary—was the main legacy from the classical tradition. The founders of Christianity, though they preached a doctrine of ultimate equality that has frequently been explosively subversive, never explicitly questioned their society's dominant mode of production. Throughout the gradual and uneven decline of slavery in Western Europe, the Church's position was profoundly ambivalent. The weight of the tradition of organized Christianity, concludes Davis, probably remained in slavery's favor. Nor, contrary to what one might have supposed, was there any inevitable confrontation with the main thrust of the Enlightenment. If all men were created equal, then some (it might be concluded) must be less than men.

There is no doubt that West Indian planters and merchant houses, especially in Liverpool, made large fortunes off the slave trade. But the argument that the traffic was crucial in the accumulation of capital for Britain's industrial revolution appears to be a good deal more tenuous. Foreign trade *in general* was less important than contemporary mercantilist thought assumed it to be, far less significant than the accumulation and investment of profits out of British agriculture. The percentage of British capital investment that can be attributed directly to the slave trade is probably between .11 and 1.11 percent (and tending toward the lower figure);[12] most of the profits went into further development of the slave trade itself and into plantations, not into new industry. Nor is there much evidence of decline in profitability in the late eighteenth century, before abolition.[13] Slavery had always been profitable and it continued to be. It was not the decline of the West Indies that caused the abolition of slavery: the end of slavery ruined the sugar plantations. The problem is not why Britain should have engaged in the slave trade, but why she gave it up.

The simplest, most direct explanation is that during the eighteenth century a gradual but profound change took place in British religious convictions in regard to slavery, and that out of this ideological shift emerged a political force powerful enough to persuade a nation to act against its own immediate economic self-interest. Such alterations in climate of opinion are by their nature difficult to trace with any precision. Two recent students who have immersed themselves in the literature—David Brion Davis and Roger Anstey—agree that such a shift took place. It came from many sources: Quakers and other Dissenters in England; the French philosopher Montesquieu; the founder of Methodism John Wesley. Davis and Anstey agree further that by about the 1770s the shift of opinion had proceeded far enough to throw the supporters of slavery on the defensive. No longer was slavery being defended as morally justifiable: its defense was that it was strategically and economically necessary. It was a nursery of seamen (abolitionists said it was their graveyard); it was economically profitable; the West Indies would be ruined; if Britain did not carry on the trade her competitors would.

These arguments continued to be persuasive. Indeed, the economic analysis of the "West India interest" was more accurate than the abolitionists', as the continuing prosperity of Cuba after the 1830s was to demonstrate. Moreover, the weight of inertia was against reform. No government, not even that of Pitt, a friend of the abolitionists, would agree to throw itself behind the campaign. The king was against it, and measures George III opposed were not as a rule presented to Parliament by governments that wished to remain in office. Abolition bills were therefore introduced as private member's motions, each member of the cabinet being left free to "vote his conscience." For some thirty-five years after the 1770s, bills of abolition were presented. Annually they were rebuffed. Not until 1806 was the deadlock broken.

The force that ultimately broke it, that transformed an ideological movement into political action, was a small band of Evangelical members of the established Church of England, led by William Wilberforce, Granville, Sharpe, Zachary Macaulay, Thomas Clarkson, the first Sir James Stephen, and a few others. Sometimes called the Clapham Sect, sometimes the Saints, they were members of the Establishment, well connected to the political elite, not rank outsiders. They were well organized and politically sophisticated in the use of the pamphlet, the public meeting, and the petition: they provided one of the first examples in British history of a successful extra-Parliamentary agitation in favor of reform. They were remarkably energetic and persistent, fanatics in the sense of possessing singleminded, narrow concentration on a cause.

What was the source of their fanaticism? It was, argues Anstey, the internal dynamics of Evangelical theology, which accentuated the religious thought of a broader spectrum of their contemporaries. They emphasized ritual sacrifice and atonement before Providence, the deliverance of the Chosen People from bondage, the duty of humanity especially to the most helpless. The slave trade and slavery became *the* national sin. And if abolition should require sacrifice and expiation (such as the £20 millions that were voted in 1833 in compensation to West Indian planters for their lost property) so much the better. For sound tactical reasons the Saints separated slavery from the slave trade, concentrating first on the trade. But there was never much doubt about their ultimate objective. Over half a century, until slavery was finally abolished in the reformed House of Commons, they pursued their goal.

It is true that their concerns were somewhat restricted, that while resolutely attacking slavery abroad they might ignore or support oppression at home. Their opponents made much of that, as of the charge that abolitionists had important connections with the *East* Indian sugar industry. In 1806 the abolitionists shrewdly changed their case. A pamphlet by Sir James Stephen (the movement's legal expert and the father of the

Colonial Office's permanent undersecretary) centered on the "foreign" trade, that is on slaves carried in British ships to the colonies of countries which were neutral in the Napoleonic war. What these ships carried might well find its way past the British blockade of Europe and enable Napoleon to prolong the war. To abolish this section of the traffic would therefore be strategically and economically advantageous. Stephen conveniently neglected to add that the foreign trade was more than half the total, an item Lord Grenville (the prime minister who was in close collusion with the abolitionists) also failed to mention when he introduced the measure into the House of Lords. This strategy worked, confusing and dividing the opposition. And, once the foreign trade had been abolished, it was comparatively easy to persuade the uncommitted members of the virtues of idealism and consistency. "One is so conditioned," concludes Anstey (who uncovered this important shift in strategy), "to expect interest to masquerade as altruism that one may miss altruism when concealed beneath the cloak of interest."[14]

A change in religious attitudes toward slavery, accentuated and articulated by a politically sophisticated and highly motivated pressure group, abolished the slave trade. All attempts to establish more "structural" explanations, to link the phenomenon directly to economic causes, have broken down. This is not to say that antislavery occurred in a vacuum. But its causes were ideological, and so were its wider effects. Davis has suggested what some of these larger implications may have been. Leaning on the Italian Communist Antonio Gramsci's conception of "hegemony"—the means by which a ruling class mystifies and justifies its power so that it rests mainly on consent rather than on the exercise of force—Davis argues that antislavery was useful both to the old political elite—the landed interests who had controlled British politics since the late seventeenth century—and to the emerging elite of industrialists.

For the political elite, antislavery confirmed the ideology of Parliamentary constitutionalism at a time of radical ferment when it badly needed demonstrating. Legal methods worked. By remaining entirely legal and peaceful, by petitioning and lobbying members of Parliament, by organizing support at the polls for friendly candidates: by such methods as these, reform could be achieved. The methods of the English "Jacobins," who attacked the very organization of society in the name of a democratic ideology imported from revolutionary France, or those of the Luddites, the machine-breakers who terrorized the countryside and destroyed property, were, by this analysis, quite unnecessary. The strategy of gradual, item-by-item reform within the established constitutional system achieved results.

For the emerging industrial elite, antislavery helped to support the campaign to create a better society at home by attacking a glaring inconsistency in the forms of labor within the Empire. In Britain a new mode of production was coming into existence: an industrial proletariat of free wage-laborers, working to the rhythm of the clock and the factory whistle instead of the sun and the seasons.[15] So massive a change as this in the habits of Britain's working people, such an attempt to substitute the voluntary work ethic and discipline for the rather shiftless, lazy mentality of "natural man," required an intense effort of propaganda. And how could the moral basis of free wage labor be sustained at home while, in another part of the British Empire, slavery persisted?

In Marx's philosophy of history, great movements such as the abolition of slavery normally reflect massive contradictions in the organization of the means of production. Such a contradiction, it seems clear, did not arise within the plantation economy itself. Nor is there much evidence that it emerged within those sections of the British economy that were directly connected to the West Indies. The contradictions which led to the abolition of slavery were, Davis suggests, indirect, emerging out of the changing configuration of British society as a whole.[16]

The Missionary Factor

Abolition was the single most significant aspect of the awakening imperial conscience in the late eighteenth century, but it does not stand alone. A cluster of new missionary societies appeared in the 1790s: the Baptists (1792), Edinburgh and Glasgow (1796), The Missionary Society, later the London Missionary Society (1797), the Church (of England) Missionary Society (1799). By the 1830s these had been joined by the Methodists, the Church of Scotland, and the Presbyterians. Maintaining the faith among expatriate Englishmen was no longer enough; from Christian salvation no color nor race was to be excluded. Closely related were the efforts of the Sierra Leone Company (chartered in 1791) to settle on the west coast of Africa liberated slaves from Britain, the West Indies, and Nova Scotia. Once there, the founders hoped, these Africans would carry into the interior the blessings of Christianity and legitimate commerce. They would transmit the conscience of the wider world. The African Association (1788) was beginning to send out exploring expeditions —scientific, commercial, strategic—in which the missionary interest was heavily involved. It was not that economics and strategy had been displaced as the basic motives of imperialism. By the early nineteenth century, they were infused with a new force of conscience.

India

Having come in the seventeenth century as traders, with no thought of conquering what was then one of the most powerful empires in the world, the East India Company had become a body of governors. With astonishing rapidity, after about 1725, the Mughal empire had crumbled, weakened from within by inflation, by feeble leadership, by successful regional challenges to central authority, by peasant wars, and by the insurgence of the Marathas in the west. India then became a prize in the "hundred years' war" between England and France, a conflict that was fought between native armies led by Europeans, with the English emerging victorious by 1763. Though the Marathas were not finally defeated until after 1800, "John Company" had emerged as the only organized power in the sub-continent. Piece by piece—here pushed on by their own rapacity, there pulled on by unstable conditions that made the annexation of "just the next piece" seem to be a necessary step if order were to be restored—the company took over Bengal and then most of the rest of India. From traders the British had become plunderers and then conquerors. Throughout this period, until rather late in the eighteenth century, anything resembling conscience is difficult to detect.

Eighteenth-century India presented a rich variety of objects for the attention of an emerging conscience. There were the fabulous fortunes that British "nabobs" managed by such dubious methods to compile. The odds against a man's hitting the jackpot were in fact extremely high; far more likely that he would die of fever within a few weeks of landing at Calcutta or Bombay. But the amount of looting that did go on was considerable, and indignant (or envious) contemporaries naturally inflated the results. British grain speculators have sometimes been blamed for the appalling famines that decimated Bengal in the 1770s. Again their effect was probably exaggerated, but it seemed undeniable that the standard of living was rapidly deteriorating. There were some rather unpleasant sides of Indian society—widow-burning or suttee, and the bands of murderous thieves from whom we have derived the word "thug"—which had probably grown worse as the bonds of Mughal society collapsed.

With conquest gradually developed a sense of responsibility. The concept of "trusteeship," which was to perform good service and adopt many forms as an integral part of the British imperial idea, is ordinarily traced to the Whig political theorist of the late eighteenth century, Edmund Burke. In his famous speech of 1783 on the ill-fated India Bill of Charles James Fox, Burke argued that "all political power which is set over men," and exercised by others, was so obviously a departure from the "natural equality of mankind," that it "ought to be some way or other exercised ultimately for their benefit." By analogy to the law of "derivative trust," he maintained that the Company must be held accountable to Parliament for its due performance of the trust with which it was vested. Under Warren Hastings, whom Burke pursued in a celebrated impeachment trial of eight years that finally ended in acquittal, the Company had notoriously abused its trust. Not moral responsibility or conscience but bribery, corruption, violence, and a general decline in the condition of the people of India had characterized his administration. Were such practices condoned in India? Might one adopt the moral standards of the less civilized country where one happened to reside? Surely not. "This geographical morality we do protest against."[17]

Several historians have rescued Hastings from a "case of mistaken identity." Imperialism without responsibility is the worst of its forms, and Hastings at least was trying to bring it under some sort of control. Burke's statement of principle is nonetheless significant. The idea that Englishmen overseas could be held accountable to some higher, collective "conscience," that imperialism must be regulated according to moral standards, was closely related to the rise of antislavery and the founding of missionary societies. It was also related to the contemporary wave of aggressive annexationism—in the Caribbean, at the Cape, in the eastern and western "appendages" of India, in Australia, in Captain Cook's reconnaissance in the Pacific—in the founding of a "second British Empire."

Davis' argument about the complex supportive role antislavery may have played in the larger ideological "superstructure" of emerging industrial capitalism has been noted. Here a simpler point may be made. Imperialism in an age of widening political participation would require an ideology that could command support from a wider public. None of those who attacked its specific abuses—not Wilberforce in his assault on slavery, not Burke in his impeachment of Hastings, certainly not the missionaries who could not hope for success in India or Africa without government support—urged that imperialism be abandoned. For all these spokesmen of the emerging British imperial conscience, the cure for the ills of imperialism was more imperialism.

That conscience is a "Good Thing" seems self-evident. But, for those who were destined to be the subject peoples of the empire, the rise of humanitarianism was a mixed blessing. Missionary movements are launched only by cultural chauvinists. The unreformed servant of the East India Company in the eighteenth century had more contact with Indian society and was probably more tolerant than his successors: for one thing he nearly always had an Indian concubine. There was indeed much in this collapsing civilization that ought not to have been tolerated. But the wholesale attacks upon Indian culture of a James Mill or a Macaulay were dubious contributions to race relations. Philip Curtin, in *The Image of Africa* (1965), argues that eighteenth-century Europeans had a more realistic assessment of African society than would be the case until the twentieth. By the early nineteenth century, however, the question of what the course of imperial history without the "missionary factor" might have been is pointless. By then, half a century after it had first emerged, conscience had become an integral part of the ideology that both criticized and sustained British imperialism.

Conscience and Early Victorian Imperialism

In British imperial history the period between the passage of the Reform Bill of 1832 and, say, the Great Exhibition of 1851 (when the technological achievements of the industrial revolution were displayed so lavishly at the Crystal Palace in London) has usually been characterized as an era of naive optimism. The first coherent attempts were made to apply humanitarian policy more broadly. Previously conscience had centered primarily on the antislavery issue, secondarily on the problem of trusteeship in India. Now the limits were being taken off.

This was true at home. Scholars still debate whether the standard of living improved or deteriorated; but times remained hard until the fifties, while continuing tension and the Chartist movement among the working classes (from whom the Reform bill had withheld the vote) demonstrated that they were unappeased. Yet what Asa Briggs calls an "age of improvement" had begun. Tory paternalists like Lord Shaftesbury and Utilitarians like Sir Edwin Chadwick were exposing shocking conditions in mines, factories, sanitation, housing, and child labor that had long been ignored. Though economists continued to favor the general rule of laissez-faire, the piecemeal accretion of legislation that was directed against specific abuses added up to an impressive pattern of government intervention. Later investigations by the journalist Henry Mayhew in the fifties, by successive royal commissions, and by Charles Booth in the nineties uncovered layer upon layer of poverty and squalor that had remained impervious to reform. Thus the Utilitarian faith that massive social problems could be "solved," if only the right remedy could be found, would appear to be pathetically naive. The charges continued to be heard —from William Cobbett on the left, from Thomas Carlyle on the right—

that Evangelical concern for poor oppressed blacks in the West Indies was simply a hypocritical evasion of more pressing problems that were being faced by workers at home. And indeed, in the half-century after the 1770s the development of the imperial conscience probably *had* run ahead of the growth of domestic sensitivity. By the 1830s that imbalance was no longer there.

The naivete of early Victorian attitudes toward the world and their role in it can easily be overstated. Did they really believe that, given free trade, a few experts, and the right sort of collaborators, they could lead India, the colonial empire, and indeed the world into a new era of happiness, prosperity, peace, and the universal rule of law? Perhaps not, but they approached that sort of optimism. Another way of putting it would be that they were making the first real attempt to make conscience the test and guide of policy and behavior. The inevitable failures could at first be blamed on insufficient time or lack of experience. As time went on, such rationalizations would naturally become increasingly difficult to maintain. After the mid-nineteenth century, the easy optimism of the early Victorians would fade.

The pressure groups who organized, sustained, and articulated the imperial conscience continued and expanded. Two of them deserve particular attention. The Anti-Slavery Society (founded 1823) by no means ceased its efforts after emancipation in 1833. Not only did the apprenticeship system that was supposed to keep freed slaves working on the plantations during the transition period have to be closely watched lest it regress back into slavery, but the society also had to be on the alert for attempts to introduce forced labor by indirect means. And the society extended its vision and goals. Its laudable object—which it would still be pursuing well after World War II—was to eradicate all forms of slavery from the face of the earth: from Cuba and Brazil (where it persisted until the late nineteenth century), from the Pacific (where it took the form of widespread kidnapping known as "blackbirding"), from East Africa and the Middle East (where the slave trade was gathering strength while the Atlantic traffic was winding down), and from all those numerous areas where domestic slavery was and is endemic. The Aborigines Protection Society, founded in 1837 under the leadership of Sir Thomas Fowell Buxton, was another organization with a huge and growing agenda: the exposure of injustice and exploitation of native inhabitants throughout the empire, including Indians in British North America, Africans at the Cape, and aborigines in Australia.

These two societies, which overlapped in objectives and in membership (they would ultimately merge in 1909), continued the techniques that had been developed in the long campaign against slavery. Notably in their own journals, but in the wider newspaper and periodical press as well, they publicized and exposed. They were usually more radical than the missionary societies, who had to survive in local political conditions in the various colonies. But they sought coordinated action with them whenever possible. To the Foreign and Colonial offices they sent hundreds of petitions. Each new foreign or colonial secretary was met by a deputation, and meetings were frequently requested on specific issues. They lobbied MPs. They raised embarrassing points at question time in Parliament. They instigated law suits, which sometimes lasted a decade or more. Sometimes they peppered away at a large variety of issues. Sometimes they concentrated their fire upon a single target. Like any organization their energy and cohesion waxed and waned. But they were remarkably persistent, and it would be rather silly to write off "Exeter Hall" (the name they acquired from their annual public meeting place) as nothing but a bunch of well-meaning but ineffective little old ladies.

Through much of the early Victorian period this organized imperial conscience was preaching to the converted. In India the perennial argument between "Westernizers" and "Orientalists" went for the time in favor of those who saw in rapid, wholesale reform along Western lines the only hope for improvement in a degenerate society. Some of the most notable experiments of the Utilitarians, writes Eric Stokes in *The English Utilitarians and India* (1959), took place in India, a marvellous outdoor laboratory where rational experiments might be carried out without the obstacles and delays they encountered at home. Whenever Lord Palmerston was foreign secretary, the abolition of the slave trade was pursued with vigor and deep conviction: not only was it a worthwhile moral objective, it was his hobby. The Whig colonial secretary Lord Glenelg, son of Charles Grant who had been a friend of Wilberforce and a Saint himself, was a strong ally of the missionary movement. His support for John Philip of the London Missionary Society is usually listed as one of the causes of the Great Trek of Boer farmers into the interior of South Africa, away from persecution. In 1835 Glenelg censured Sir Benjamin D'Urban, governor of the Cape colony, for his aggressive policy and methods of warfare against Africans: "Whether we contend with a civilized or barbarous enemy, the gratuitous aggravation of the horrors of war on the plea of vengeance or retribution, or on any similar grounds, is alike indefensible."[18]

Like other colonial secretaries, Glenelg soon departed. The permanent undersecretary, Sir James Stephen, son of the abolitionist who had been so important in 1806, remained. The man's tenacity and his devotion to the idea that colonial policy and the laws of colonial legislatures ought to be based on justice and morality were remarkable. Stephen is the most outstanding example of how the Victorian imperial conscience was institutionalized, of how it became a routine part of detailed decision making.

Unfortunately conscience rarely pronounced with a united voice. Whose conscience? Suppose conscience should point in opposite directions? A Westernizer like Macaulay, who argued that Western education alone could move India forward; an Orientalist like Burke, who maintained that the exercise of the trust must remain faithful to India's own heritage and "constitution": both sides of the debate over India undertook moral defenses of their contradictory positions. Similarly, in the thirties and forties a struggle was joined between the Colonial Reformers, led by Edward Gibbon Wakefield, and the friends of aborigines, led by Sir Thomas Fowell Buxton.

Like Burke, the Colonial Reformers appealed to the concept of the trust. What Wakefield called the "waste lands" of the empire were a sacred trust, the birthright of the British working man, the means by which those whom the competitive market system had squeezed out might begin afresh, where the "condition-of-England" question might be solved. Wakefield's scheme of systematic colonization—in which what he called a "sufficient price" for colonial land would automatically control the flow of migration from Britain and counter the labor shortage that is a chronic condition of new societies—was framed for empty continents, for "virgin lands." There are no "natives" in Wakefield's books. They have been miraculously whisked away.

When critics argued that the colonization scheme would not work, Wakefield replied that it had never been tried. America might have used it, thereby preventing the development of the social levelling that was described by Alexis de Tocqueville's influential *Democracy in America:* but there they all but gave the land away. So might Australia, except that so much of it had been ruined by the transportation of convicts. The next colony would clearly be New Zealand, and the Colonial Reformers claimed it for their own.

But, objected Buxton's Select Committee of the House of Commons on Aborigines, New Zealand was not empty. Polynesians lived there. Presumably the place belonged not to Wakefield, nor even to the distressed British working man, but to the Maoris. Was not their protection also a sacred trust? Great Britain in former times had "countenanced evils of great magnitude." For these "evils of an ancient date" she had atoned. But "the oppression of the natives of barbarous countries," continued the report of the Committee, apparently forgetting the systematic elimination of the natives of North America and Australia, was comparatively recent. All over the world aborigines were dying out from disease and liquor. Europeans were murdering them, or they were killing each other off with European guns. Systematic colonization and the rights of aborigines were in conflict, and a choice must be made:

> He who has made Great Britain what she is, will inquire at our hands how we have employed the influence He has lent to us in our dealings with the untutored and defenceless savage; whether it has been engaged in seizing their lands, warring upon their people, and transplanting unknown disease, and deeper degradation, through the whole regions of the earth; or whether we have, as far as we have been able, informed their ignorance, and invited and afforded them the opportunity of becoming partners of that civilization, that important commerce, that knowledge and that faith with which it has pleased a gracious Providence to bless our own country.[19]

The language of this report—its emphasis on Providence in having chosen Great Britain for a sacred mission in the world, on the need to atone for past sins, on the day of judgment when the nation would be called to account—is characteristic of this early Victorian period. (So, of course, is the language of Wakefield, in which conscience is perhaps rather less conspicuous.) That commerce, the Christian faith, good government, and enlightenment all formed a self-sustaining cycle, and that Britain had the obligation to exercise moral leadership throughout the world: like other ideologies, the early Victorians' "imperialism of free trade" was composed, layer upon layer, of self-interest, elaborate mystification, and sincere belief.

The lines of this ideology emerged most distinctly in West Africa. There, despite Britain's own abolition, her diplomatic efforts with other European powers, and her naval squadron, the slave trade persisted. Behind this persistence, argued Buxton in *The African Slave Trade and the Remedy* (1839), lay basic economic facts. Labor values in the New World were perhaps ten to fifteen times higher than they were in Africa, and the slave trade would endure until that enormous disparity was reduced. Legitimate alternatives (such as the growing trade in palm oil, which was brought down from the interior along the same routes that had brought the slaves, and was needed in Europe for soap and machine oil) must be developed; and since white men could not live permanently in the area, this must be done by African leadership. The economic and humanitarian factors were thus completely complementary. As Buxton put it in proposing what was to be a disastrous expedition to open up the Niger river: "We take a plow with us; but let it be remembered that in Africa the Bible and the plow go together."[20] MacGregor Laird, a member of a Liverpool ship-building firm who explored the region as a young man, dreamed of the Niger as a throbbing commercial artery like the Mississippi. When he applied for postal contracts to go up the river in the 1850s, his language was like Buxton's—and he meant it. David Livingstone would pursue the same formula in attacking the Arab slave trade in East Africa: good trade must drive out the bad.

In West Africa the problem was relatively simple. Legitimate commerce in palm oil, peanuts, and cotton was needed if the slave trade were to be curtailed, while European susceptibility to disease made a partnership with liberated slaves and educated coastal Africans essential. In the West Indies the problem was more complicated. There the former slaves were refusing to work for wages on the plantations, confounding the abolitionists' promises that free labor would be more efficient than slavery. While Cuban sugar prospered, Jamaica and Trinidad floundered. Not without strong protests from the Anti-Slavery Society, the Colonial Office agreed to taxation. In tropical countries, observed the colonial secretary, the third Earl Grey, a subsistence standard of living came so easily that only by artificial means could primitive man be persuaded to work for money. Once possessed of money, the worker would be caught up in a cycle of improvement. His wants would increase, and he would be introduced to the "dignity of disciplined labor." It was the same argument that factory owners had been using about English laborers, and it would be employed by Cecil Rhodes in South Africa and yet again by Lord Delamere in Kenya in the twentieth century. Governors, local legislatures, and the Colonial Office all confronted the chronic "underdevelopment" of the Caribbean with an impressive lack of imagination. Little or no thought was given to diversification—one might think for instance that islands would be good for fishing—but sugar colonies they had always been, and sugar colonies they would remain.

Reluctantly the Colonial Office also sanctioned the indentured service of Indian coolies, which Hugh Tinker has recently castigated as *A New System of Slavery* (1974). So in a way it was. Forced labor is forced labor. And the indentured labor system (with its ten-year contract, nearly always renewed because a paid return passage was not guaranteed until after twenty years of service, and with the local law-enforcement authorities working on the side of the employers) had many of the features of outright servility. How did the British manage to tolerate the introduction of coolie emigration less than a decade after emancipation? Mainly for economic and political reasons: the demands of colonial legislatures, who could make things extremely awkward by refusing to pass money bills, and the pressure of well-connected planters such as W. E. Gladstone's father; the need to increase the revenue so that colonial budgets could be balanced. One could of course argue that the coolies had been pushed out by intolerable conditions at home, and that the system was relieving population pressure in India. In addition, an elaborate network of protective officials, legal safeguards, and regulations was constructed, supposedly controlling every phase of the coolie's recruitment, passage, employment, and return. These regulations were often evaded, and in Tinker's view they affected only marginally what remained essentially an oppressive system of forced labor. They did however salve conscience. One might, with some justification, cry "hypocrisy." But Sir Frederic Rogers (who became permanent undersecretary at the Colonial Office in the 1860s) spent much of the late fifties negotiating a treaty with the French under which, in exchange for the French agreement to abandon their recruitment of African slaves who would then become "free" indentured workers in French colonies, they would be allowed to recruit coolies in British India. Rogers' concern was to protect the regulations, lest "loss of life may be inflicted on thousands of people by a false step. I get rather nervous and shaky when I think of this part of the matter."[21] His nervousness was genuine.

The early Victorian period was in many ways a normal period of British expansion. Industrialization proceeded. The railway boom in Britain would soon be over, and the export of rails and locomotives would become one of the most important sources for the accumulation of overseas capital. Cotton exports were facing stiff competition from the United States and Europe, and the need for new textile markets and additional sources of raw cotton was a powerful force in expansion. There was plenty of work for the soldier: wars with Sikhs and Afghans, against Malay pirates and "headhunters" of Sarawak, against Kaffirs in South Africa, against China. When Gladstone in 1840 denounced the China war—and since hostilities had grown out of Chinese efforts to halt the British trade in opium from India, he perhaps had some justification —he had to be reminded that "our empire in the East was founded on the force of opinion; and that if we submitted to the degrading insults of China, the time would not be far distant when our political ascendancy in India would be at an end." The war went on. When it was over Britain acquired Hong Kong. And so it went.

Early and mid-Victorians often said, and sometimes meant, that they were fed up with the colonies they had, and wanted no more of them. An anti-imperialist posture was consistent with the campaign for international free trade, which was argued as an affair of conscience by such members of the Manchester School as Richard Cobden and John Bright. But one of the most powerful forces in human affairs, inertia, was against them. The technological gap between Western and non-Western peoples continued to widen, and it therefore became increasingly easier for aggressive men on the spot to act on their own. Inertia, again, made it easier for the government to accept a fait accompli than to reject an annexation scheme in advance. Without any particular plan or design, the empire continued to grow.

Until at least the 1880s, however, the "colonial question" remained the conflict between colonization and the rights of aborigines in settlement colonies of the temperate zone. Colonial Reformers could attend to the dictates of Providence. They had before them the example of the American Revolution. How, in good conscience, could they permit that dreadful saga of the last century to be repeated? "The normal current of colonial history," wrote one of them, "is the perpetual assertion of the right of self-government."[22] Beginning in the 1830s, first Canadians, then Australians, New Zealanders, and South Africans had demanded "responsible" self-government. The British climate of opinion moved with them. As Gladstone said in 1867, while the "mother of Parliaments" was deliberating the British North America Act that still serves as the basis of the Canadian constitution, his generation might review the transfer of power with some pride.

Little enough was said about aborigines in the discussions of the Australian and Canadian constitutions, native reservations and demographic decline having "solved" the problem. In New Zealand and South Africa they could not so easily be disregarded, for Africans and Maoris were both numerous and warlike. Colonial Reformers claimed that systematic colonization would be good for them; unregulated anarchy harmed them most. The two positions—colonization as a remedy for the "condition-of-England" question, and the obligation to guard aboriginal interests—were nicely balanced in the instructions that were given to Captain William Hobson, who was sent to negotiate with the Maoris. New Zealand was not to be annexed without their full and free consent. Something along those lines seemed to have preceded the celebrated Treaty of Waitangi of 1840, by which the islands of New Zealand were ceded to the crown. In the next few years, as white settlement increased and as the Maoris grew more resentful and turbulent, it became apparent that the inherent conflict of interest between settlers and aborigines could be reconciled, if at all, only by a strong governor of genius.

Such a man, with all his faults, was Sir George Grey, the greatest of the mid-nineteenth-century colonial governors. With him we come to the phenomenon of the "proconsul": men such as Sir Thomas Munroe, the Lawrences, Lord Curzon, and Lord Hailey in India; Sir Stamford Raffles and Sir Frank Swettenham in Malaya; Lord Lugard and Sir Donald Cameron in Nigeria; Lord Cromer in Egypt; Lord Milner in South Africa. These men were authoritarian, impatient of any authority but their own, colorful even charismatic figures who projected their personalities to the British public and to their darker subjects as well. Maori chiefs hailed Grey as a great white chief; long after his retirement Nigerian emirs would gather in Lugard's garden outside London. The proconsuls used pageantry freely, putting on elaborate shows that may well have appealed to the imaginations of primitive peoples and certainly appealed to their own. Their pens were skillful and they used them often. Grey's dispatches are masterpieces of subtle obfuscation; Cromer wrote what for many years remained the standard work on modern Egypt; and I. F. Nicolson, in *The Administration of Nigeria* (1969), has demonstrated the brilliant mastery of Lord and Lady Lugard in the arts of propaganda. The proconsuls claimed to understand the native as no one else could, and thus the right to speak for him. These were masculine, masterful men, with whose domains the sedentary and ill-informed bureaucrats in London simply must not meddle.

The proconsul flourished in the British Empire because he was indispensable. The great problems might or might not be resolved by the masterful genius on the spot. London obviously could not. In the age of sail, six months at least elapsed before a reply to a letter could be received from the Cape, a year from India, eighteen months from New South Wales. Steam halved that figure by mid-century, and by the 1890s the telegraph reduced it to a matter of days or even hours. Even so, local knowledge remained indispensable. Proconsuls became adept media experts, employing the telegraph skillfully to build up a sense of crisis. The Colonial Office found the proconsuls trying, but could not do without them. The image of mastery they projected—some of it bluff, some of it based on solid achievement—enabled their superiors to assure themselves and the British public that the best possible job was being done.

To Sir George Grey, "the man of our times who has displayed the most special talent for the conduct of native affairs,"[23] was entrusted the task of resolving the apparently irreconcilable conflict between colonization and aboriginal interests. He grappled with it first in New Zealand (1845–52), then in the Cape Colony (1854–60), and again during the Maori wars in New Zealand (1861–64). Grey's policy was "amalgamation" of the races, by which he meant not racial mixture (though in fact that did not horrify him) but the interlocking of white and native peoples into an interdependent economic and social relationship. No doubt about which group would be dominant: the "barbarous race" would become a "part of ourselves" in the shape of "useful servants, consumers of our goods, contributors to our revenue; in short a source of strength and wealth for this colony [the Cape], such as Providence designed them to be."[24] Another way of putting this would be that natives were to be exploited. But if they did not contribute economically, Grey retorted, then the aborigines would simply be eliminated as they had been in America and Australia.

Grey pursued amalgamation by building schools and hospitals that would demonstrate the superiority of civilization, by allying with missionaries (whom he described as effective government agents), by establishing courts to which natives might bring their disputes, and above all by asserting his own personality in place of the crumbling authority of the chiefs. In New Zealand, according to his biographer James Rutherford, his measures had affected perhaps one-third of the Maoris by the end of his first governorship in 1854: less than he claimed, but a fair beginning.

In South Africa, which was so much larger and so much more complicated, Grey achieved far less. In fact he was not sent there to solve the "native question," but to remain aloof from conflicts between Boers and Africans in the interior, the Colonial Office having decided that nothing but headaches and expense were to be gained by intervening. In 1854 the British had even abandoned the recently annexed Orange River territory (later the Orange Free State), one of the few such retreats until after World War II. (This policy had been strongly denounced by David Livingstone and the London Missionary Society, who pleaded that Africans must be protected from enslavement and mistreatment by the Boers.) Hardly the man to implement such a passive policy, Grey proposed a federation of all the Boer and British settlements, as well as an active policy of "amalgamating" the Africans.

In both colonies the conflict of interests inherent in the colonial situation moved ahead. No policies, and not even Grey's dominating personality, could really control the reactions to conquest. In South Africa in 1857 came the strange and tragic "cattle-killing," in which members of the Xhosa tribe (acting on the instructions of a prophet figure) destroyed their crops, killed their cattle, and then starved by the thousands. This incident broke the power of the Xhosa, and the stream of men looking for work on the farms of the Cape colony was an important step toward the loss of African economic independence. More wars were to be fought—

the fiercest being against the Zulu in Natal in the late 1870s—before white supremacy would be secured.

During Grey's absence in South Africa the situation in New Zealand deteriorated, and the Maori wars began in 1861. Ostensibly they grew out of a disputed land transaction, but the causes were much broader. Having suffered grievously from disease and social disintegration, the Maoris feared the loss of their racial identity. Historically a politically fragmented people, they tried to organize themselves in the Maori King movement. With bravery and skill that won the British army's respect, they fought on against overwhelming odds for a decade. Finally, in the last stages of the wars, came a reaction of despair, a secret society that consciously practiced the most barbarous of customs: a defiant rejection of European culture. It seems very doubtful whether Grey's presence or absence was all that important. The Maoris were reacting not against particular personalities, policies, or even specific injustices so much as against the main fact of European domination.

The British government's response was to give the responsibility for "native policy" to the self-governing settlers. When conscience protested, the Colonial Office had answers ready. To pretend that Downing Street could really control race relations thousands of miles away was utter foolishness. Colonial politicians would in fact be in control, and one might hope they would act more responsibly if the lines of power were made clear. Besides, it was frequently charged that the frontier wars were "got up" intentionally so that local speculators might gain large profits by supplying British troops, all at the expense of the British taxpayer. Bring home the troops, and wars would soon cease. Self-government and self-defense, said the Select Committee of the House of Commons on Colonial Military Expenditure in 1861, must go together. Self-governing colonies should develop their own militias or, if British troops were to be provided, must agree to pay for them. New Zealand had received responsible government in 1856, before the full adoption of this policy. Throughout the Maori wars the Colonial Office attempted to apply it, and in 1869 (over much protesting from the colonists) the last regiments were withdrawn. The Cape received responsible government in 1872, but the concession was denied indefinitely to Natal, who would need a strong imperial force to guard them against the powerful Zulu.

By the 1860s Great Britain had no "native policy." Instead she had developed a defense policy. In the three decades since the report of Buxton's select committee on aborigines there could be no doubt that the wind had blown in the direction of the settlers. Better organized, more articulate, possessing in representative institutions powerful instruments that could bring government to a halt if they chose, the settlers had their way. Native affairs were included under responsible government, and the usual proviso that laws affecting native interests must be reserved for the consideration of the Colonial Office proved quite ineffective. For a time the vacuum had appeared to be filled by a colorful, masterful proconsul. Events had been permitted to take their course, the stronger party on the spot allowed the initiative. In 1861 the recently retired permanent under-secretary at the Colonial Office, Herman Merivale, explained laconically: "It cannot be doubted that a consistent and regulated system of management of the natives by the home executive would be better, as regards justice towards the natives, than the arbitrary will of the settlers. Unfortunately no such system has ever been established by us, or seriously attempted."[25]

The former permanent undersecretary of the India Office, John Stuart Mill, said much the same thing in *Considerations on Representative Government* (1865): the government of one people by the free institutions of another was quite impossible; only a despotism could hope to work. But that way led to a repetition of the American Revolution, for which the mid-Victorians had no stomach.

The traditional interpretation has been that the "humanitarian factor" declined sharply after about 1850. Yet David Livingstone's great popularity and success came after his celebrated speech at Cambridge in 1857. The foundation of the Universities' Mission to Central Africa (1859) was a direct result. Generally, but particularly among Nonconformists, subscriptions for foreign missions rose. The number of missionaries also grew considerably, and their training became more systematic. Only in the late nineteenth century can Protestant missions be said to have begun to carry the Gospel "into all the lands." And in the campaign of the early 1890s to retain Uganda, which the Liberals showed signs of giving up, the British conscience could still display the organization, skill in propaganda, and zeal that had gained abolition in the thirties.

Conscience had not disappeared. It had, to borrow a term from the German sociologist Max Weber, been routinized. In the 1830s Sir Henry Taylor, the senior clerk at the West India desk in the Colonial Office, was a firm advocate of emancipation, with reason regarded by the planters as a foe. By the late fifties, in a memorandum typical of many others, he wrote on the back of a "memorial" from the Anti-Slavery Society: "This production is a specimen of those which the Anti-Slavery Society has been accustomed to send forth of late years and an evidence of the condition to which it has fallen. Since the great British Anti-Slavery objects have been accomplished, the men of note and ability who used to govern the operations of the Society seem to have become inactive, and the paid servants of the Society prepare papers such as these which seem as if they cd. not be written in sincerity and were rather written by way of doing something to earn a salary and make a show of business to be done."[26]

The West Indian problem having apparently been solved for ever, the colonial secretary need not waste his time on charges that all was perhaps not well there. Taylor may have been right in arguing that routinization had sapped the energy of a once-vibrant philanthropic society. The disease had certainly infected the Colonial Office. At the Foreign Office and at the Admiralty the reports of the West (and now East) African naval squadrons were still being inspected. But Palmerston was not there.

The climate of opinion was changing. A series of shocks were being administered by non-Western peoples to the early Victorian presumption that, as Christianity, free trade, and good government were self-evidently a boon to the whole human race, the lesser breeds would welcome their ministrations. These hopes were dashed by a succession of risings and rebellions, serious enough individually, and collectively a crisis.

The fifties opened with yet another "Kaffir" war in South Africa—the ninth or the eleventh, depending on the count. This time two years and a million pounds were required to put down the Xhosa, and "economists" in Parliament turned savagely against the interventionist policy of Governor Sir Harry Smith and the colonial secretary, Lord Grey. By 1854, as has been mentioned, the British had renounced their annexation of the Orange River territory. Henceforth they meant to follow a policy of strict neutrality, and if "the natives should choose to slaughter each other and the Boers & Missionaries choose to assist them, we can't prevent their doing so."[27] The diamond and gold discoveries of the years after 1870 would change all that, adding a powerful economic element to the strategic and humanitarian considerations that already existed. For the time being, however, conscience had been set aside.

After the Kaffir war there was a brief respite—thankfully, since at the time Britain was fighting in the Crimea her only war against a European power between the defeat of Napoleon and 1914. But in 1857 the situation exploded. The Indian Mutiny, the "affair of greased cartridges" that touched off grievances among some upper-caste Hindus, Muslims, landlords, and regional groups, became almost a national revolt across North India. Not until 1859, after a savage conflict with numerous atrocities on both sides, was "order" finally restored. The administrative machinery of the government of India was shaken up: the East India Company was abolished, a secretary of state for India was created, and the army was reformed. According to all authorities, bitterness, hatred, and distrust replaced a paternalism that had sometimes been genuinely benevolent as the dominant mood of the British in India.

Simultaneously there was war with Persia and with China. The latter conflict was denounced in Parliament—there was some question, apparently, about whether the *Arrow,* whose British flag the Chinese were supposed to have insulted, had been properly registered to fly that flag at all —but clearly the local authorities must be supported and the honor of the flag defended. This time, thought Lord Elgin, the Chinese must be taught a lesson they would remember. In that he succeeded, for he burned the Summer Palace in Peking. Nothing could be more symbolic of the distinction Victorians made between civilized and "semi-civilized" peoples, for Elgin had deservedly won a high reputation for his part in the introduction of responsible government into Canada and for his good relations with the French-Canadians. As K. M. Panikkar observed, in *The Age of Western Dominance* (1953), Europeans have repeatedly demonstrated by wanton destruction of priceless artistic creations a peculiar insensitivity to expressions of beauty on which their civilization supposedly places so high a value. There would be time for all that later. "At present," announced *The Times* rather grandly in August 1857, England was "in conflict with the Eastern world. From Aden to Hongkong the British flag has been unfurled, and at various spots throughout this great section of the globe the inhabitants of these little islands are actually engaged in hostilities with well-nigh one-half of the human race."

In the 1860s came the Maori wars. And in 1865 followed Governor William Eyre's (at best) overenergetic suppression of an alleged rebellion in Jamaica. After what could at most be described as a riot of peasants, which was easily put down, 1000 homes were burned, 500 blacks were killed, and many others were flogged. Martial law remained in force for months. A mulatto member of the legislature was executed on the strength of hearsay evidence which the reviewing judge declared should never have been admitted even in the most informal of military tribunals. Meanwhile the English ruling class had been divided on the American Civil War, and was mainly pro-Southern at least until the Northern victory had clearly become inevitable. It was long supposed that the working classes of Lancashire, in opposition to their own economic benefit (for the war stopped the flow of cotton from the South and created severe unemployment), were staunchly for the North; but recent research has put this in question. British opinion was sharply against the Freed-man's Bureau and other attempts to reconstruct the South. Many a separate peace, then, had been made with Negro slavery.

The organized British conscience did not vanish: the Victorian imperial idea would have been difficult to sustain if it had. But this succession of crises had bred a hard sense of toughness closely akin to the *realpolitik* that we usually associate with the Germany of Bismarck. By the sword the empire and the greatness of Britain had been built; by the sword, not by the alleged affections of their subject peoples, they must be maintained. Now was no time for "maudlin humanity." Officers returning to India in the summer of 1857 were informed that the country would support them in their just and terrible reprisals, "however stern may be the measures which they may think it proper to employ." It was, continued *The Times,* "no question of fair warfare, and of sheathing the sword once the battle is over."

Indeed it was not. Native Indian soldiers had mutinied and murdered savagely. Officers were shot in the back while addressing troops they had commanded for years; when mutinous soldiers refused the order to shoot down women and children in Cawnpore, butchers were sent in to slaughter them; women suffered a fate so horrible "that even men can scarcely hint to each other in whispers the awful details." William H. Russell, *The Times'* special correspondent who had just exposed the scandal of the British army's lack of preparedness in the Crimean war, went out in 1858 to investigate the atrocity stories. Many of them, he concluded, were true, He also saw and heard of many equally shocking examples of "frightfulness" that were being done by the British and their native allies. Mutineers who surrendered on the promise of a fair trial were summarily executed. Trees were decorated with hanging bodies. Muslims were tied up inside pigskins (which are "unclean" in the Islamic religion) before being killed. Both sides, Russell concluded, were carrying on "Oriental warfare" with shocking vengeance and ferocity. "The peculiar aggravation of the Cawnpore massacres," he wrote, was "that the deed was done by a subject race—by black men who dared to shed the blood of their masters, and that of poor helpless ladies and children." The violence of the Mutiny was fed from many sources: "Here we had not only a servile war and sort of Jacquerie combined, but we had a war of religion, a war of race, and a war of revenge."[28]

Even more disturbing, in a way, was what Russell thought he could detect about the normal methods and structure of British rule in India. Collaboration was clearly essential to its endurance. Even during the Mutiny itself, native Indian troops did much of the fighting; natives cut the grass for the horses and elephants, prepared food for the troops, and made camp each evening. Without them it was hard to see how a British regiment could have stirred. Yet he saw no evidence whatever that British rule was based on affection or appreciation. Instead he everywhere encountered the use of force. And in the eyes of the women and children he passed on the road he saw unmistakable hostility.

The language and attitudes of respectable civilians, quite as much as violence in the field, revealed the growing tide of race prejudice. In the thirties the Buxton committee had noted with alarm the decline of aborigines wherever Europeans seemed to be settling. In the "Kaffir war" debates of the early fifties a view that might be called Darwinism before Darwin was being expressed:

> Did not the history of colonisation tell . . . that wherever he found the white man, and more especially the Anglo-Saxon, by the side of the aborigines—whether it was in North America, in South Australia, in New Zealand, or in South Africa—the inferior man vanished before him? . . . The savage was a degraded being, and the question was, could he be raised to the state of civilization of the man placed by his side? All history said that was impossible, and those men would vanish before the face of the white man. Let the British people make up their minds whether to colonise or not. He was prepared to say colonise: . . . the end justified the means.[29]

The language of letters from Anglo-Indians with which *The Times* saw fit to fill its pages during the Mutiny, based on second-hand reports of atrocities which there had been no opportunity to verify, could be repeated ad nauseum. Some called for the utter destruction of Delhi (which the mutineers had "restored" as the capital of an independent India) together with all its inhabitants, whether guilty or not. In June 1857 Macaulay noted that the nation was enraged "to a degree unprecedented within my memory. Peace Societies, Aborigines Protection Societies, and societies for the reformation of criminals are silent. There is one terrible cry to revenge."[30] This assessment, which has often been quoted as authoritative, was not in fact quite true. The Aborigines Protection Society argued that Britain's search for military prestige in Asia was ultimately responsible for the Mutiny; they deplored the tone of the British and Anglo-Indian press; they applauded the relatively judicial statements of the governor-general, "Clemency" Canning; and they printed early reports of British atrocities. Still, Macaulay's generalization was on the whole accurate.

Again, in the Governor Eyre controversy of 1865–67, the disturbing thing was not so much that a colonial governor had given way to panic—

he claimed to be preventing a recurrence of the Indian Mutiny—but the eminence of the individuals who publicly defended him against John Stuart Mill's Jamaica Committee. These included Charles Kingsley, Thomas Carlyle, and John Ruskin. As in the Mutiny, the language of controversy exposed a racism that had been only implicit in the generation that had emancipated the slaves. "The terrible Indian rebellion has sown evil seeds enough in the military as in the civil system," wrote a member of the Jamaica Committee. "It called out the tiger in our race. . . . That wild beast must be caged again."[31]

In this fevered atmosphere, Charles Darwin's *Origin of Species* (1859) was written and received. As is well known, he did not advance evolution as a principle but identified natural selection as the primary mechanism of biological change. The idea that "most favored races" were the "fittest" and therefore "survive" in the everlasting "struggle for existence" was, by at least the early nineteenth century, an implicit British and European assumption. As Darwin observed, he borrowed the idea from T. R. Malthus' famous essay on population. Authorities agree that in the late nineteenth century—the age of Count Gobineau, of Treitschke, of Houston Stewart Chamberlain, of Karl Pearson and the eugenics movement (which advocated strong measures to check the "deterioration of the race")—the general nastiness of European racist ideology increased, though only in the Nazi movement would it reach its logical and terrible conclusion. How much Darwin's writings had to do with this surge of Social Darwinism is still debated. Rather, Darwinian concepts and language could be and were mobilized to support all sorts of contradictory positions. Darwin surely had far less effect on the climate of Victorian racial opinion than did events such as the Indian Mutiny and the Jamaica rebellion. It may be that the mounting stridency of late Victorian ideology was a reaction to an increasingly hostile and difficult world, a world in which British and white supremacy could no longer so easily be taken for granted.

The effects of the change in attitudes were felt all round an empire in which the British representatives were becoming more exclusive and more insulated from contact with subject peoples. Rapid transportation by steamship and, toward the end of the century, the revolution in tropical medicine enabled larger numbers of English women to make semi-permanent homes in areas where they had been absent. Once nearly universal, concubinage came to be frowned upon, if not exactly rare. As so often happens, changes in conditions coincided with the shift in prevailing attitudes. In West Africa, for instance, Buxton's vision of a partnership with educated Africans that would build a thriving Christian country was gradually abandoned—except by the educated Africans. The African bishop Samuel Crowther resigned under pressure from his white colleagues; gradually but relentlessly the missionary hierarchy became lily white. Africans were forced out of all but the very lowest rungs of the civil service. Ironically, by the 1890s when Sir George Goldie's Royal Niger Company began to move into the interior, the only people in the region who possessed anything resembling a coherent Imperial idea were black.[32]

Racism, then, rose in the last half of the nineteenth century. It would not, however, be accurate to say that conscience declined as well. The sixties and seventies, indeed, saw the crest of the Nonconformist conscience as a force in British politics, a force to which Gladstone appealed very successfully in the famous Bulgarian agitation and in his Midlothian campaigns in Scotland in preparation for the Liberal victory in the general election of 1880. Gladstone charged his Conservative opponents with supporting tyranny around the world, with possessing a policy utterly devoid of moral principle or humanitarian concern. In Afghanistan, Burma, the eastern Mediterranean, and Zululand this deplorable pattern was the same, and British honor must be rescued from it. Gladstone fought the election on the platform of conscience, and he won handsomely. Somehow, the British climate of opinion was sustaining *both* an increase in racism and an enormously successful appeal to conscience as a practical political weapon.

Conscience and the "New Imperialism"

The rise of explicit racist ideology in the last half of the nineteenth century was a long-term development. No sudden spurt occurred shortly before 1885 that would account for the frenzied diplomatic activity that resulted in the partition of Africa and the Pacific. Continuity is the dominant pattern. Through the 1880s and beyond, the "colonial question" still meant what it had to the generation of Gladstone and Disraeli, the sometimes strained but generally improving relations between the mother country and her self-governing white settlement colonies.

What created the "new imperialism" is still being debated. Some point to a decisive alteration in the basic structure of the British economy, especially to what at the time was generally called the "great depression." Rather suddenly, in the early 1870s, Britain's economic and therefore political future became a matter of great concern. The country was rapidly losing her lead as an industrial power, and she perceived the raw materials and export markets of the world to be a finite and fast-closing system. The surge in overseas activity, then, may have been in fear of becoming a small and inconsequential country in the world, as the Dutch before them had become. The future would belong to large countries: the German Empire, the United States, and Russia. Only by thinking imperially, by binding Britain and her white colonies together in some sort of unity, could she avoid a slide into obscurity.

Others argue that the change came in European politics, the most decisive trigger being Germany's sudden claim for colonies in 1884–85. Imperialism had been largely a British monopoly, but that was no longer true. Growing national competition within Europe had its repercussions in the scramble for territory overseas. Colonies came to be regarded as essential accoutrements of successful nation-building.

Finally, the change may not have come about in Europe at all, but in the peripheral regions. In the classic and controversial interpretation of Robinson and Gallagher, *Africa and the Victorians* (1961), the trigger was Gladstone's reluctant intervention in Egypt in 1882, undertaken in order to guard the Suez Canal against a nationalist uprising. This event hastened the decline of the Turkish Empire in the eastern Mediterranean, and destroyed a gentleman's agreement that supposedly had existed with France not only in Egypt but elsewhere. The rising friction between Britain and France gave Bismarck an opening, and he entered his claim for colonies in the hope of keeping his rivals apart. Suddenly the approaches to India had become extremely vulnerable. And India—a valuable trading partner and recipient of British investment, and strategically crucial because its taxpayers paid the cost of about one-third of the imperial army, a branch moreover that was not within the scrutiny of Parliament —must be protected. Britain moved into Africa, then, in order to protect the routes to India. Despite the greater wealth and economic potential of West Africa, Britain's prize objective became East Africa, which controlled the headwaters of the Nile and thus the Suez route. Attitudes to empire, in the view of Robinson and Gallagher, were remarkably continuous until the 1890s, that is until after the period of the scramble. The excited talk that then became so prevalent about the great economic benefits of "undeveloped estates" was largely an exercise in rationalization after the fact, an attempt to justify the annexation of what had earlier been regarded as rather unprofitable territories. Imperialist ideology was not a cause but an effect of imperialist diplomacy.

To the organized British imperial conscience, the momentum of this new imperialism seemed awesome and inevitable. The twice-yearly journal of the Aborigines Protection Society was hard pressed to keep up with the rush of expeditions and acquisitions. Economic and strategic interests were so mighty, the self-appointed guardians of aborigines so weak and helpless. With an active membership of less than a hundred and an annual income of between three and four hundred pounds (which might be compared with Cecil Rhodes' private fortune, estimated as high as £540 millions), they could not have hoped to block the scramble. And that, after all, they did not really want to do. They were not, they declared repeatedly, enemies of colonization. The real opponents of the imperial idea were those who mistreated natives and drove them into rebellion, those who gave empire a bad name. Year after year at their annual meetings the speaker in the chair (who was usually an outsider, presumably invited in the hope of winning a powerful new friend) would note that "one of the principal missions of the Anglo-Saxon race [is] to open up and fill the unoccupied spaces of the world." If members of the audience disagreed, they did not say so. The scramble for Africa was too strong to be resisted. And the assumption by Great Britain of the responsibility to lead the benighted and backward portions of humanity toward civilization and Christianity might even be desirable.

How, except by opening up Africa to European commerce, could the dreadful Arab slave trade be stopped? How else could those barbarous and cruel native customs that missionaries were discovering be eliminated? How else could the evil, debilitating, and growing trades in arms and liquor be curtailed? Buxton and Livingstone had maintained that the development of legitimate commerce held the only hope for Africa. Was there any reason to disagree?

The friends of native interests sought not to oppose imperialism in general but to expose and check its worst abuses. They welcomed the initiative of King Leopold of Belgium, who proposed international cooperation in the Congo region; they condemned the "exploration" by means of flogging and shooting up villages as conducted by his lieutenant, Henry M. Stanley. Only gradually did they turn to expose the general pattern of atrocities that emerged in the Congo Free State. They applauded the civilized way in which the conference called by Bismarck in Berlin in 1885 divided up most of Africa among the European powers: such a welcome exception to the militarist way the world seemed to be going. On the whole they favored outright governmental annexation and hence responsibility. Their attitude toward Sir William Mackinnon's Imperial British East Africa Company (in which substantial "humanitarian" interests were involved) was cautious but generally favorable. Toward Sir George Goldie's Royal Niger Company and Cecil Rhodes' British South Africa Company they were more or less continually hostile, though a member of the board of directors of the latter (the Duke of Fife) was invited to take the chair at the annual meeting in 1891: surely a case of the cat among the canaries. They made good use of the Matabele (or Ndebele) War of 1893, and still more of the rebellion of both the Ndebele and the Shona three years later, to launch a sustained attack on Rhodes and the administration of his country. They were unhappy about the role of Lugard's mercenary army in taking over Uganda, but they favored its retention as a means of combatting the slave trade.

Whether or not missionary pressure for government intervention was an important cause of the scramble—Roland Oliver, in *The Missionary Factor in East Africa* (1952), says no; H. Alan Cairns, in *Prelude to Imperialism* (1965), a study of European attitudes in Central Africa, says yes—the organized British imperial conscience shared many of the assumptions and some of the rhetoric of the new imperialism. And, in truth, given the overwhelming superiority of the West in technology and power in the late nineteenth century, some sort of political domination probably was inevitable. If so, direct government responsibility was certainly preferable to indirect imperialism on the cheap through chartered companies. Better to formalize the colonial relationship, to bring it under the control of the Colonial Office, to make it the official responsibility of ministers of the Crown who could be questioned by members of Parliament who must be elected by the British public.

Conscience and the Boer War

Queen Victoria's reign ended in the midst of what was intended to be a small war to subdue the Boers in South Africa. Instead it dragged on, exposed the military weakness of an army that had become used to cheap victories against outgunned native opponents, and divided British opinion to a degree that invites comparison with the bitterness of the American debate over the Vietnam war in the 1960s. The Boer War was brought on by a conflict between obstinate men: President Paul Kruger of the South African (Transvaal) Republic on one side; on the other the British High Commissioner Sir Alfred Milner and the Colonial Secretary Joseph Chamberlain. The immediate cause was the denial of the franchise to British miners and other immigrants of Johannesburg. This was the excuse for Cecil Rhodes' planning of the Jameson Raid of 1895, intended to overthrow Kruger's government and achieve a federated South Africa by force. Milner determined that the Boers must either be faced down diplomatically or defeated militarily: what was ultimately at stake was British supremacy in southern Africa.

Native policy was never an important cause of division. As the Aborigines Protection Society noted at the time, the attempts to use it in justification of the war were profoundly hypocritical. In theory, there was a substantial difference between the principle of the Cape Colony's supposedly color-blind franchise (on which the mid-Victorian Colonial Office had insisted when it agreed to local self-government) based on property and educational qualifications, and the rigidly racialist doctrine of "no equality in church and state" that underlay the constitutions of the two Boer republics of the Transvaal and the Orange Free State. In practice, very few Africans voted in the Cape, and none at all in the other English-dominated colony of Natal. Moreover the rise of the British-controlled mining industry—the diamonds of Kimberley, the gold of Johannesburg—had done far more than the Boer farmers to lock Africans into a position of subserviency as an unskilled labor force of migratory workers.

Conscience was heavily on the side of the Boers. They were like the Irish, a people of European stock who were being bullied and denied self-government by an overbearing and militarist imperialism. They fought courageously, tenaciously, and well, demonstrating what valuable allies they might become if treated properly. Instead, a harsh and indeed impossible ultimatum had been given them, their country had then been invaded and devastated, their women and children had been rounded up and herded into concentration camps (a term that was invented in this war) where the sanitation facilities and death rates were appalling. World opinion almost universally condemned the war, and the "pro-Boers" agreed with them: British imperialism had gone mad. In this divisive atmosphere outright denunciations of imperialism became more frequent, most notably John A. Hobson's *Imperialism: A Study* (1902).

To the pro-Boers the moral issue seemed self-evident and imperative. They were therefore disappointed and surprised when the working classes, whom Gladstone had once mobilized so successfully, did not unite behind their crusade, even when Hobson informed them that surplus capital for overseas investment existed only because underconsumption at home took that money right out of their own pockets. But Hobson's analysis was complicated, and the underconsumptionist thesis was cancelled by the counter-argument of "social imperialism," whose advocates maintained that imperial markets and raw materials (which without annexation would be taken over by competitors) created opportunities for employment. How except by imperialism could the tiny British Isles support a large and expanding population?

According to Richard Price in *An Imperial War and the British Working Class* (1972), the failure to build a strong base of popular

support was the fault of the pro-Boers themselves. They did not systematically emphasize issues with which the working class could intimately
identify. The organization and intensity of Nonconformity had clearly
waned, and it was by no means united against the war. Above all, no
great popular figure stepped forward to fill the position Gladstone had
occupied so long.

In the perspective that is afforded by the development of South African apartheid in this century, the role of conscience in the Boer War
may appear to have been mistaken. Only by ignoring the 75 percent of
the population who were black could the parallel between the Boers and
the Irish be maintained. It is difficult to believe, however, that Britain
could have delayed indefinitely the march to white self-government. And
the hope that inclusion within the larger Commonwealth might liberalize
Afrikaner (i.e., Boer) attitudes seemed until after World War II to have
some justification.

Conclusion

By Queen Victoria's death in 1901, the imperial conscience had been
in existence for more than a century. Like the statements of the spokesmen of conscience, this essay has had much to say about failures. Conscience had not prevented vast global exploitation, massive displacement
of whole populations, the destruction of most of the world's "primitive"
societies, and a constant succession of conflicts that may have been small
wars for the British but were very large indeed for their native opponents. Conscience may have helped prevent Africa's going the way of the
Americas and Australia, though the greater effectiveness of African resistance and the fact that so much of the continent lies outside the temperate zone were considerably more important brakes upon expansion.
The simple fact is that Africa could not be exploited without Africans.
What, then, had been achieved?

For one thing, the abolition of slavery. Granted all that one may say
about the complexity of motives, and taking into account the substitute
forms of indentured service and indirectly coerced labor that so often
succeeded it, slavery was never reinstituted. Abolition was a momentous
achievement of enduring significance, a true turning point in the history
of the world. Second, the imperial conscience had evolved and nurtured
the concept that British behavior overseas as well as at home ought to be
conducted according to moral principles. The exceptions were of course
numerous. But the governing classes were for the most part brought

round to the notion that the concept of trusteeship was integral to the imperial idea.

All of the elements of the doctrine of trusteeship, to which Sir Frederick Lugard was to give classic form in *The Dual Mandate in British Tropical Africa* (1919), were already explicit in British imperial ideology by the death of Queen Victoria. No people, agreed Lugard, the Labour leader J. Ramsay MacDonald, and the pro-Boer Hobson, had the right to lock up substantial portions of the world's resources. Primitive peoples lacked the technology, knowledge, and organization to develop those resources. Colonization was therefore morally justified as well as inevitable. Yet the mandate could and should be dual. The interests of colonizers and colonized need not conflict. The government of backward peoples could be conducted so as to benefit the ruled as well as the rulers and the working classes at home.

The doctrine of trusteeship had been created and integrated as an essential component of British imperial ideology. A. P. Thornton, in his excellent and provocative studies, *The Imperial Idea and its Enemies* (1959) and *Doctrines of Imperialism* (1965), has shown how this ideology had constantly to be refurbished and modernized as it fought its battles against British socialism, American liberal anticolonialism, Asian and then African nationalism, and after 1917 international communism led by Moscow. An entirely negative, selfish sort of ideology would not have survived in this fierce competition. Large numbers from several generations of Englishmen would not have been attracted to it. First the white man's burden, then trusteeship, then partnership, and finally the grand concept of independence within the Commonwealth of Nations: in all of these phases the ideology had positive substance as well as what Marxists call mystification. The imperial idea was a flexible, absorptive, tough ideology capable of adapting with the times. It is easy, these days, to underestimate its former effectiveness.

At the height of the frenzy of the Indian Mutiny the pacifist free trader Richard Cobden had wondered whether empire and constitutional liberty at home would in the long run continue to be compatible. "How," he asked, "are we to maintain despotic sway in future over 100,000,000 of Asiatics (for it must be undisguised despotism henceforth) and preserve our own freedom at home?"[33] Cobden wrote this at a time when savage conflict had made the essential elements of the colonial situation unusually clear. Mystification had been swept away at Cawnpore. Cobden was mistaken, however, in supposing that despotism would continue to be undisguised. Within a decade of the Mutiny it had again become common to point to the small number of Englishmen who managed to rule India's millions, and to conclude that only the implicit loyalty of their subjects, won by an unspoken recognition of Britain's "great work" out there, could explain this. Despotism would certainly continue. But it would again be partly submerged beneath layer upon layer of mystification.

Cobden's fear that imperialism would poison British domestic politics and destroy constitutional liberty also proved to be largely unjustified. The Indian Mutiny and the Boer War did inject a kind of poison into the British political atmosphere. How Britain managed to remain liberal at home and imperialist abroad is a serious problem for the student of Victorian politics and society. But the general pattern seems clear enough. Though there were a lot of them, the imperial conflicts were in fact "small wars" that did not greatly tax British resources or civilian manpower. Small numbers of Englishmen fought them, and these were a profession and a class apart. The Boer War was a significant exception; and the turmoil it created shows what might well have happened in British society if Africans and Asians had been able to mount more effective resistance. The relative ease with which Britain waged these wars was, in turn, a function of the tremendous gap in technology between Western and non-Western peoples that widened so enormously in the late nineteenth century. The Victorians were lucky.

Notes

1. Ronald Hyam and Ged Martin, *Reappraisals in British Imperial History* (1975).

2. Quincy Wright, *A Study of War,* 2nd ed. (1965), p. 650.

3. Brian Bond, ed., *Victorian Military Campaigns* (1967).

4. Charles E. Callwell, *Small Wars: Their Principles and Practice,* 3rd ed. (1906), pp. 25–26.

5. Quoted by Terence Ranger, *Revolt in Southern Rhodesia, 1896–97: A Study in African Resistance* (1967), p. 328.

6. Francis Jennings, *The Invasion of America* (1975).

7. Peter Wood, *Blacks in Colonial South Carolina* (1975). I owe the suggestion about the real meaning of Darwinism for the student of history to Mr. Wood.

8. Immanuel Wallerstein, *The Modern World-System: Capitalist Agriculture & the Origins of the European World-System in the Sixteenth Century* (1974).

9. *Ibid.*

10. This is not to dispute, in the slightest, the analysis of the origins of American racism in Winthrop D. Jordan, *White Over Black: American Attitudes toward the Negro, 1550–1812* (1968).

11. Roger Anstey, *The Atlantic Slave Trade and British Abolition, 1760–1810* (1975), p. 53.

12. *Ibid.*

13. See Seymour Drescher, *Econocide: British Slavery in the Era of Abolition* (1977).

14. Anstey, *The Atlantic Slave Trade,* p. 408.

15. See Edward P. Thompson, "Time, Work-Discipline, and Industrial Capitalism," *Past and Present* 38 (December 1967): 56–97, and his great book, *The Making of the English Working Class* (1963).

16. David B. Davis, *The Problem of Slavery in the Age of Revolution, 1770–1823* (1975).

17. George Bennett, ed., *The Concept of Empire: Burke to Atlee, 1774–1947* (1953), pp. 51–52.

18. Kenneth N. Bell and William P. Morrell, eds., *Select Documents on British Colonial Policy, 1830–1860* (1928), pp. 462–77.

19. *Ibid.,* pp. 545–46.

20. Thomas Fowell Buxton, *The African Slave Trade, Part II: The Remedy* (1839), p. 192.

21. Letter to his mother; George E. Marindin, ed., *Letters of Frederic, Lord Blachford* (1896), p. 194–95.

22. Charles B. Adderley, *Review of "The Colonial Policy of Lord J. Russell's Administration," By Earl Grey, 1853: And of Subsequent Colonial History* (1869), p. 3.

23. Herman Merivale, *Lectures on Colonization and Colonies* (1841; 1928), p. 515 (footnote added to 1861 edition.)

24. Great Britain, Parliamentary Papers, 1854–55 [1969] 38, 52.

25. *Lectures on Colonization,* p. 518.

26. Great Britain, Public Record Office, CO 318/18.

27. Sir William Molesworth, CO 48/367.

28. William H. Russell, *My Indian Mutiny Diary,* edited by Michael Edwardes (1957), p. 29.

29. J. A. Roebuck. Great Britain, 3 *Hansard's Parliamentary Debates, 116,* 272–75.

30. Quoted by Bernard Semmel, *The Governor Eyre Controversy* (1962), p. 21.

31. *Ibid.,* pp. 131–32.

32. John E. Flint, "Nigeria: The Colonial Experience from 1880 to 1914," Lewis Gann and Peter Duignan, eds., *Colonialism in Africa,* 5 vols. (1969–), I: 220–60.

33. Letter to John Bright; John Morley, *The Life of Richard Cobden* (1893).

THE CONSERVATIVE CONSCIENCE
Peter Marsh

T HE WELL-EDUCATED, widely-read Conservative, who is well assured that all good things are gradually being brought to an end by the voice of the people, is generally the pleasantest man to be met," Trollope reflected. "But he is a Buddhist, possessing a religious creed which is altogether dark and mysterious to the outer world. Those who watch the ways of the advanced Buddhist hardly know whether the man does believe himself in his hidden god, but men perceive that he is respectable, self-satisfied, and a man of note."[1]

In the eyes of detached observers, the conscience of Victorian Conservatives was a puzzling paradox. Even in the heyday of Disraeli, it was hard to cast aspersions on the often religious earnestness and quiet philanthropy of the country gentlemen and men of suburban property who formed the Conservative party's rank and file. But their set of values seemed ethically defective and socially unrealistic. In an age when conscience was increasingly conceived of in individual terms, and when at the same time it seemed to require increasing sensitivity to men of all classes and creeds, the Conservative's conscience remained cloistered. His deepest commitments were to the concrete institutions and interests which inspired and protected his values—institutions and interests to which he remained loyal even though they were in varying degrees exclusive.

The distinguishing characterisic of the Victorian Conservative ethic was this commitment to institutions and to their undergirding interests. In the twentieth century, Conservatives, perhaps recalling the example of Sir Robert Peel[2] or moved by the myths which grew around memory of Disraeli and Lord Randolph Churchill, would adopt more elastic, less tangible objectives. But their Victorian forefathers had rejected Peel and later turned from the excitements of Disraeli and Lord Randolph Churchill to the more comfortable embrace of Lord Salisbury. The conscience of Victorian Conservatives was cast in an older, pre-liberal, collective rather than individual mold; and though it proved sufficiently adaptable to entrench them in power for most of the final fifteen years of the nineteenth century, never was their commitment to institutions and interests more apparent than then.

Their ethic was nonetheless conscientious for being cloistered. The institutional commitments of Conservatives were threefold: to Church, to land eventually broadened to include all property, and to party. And they invested all three with varying degrees of moral import. The investment was obvious in the case of the Church, by which they meant the Established Churches, especially the Established Church of England and Ireland. Conservatives relied upon the clergy not merely to preach true religion, but also to foster harmony among classes (and between England and Ireland), to inspire philanthropic giving, to care for the material well-being of their parishioners, of widows, orphans, the sick, the aged, and the destitute, and to serve as England's educator from the elementary level to the universities. They relied for these services upon the Church, and disputed the competence as well as the right of the state to provide them. The churchmanship of many Conservatives was undoubtedly inert, little more than an excuse for warding off unwelcome action by the state rather than a commitment to give the Church generous, active support. But, taken as a whole, Victorian churchmen, among whom Conservatives were predominant, gave to their Church with a generosity nothing short of spectacular. Conservatives in Parliament also defended the rights of the Established Church and its provision of social services tenaciously. Sometimes their actions, particularly when Irish Roman Catholicism was involved, displayed ugly prejudice, but that seemed to be inseparable from the highest good they knew. And they persisted with their support for Anglican elementary education right past the end of the century even though it strained their alliance with the Liberal Unionists who held the balance of power.

Until the last twenty or thirty years of the century, the Conservative party was identified, either wholly or by its core, with the landed interest. The ownership of land was more obviously an interest than an ethic. It was certainly as an interest, a privileged, selfish interest, that Richard Cobden and the Anti-Corn Law League attacked it in the 1830s and '40s. Cobden charged that the owners of land used their entrenched position in Parliament to keep up the cost of wheat and hence of bread in face of massive poverty, unemployment, starvation, and the difficulty of British manufacturers in contending with cheap foreign competition. Cobden's agitation helped to convert the leader of the Conservative party, Sir

Robert Peel. But the bulk of the party clung to agricultural protection as the custodians of a pre-industrial tradition which envisioned the ownership of landed estates not merely as an economic interest but as conveying well-defined, beneficent social responsibilities. In this tradition, the landed estate was also conceived of as the indispensable counterpart of the ecclesiastical parish, and as the base which provided England with good governors, freed by economic security from the distracting necessity of pursuing their own livelihood through commerce or industry. As the industrial revolution and the growth of cities tore up the rural fabric of English society, these traditional conceptions became less a reflection of reality than an idealized, romantic memory. Still, the tradition was influential, particularly through the Young England movement of the 1840s, in sharpening Conservative concern about the callous treatment and terribly long hours demanded of the laborers in the new mills and deepening mines, and about the demoralizing, disease-infested tenements into which the inhabitants of the swollen cities were piled. Though this concern produced more indignant rhetoric than remedial action, it contributed to the enactment of some legislation, notably the Ten Hours Act of 1847, which limited the hours of labor of women and children in textile mills, and to a spate of social legislation during Disraeli's second Ministry in 1875–76 unmatched at any other time in the century.

By then the Conservatives had lost the battle to preserve the political and economic dominance of land and were adapting themselves to the loss by widening their commitment to embrace all forms of property. The split of 1886 in the Liberal party over Home Rule for Ireland, and the alliance of Liberal Unionists with Conservatives, came close to completing the process. The consolidation of the interests of property under the wings of the Conservative party weakened its broader social sensitivities. There was less ethic and more interest in the Conservative commitment to property than in the superceded commitment to land. As Young England had argued years before, the social obligations involved in the ownership of property generally were more vague and hence less effective than those attached by tradition to the ownership of land. The old tradition still helped to sustain a trickle of social legislation, particularly in the field of housing, but little more than a trickle. Lord Salisbury evoked the old tradition of Conservative social concern often just to cast the Liberal preoccupation with political reform in an unbecoming light. Despite his talk about the benefit which all classes would reap from his government's refusal to disturb the confidence of potential investors in the economy, the Conservatives were closer to being a class party at the end of the century than their Tory predecessors had been at its beginning.

The ethical significance of the Conservatives' third institutional commitment—their commitment to party—was disputed if anything more seriously than the idealism associated with the ownership of land. Traditional associations, which supported a romantic view of landed estates, worked against a high view of party. Though the Tory party possessed better organization and a stronger sense of its identity in the eighteenth century than is commonly assumed,[3] conventional wisdom, reaching back to the scarring experiences of the seventeenth century, had identified parties with factions pursuing selfish ends rather than the well-being of the country as a whole. The argument that country should come before party was hard to resist and always seemed particularly pressing at moments of national crisis. In the century following the defeat of Napoleon at Waterloo, these crises tended to arise over domestic rather than foreign affairs, and they commonly involved tensions between England and Ireland. They drove most nationally responsible leaders to look for nonpartisan, consensual solutions. But the solutions they offered—Catholic emancipation in 1829, repeal of the Corn Laws in 1846, some measure of self-government for Ireland in 1885—invariably entailed the abandonment of arrangements in which the Tories or Conservatives of the day still believed. Tory resistance was weakened in 1829 and 1846 for lack of a widely accepted, conventional rationale for insistence upon partisan commitments. The opposition put up by Ultra-Tories in 1829 and by Protectionists in 1846 was instinctive rather than well considered. It was not until 1885 that English revulsion at the prospect of Home Rule enabled Lord Salisbury to work out a way of reconciling respect for the instincts of his party with the need for a viable response to the current crisis and for enough electoral and Parliamentary support to sustain a government.

But the case for investing loyalty to party with binding moral force was firmly rooted in the realities of British politics as transformed by the Reform Acts of 1832, 1867, and 1884. By giving the vote to the entire middle class, then to a large portion of the working class, and eventually to three-fifths of all adult males, the Reform Acts created a popular though not yet fully democratic political order which greatly increased the debt of leaders to followers. New forms of constituency organization and Parliamentary consultation had to be developed to mobilize the electorate and to translate its votes into reliable majorities in the House of Commons. The political parties built machinery to meet this need, and their expectations grew accordingly. The right of leaders to trample upon the expectations of those whose exertions raised them to office became increasingly open to question. Conservatives had few doubts about the answer. Their leaders could differ with that answer only at great peril.

Sir Robert Peel was brought up fully sharing his family's particular appreciation of the institutional order which Tories treasured. Though old, that order was, by European standards, impressively elastic and hence capable of winning the allegiance of new segments in a changing society, as Peel's own family proved. He was the grandson of a yeoman farmer who, through bold financial and mechanical enterprise, turned himself into a rich textile manufacturer. Peel's father went farther, creating one of the large textile fortunes which marked the industrial revolution, and he promptly used his wealth to join the dominant landed classes by acquiring his own broad acres, a seat in the House of Commons, and a baronetcy. In Parliament the first Sir Robert Peel enrolled himself within the party of the then prime minister, William Pitt, on the eve of Britain's long battle against Revolutionary and Napoleonic France. In religion, the Peels were firm adherents of the Protestant Established Church of England. Young Robert received the education of a gentleman commoner at Harrow and Oxford, where he achieved unprecedented academic distinction and imbibed still more deeply the convictions and commitments summed up in the loyal toast to Church and King. With the family fortune more than secure, Peel was free to enter Parliament two years after leaving Oxford. Within another two years, fulfilling the expectations of his father, he began his apprenticeship in the service of the Tory successors of Mr. Pitt as a junior minister.

For six years, from 1812 to 1818, Peel's assignment was to uphold the most beleaguered outworks of English and Anglican ascendancy as Chief Secretary for Ireland. His performance in that office attracted particular attention. For, since 1800 when Pitt had been driven temporarily from power over his proposal to combine full political rights for Roman Catholics with legislative union between Great Britain and Ireland, the issue of "Catholic emancipation" had created an enfeebling division within the Tory party. Many of its abler men, particularly among the young and rising, favored the reform. By the competence which he displayed in the governance of Ireland as well as by staunch support for the Protestant constitution, Peel emerged from his term in Ireland as the most promising young champion of the Protestant cause. In an allusion to the aggressively Protestant Orange Order in Ireland, he acquired the nickname of "Orange Peel." And he won the high honor of election as Member of Parliament for the University of Oxford, whose electorate consisted largely of clergymen of the Established Church.

But the need to maintain an army of at least 20,000 in Ireland, upon which Peel insisted, and the regular, widely scattered break-downs of law and order in England with which he had to deal during the 1820s as Home Secretary, amply indicated that the old constitution was too rigid to encompass the social changes and popular demands which accelerated after the victory at Waterloo. Peel spent his career responding to waves of popular agitation, actual or expected. In doing so, his notion of the order which he wished to conserve grew more conceptual than institutional, while the code of ethics by which he regulated his conduct became internalized—a matter of personal honor regardless of party.

This gradual transformation came about through the working upon Peel of a conscientious attitude toward the work of administration, an attitude which he imbibed during his apprenticeship in Tory Ministries and refined through his own powers of intellect. The practice of government by the Tory ministerial elite, led from 1812 to 1827 by Lord Liverpool, was inextricably bound up with their philosophical commitments and constitutional concerns. The experience of the French Revolution had burned deeply into their minds an aversion to attempts at reconstruction or reform on the basis of theory or idealism. Although the same experience deepened their veneration for the existing order of Church and State, they shied away from philosophical argument in its defense. They relied instead on the empirical arts of attentive, cautious, capable administration. They sought to resist the far-reaching proposals of theorizing reformers with carefully observant, piecemeal response to particular abuses.

Peel had brought this technique to a new height of refinement by the time he left Ireland. There he developed a method of administration characterized by "the collection of factual information by means of carefully prepared series of specific questions to the men most likely to have access to the knowledge he wanted; the testing of generalities, opinions, and advice by reference to the facts; the prudent choice of agents; caution and scepticism in coming to a decision; and energetic action once the decision was reached."[4] At the Home Office he responded to the demand of humanitarian penal reformers for reduction in the vast number of crimes for which death was the prescribed punishment. He could see that reform was needed because excessively severe punishments failed in practice to deter crime and often induced juries to acquit those whom they regarded as minor offenders. But Peel acted to reduce the severity of the

law with greater circumspection and with greater concern for enforce-
ment than even the moderate Whig Opposition wished. In true administrative spirit, he placed his reforms in the context of a consolidation and
codification of the penal code. To ensure that his proposals would work,
and also to obviate diehard opposition, he worked with the leaders of the
legal establishment in framing his bills. And his most distinctive contribution was to give London a police force to prevent infractions of the
law.

In spite of the conservative intent and style of this administrative approach to government, it had three liberalizing elements within it. The
Tory ministerial elite wished to demonstrate that the existing constitutional order could provide good government in the interests, not just of
the landed classes and the Established Church, but of the whole society.
Their administration clothed a disinterested, altruistic intent. The effect
of this ethic was reinforced by another, constitutional concern. One
weakness in the existing political order of which the Tory ministers were
acutely aware was the difficulty of maintaining a strong executive *vis-à-
vis* Parliament. Throughout the first two thirds of the nineteenth century, British ministries lacked many of the powers of patronage on which
their predecessors relied to assure themselves of a majority in the House
of Commons, and they did not possess the support of disciplined parties
on which their successors depended. The reduction in patronage, a process which continued until by 1870 virtually complete, was in itself an
exercise in political altruism. The cultivation of parties in and out of Parliament, on the other hand, implicitly challenged such altruism. But that
problem lay on the horizon. Meanwhile ministries had to struggle,
against running criticism in Parliament and periodic waves of unrest in
the country, to vindicate their title to govern. This struggle not only
heightened the need for governments to demonstrate their disinterested
concern for the general welfare. The weakness of executive power also
gripped Tory statesmen with a sense of their responsibility to ensure that,
somehow or other, the country was provided with a government or, as
they preferred to put it, that the King's (or Queen's) Government was
carried on, even if that involved the enactment of reforms which went
against their grain.

Finally, the anti-philosophic pragmatism with which Tory ministries
sought to uphold the order of Church and State exposed that order to
pragmatic assault. Paradoxically, the Tory ministers' aversion to abstract argument, and their reliance on empirical administration to defend
a concrete order, loosened their commitment to the philosophical principles embodied in its outworks and made their conception of its essence

more and more ethereal. Peel's powers of intellect, and his contempt for uninformed, unreflecting prejudice, made him particularly susceptible to all of these liberal potentialities in Tory statecraft.

He had no time for proposed reforms for which there was no practical need or urgent popular demand. As befitted the Member of Parliament for the University of Oxford, Peel tried in the spring of 1828 to prevent the dismantling of one of the old order's theoretically vital defenses, the Test and Corporation Acts. The Corporation Act in particular debarred from civic office the Protestants in England who did not conform to the Established Church. The terms of the alliance between the Church of England and the state, which placed bishops in the House of Lords and turned Parliament into the Church's legislature, logically required an exclusively Anglican Parliament. At the same time, the English Nonconformists had little practical grievance on this score, because Acts of Indemnity had long been passed to excuse those who violated the Test and Corporation Acts. And though Nonconformists worked concertedly upon the suggestible Whigs to press in Parliament for repeal of the Acts, there was no extraordinary agitation in the country to reinforce the demand. Peel therefore defended the status quo in his customary pragmatic manner; and while his efforts did not succeed, they left his reputation (now that Lord Liverpool had retired) as the foremost defender of the privileged position of the Church of England unimpaired. In the autumn of 1828, ardently Anglican, anti-Catholic Lancashire hailed him at a succession of semi-public dinners given in his honor.

But already the acids created by the interaction of the administrative ethic and popular agitation were at work, corroding Peel's commitment to the Protestant constitution. In a by-election in midyear for the Irish constituency of County Clare, Daniel O'Connell, leader of the nationalist Catholic Association, challenged the government's candidate, Vesey Fitzgerald, a popular landowner sympathetic to the demand for Catholic emancipation. Though Fitzgerald was the most attractive candidate that the government could run, O'Connell defeated him by a vote of more than two to one. The success of O'Connell demonstrated the command which the Catholic Association had over the Irish electorate, and did so all the more powerfully because O'Connell's supporters, with conspicuous discipline, refrained from the rioting and drunkenness common at election time. Catholics could vote; but because of an oath rejecting central Catholic doctrines which was required upon entering Parliament, they had not previously run for election. O'Connell shattered this convention. And while he could not take his seat in the House of Commons, his election for County Clare gave rise to the prospect, at the next general election, of Catholic candidates successful in a host of Irish constituencies. Their inability to take their seats would then, in effect, destroy the legislative union between Ireland and Great Britain and inaugurate a clash of the utmost seriousness between the two islands.

Since the beginning of the year, the government had been led by the Duke of Wellington as prime minister, with Peel as leader in the House of Commons. The Clare by-election confronted the ministry with an urgent, practical challenge to which there could be only two responses. The government could defy the challenge and arm themselves to crush the upheaval which would inevitably ensue in Ireland. But Parliament had been so closely divided on the issue of Catholic emancipation, and also tended to respond so uncomfortably to forcible repression of unrest in England, that this course did not seem politically feasible. It was likely only to weaken the government at a time when it would need maximum strength. The remaining alternative, to eliminate the anti-Catholic oath, in other words to concede Catholic emancipation, posed a painful moral dilemma. The Duke of Wellington might be able without loss of character to propose Catholic emancipation, for the principle of government with which he was associated was authoritarian more than Anglican. Not so Peel. The expectations not only of his constituents at Oxford but, as the Lancashire festivities demonstrated, in the country at large would be violated if he remained leader in the Commons for a government which proposed Catholic emancipation.

Peel's immediate reflex was to offer Wellington his resignation. At the same time, he recognized that the practical logic of the situation required Catholic emancipation. By resigning office while continuing to speak in support of the government when it proposed the change, he could reconcile the just expectations of his constituents with his own administrative understanding. But he also recognized that the current executive, weaker than ever since the departure of Lord Liverpool, would probably prove unable to push Catholic emancipation through Parliament if he resigned. No viable alternative ministry could, in all probability, be formed in the present Parliament. And a general election under current circumstances would unleash dangerous religious passions, to say nothing of the outcome in Ireland. Foiled of an opportunity to leave the government before the crisis erupted,[5] Peel stayed on; and though for many months his letter of resignation remained in Wellington's hands, Peel entered with Wellington into the business of considering how and in what shape Catholic emancipation should be granted. To add to the surprise, Peel's influence within these deliberations made the eventual bill much more thoroughgoing than had previously been contemplated. Previous proposals for Catholic emancipation had been coupled with provisions to give the state some compensatory control over the Roman Catholic Church, whether through arrangement with the papacy or by making the Catholic clergy financially beholden to the state. Peel, through a mixture of Protestant repugnance at dealing with Roman Catholicism and administrative recognition that such guarantees would prove ineffective, kept them out of the bill which the government introduced.

Trust in Peel never entirely recovered from the shock which he gave by proposing Catholic emancipation to Parliament in 1829. He immediately exchanged the nickname of "Orange Peel" for "Lemon Peel." His constituents at the University of Oxford threw him over. He had to re-enter Parliament as Member for the pocket borough of Westbury, and even there the unenfranchised citizenry made their Protestant anger brutally plain. Though the government passed its measure, Ultra Tories, furious at the betrayal and confident that they could have put up a stronger resistance if the electorate of Protestant England had been broader, began to flirt with the Whig Opposition and with Parliamentary Reform. Their votes helped to throw Wellington's government out in 1830, placing Peel on the unfamiliar benches of Opposition.

He was immediately confronted by a drastic transformation of the constitutional order, precisely the kind of upheaval that he had long sought to preclude. The Whig Ministry of Earl Grey, which succeeded Wellington's, introduced a Parliamentary Reform bill to enfranchise the entire middle class and to redistribute fully a quarter of the constituencies for election to the House of Commons. The magnitude of the proposed change staggered the Commons but excited the country, to which, when subjected to a narrow Parliamentary defeat, the government appealed through a general election. For the first time, the terrible power of the *vox populi* was called upon to decide the course of state. It made its demand for the Reform bill overwhelmingly clear. As much intimidated as strengthened by the power which they had unleashed, the Whigs forced their bill into law over the reluctance of William IV and the hostility of the House of Lords.

Peel was anxious to preserve what he could of the institutions and values of the old order in the storm which attended and persisted after the enactment of the great Reform bill. But, like the kingdom generally, Peel personally could not follow his former charts. The two axes by which he had hitherto plotted his course were the task of administration and the demands of the country. Deprived of executive power, he resorted to cultivation of intermediate, partisan relations in which he had previously put less store. Out of persisting loyalties and new fears in the

1830s, he built the Conservative party. Through general statements on public policy and constructive conduct in Opposition, through new devices for electoral and new facilities for Parliamentary organization, and through more systematic use of customary means of consultation with colleagues on the front bench, with sympathizers on the back benches and with leaders in the House of Lords, he drew together a political army of varied colors.

It contained four elements indispensable for victory. Its core consisted of the old Tory interests of Church and land. Now that the electorate had been reformed, this core could not by itself win power. Peel added to it groups which had supported the Reform Act but grew uneasy at the pace and direction of the other changes to which the Reform Act threatened to lead, particularly to reduction of the material resources and social functions of the Established Church. These groups included men of property in the provincial towns and eminent Whig defectors in Parliament like Lord Stanley (who later became fourteenth Earl of Derby) and Sir James Graham. Stanley and Graham soon joined the third element, survivors of the ministerial elite of the 1820s, whose ranks Peel freshened with talented young recruits such as Gladstone. The final indispensable element was Peel himself. For calm wisdom, steady determination, breadth of experience, and lucidity in debate, Peel acquired a reputation unmatched by anyone else in Parliament. Although in the general election held in 1832, right after the passage of the Reform Act, the Tories or Conservatives were reduced to form the smallest of the three major groups in the House of Commons, smaller even than the motley contingent of Radicals, within nine years Peel and the Conservative party secured for themselves a commanding majority.

But after five more years back in office, Peel broke the party which he had put together; and the party in turn broke him. The growth of the party in the wake of the Reform Act gave rise to internal expectations that complicated the task of providing the country with altruistic, disinterested government; and Peel refused to subordinate his personal, massively informed, acute judgment of what that task required to the untutored instincts of the party which restored him to power. He was aware that the development of political parties produced a tension between what a leader owed his party and what he owed his country. But he did not fully recognize the new force of the tension. The character of Parliamentary politics after 1827 further clouded his perception of the increasing importance of parties. Once the collapse of Lord Liverpool's health in 1827 forced him to retire, the party of Mr. Pitt, which Liverpool had painstakingly reassembled, began to crumble. Every government after that time, whatever shade of Tory, Whig, or Conservative, relied for its Parliamentary support upon a variety of groups or factions which did not readily cohere and also fluctuated from issue to issue. The Conservative party was itself just such a variety of groups. And though the instincts of its landed and Anglican core were fairly predictable, they did not exhaust the range of reflexes within the party. The limits within which its leader was free to maneuver were therefore wide.

But however wide, the confines of party made Peel uneasy. From the outset of his leadership in the 1830s, he attempted to minimize the risks of a clash between the requirements of the party and the dictates of good government by imbuing the party with his own spirit and also by reserving, repeatedly and publicly, his freedom to act as he himself thought best. Those efforts were not enough. His precepts and pleas neither weakened the commitment of the Tory core of the party to land and Church nor dispelled the impression, particularly strong after the general election of 1841, that he was returned to power in order to protect those interests. After the election, back in the harness of administration, and responsible for the well-being of the country during the most searing economic depression of the nineteenth century, Peel reduced his consultations with the Parliamentary party to a disenchanting minimum. He also shaped the policies of his ministry with Olympian dispassion, as his powers of informed observation and analysis dictated, undeflected by the prejudices, pledges, and special interests of his partisan supporters.

Public agitation, his administrative talents, and, by reaction, the demands of the party all pushed Peel toward a more elastic, institutionally less encrusted conception of the order of society he wished to foster and toward a correspondingly more individual, institutionally less inhibited code of political ethics. Three extra-Parliamentary agitations bombarded the civic order of the United Kingdom in the years of Peel's ministry. Two of them, provoked by the depression in the still strange and immature industrialized economy, arose simultaneously in the larger island. Those who rallied behind the radically democratic demands of the People's Charter were divided by regional interests, by ultimate objectives, by a variety of particular panaceas, and by a tactical dispute over reliance upon physical or moral force; but Chartism still constituted the largest mobilization of working-class anger in British experience. The Anti-Corn Law League mobilized more effectively the anger of the urban, mercantile, and industrial middle classes against the continuing sway of the landed interest embodied in the tariffs protecting the price of grain. The third agitation came from Ireland. Having won Catholic emancipation, O'Connell now focused Irish discontent upon a demand for repeal of the

Act of Union; and the memory of his skill and daring in the past disguised the fact that he was losing his grip.

The suffering inflicted by the economic depression, and the class conflict from which Chartists and the Anti-Corn Law League stripped away all disguise, produced a rapid acceleration in Peel's thought about the administrative field which was already uppermost in his mind—finance. One of his chief charges against the Whig ministries of the 1830s had to do with their inept, hand-to-mouth handling of finance and with the resulting budgetary deficits. In his first budget in 1842, tackling the problem with masterful resource, he resurrected the income tax, hitherto reserved for the emergency of war, and compensated for this unwelcome novelty by reducing a wide range of tariffs. There was nothing essentially doctrinaire about the budget. Though it liberalized the Corn Laws, it retained them at a level tolerable to his party; and the step toward generally freer trade was in keeping with the trend of Tory as well as Whig ministerial financial policy over the previous twenty years. But, almost immediately, his observation of the social impact of the depression, at its most acute in 1842, began to turn his adherence to the financial policy of the budget into a philosophical, even a moral commitment to reduce the cost of living. His observation and analysis of the economic impact of the budget consolidated that commitment. The price of wheat remained above the level at which the new Corn Law could come into effect, while the reduction in other tariffs seemed to have the effects he looked for. By 1845, Peel was a convinced free trader. He concluded that the Corn Law was economically unnecessary and a political liability. The Corn Law gave British wheat protection which it did not seem to need, and stood exposed, now that other tariffs had been pared down, as an infuriating symbol of landed-class privilege.

Meanwhile, O'Connell's agitation for repeal of the Act of Union had thrust Ireland to the fore in the mind of the prime minister, advancing in another way his emancipation from the old Tory mold. Until the staple potato crop in Ireland was stricken with blight in 1845, the unrest there was not as grave, nor its leadership as tenacious, as in England. It was, nevertheless, quite strong enough to loosen the nature of Peel's commitment to Protestantism and the union of Church and state: "the attack upon the Church of Ireland," he told his Cabinet, "can only be staved off by liberal concessions."[6] No longer repelled by Protestant prejudice from injecting the state into the affairs of the Roman Catholic Church as he had been in 1829, Peel now proposed to alleviate Irish Catholic disaffection by increasing and making permanent the state's financial contribution to the Catholic seminary at Maynooth.

This proposal exhausted the patience of Conservatives. Peel was forced to rely on Whig votes to pass the Maynooth grant over the angry opposition which half of his own party in the Commons put up. Protestantism and the alliance between the state and the Established Church of England and Ireland were as deeply imbedded in Tory values as was land, and they ranked even more highly than land among many urban Conservatives. The difference of opinion between Peel and the rank and file of his party was no longer, for most of them, merely a matter of differing political calculations about the way to a common end. They agreed on ends now only at an intangible, ethereal level, far above the clash of concrete partisan commitments. The Conservative rebels identified those ends with the pre-eminence of the landed order as they knew or idealized it and with the existing relationship between Church and state. Peel had moved beyond that identification. In doing so he transgressed the outer limits of his party's tolerance, and hence violated the obligation of loyalty to those who had raised him to the premiership in the first place. That obligation had acquired new force in the 1830s; the pressures with which the party confronted him in the 1840s destroyed its hold upon him; and he replaced it with absolute insistence on the obligation of a minister to be true to his own convictions and to give the Crown the best advice he knew about the needs of the country.

There was high drama in 1846 when Peel finally, irrevocably, split his party by proposing to repeal the Corn Laws. But the events of that year did little more than crystallize already familiar patterns of response. Peel's proposal, which he intended to make anyway before the natural life of the current Parliament expired, was precipitated by the potato famine in Ireland. In fact, repeal could do little for the starving Irish. They could not afford even cheaper wheat. There were no adequate means of transport to carry wheat to the remote areas where the shortage of food was most acute. In any event, Peel proposed to phase out the Corn Laws over three years, too long if Irish starvation was his major concern. It was, indeed, no more than a pressing pretext. The distress which induced Peel to act lay, not in the reality of famine in Ireland, but prospectively in England, where the Anti-Corn Law League would use the Irish spectacle to whip up class hatreds. Peel entirely succeeded in dispelling that threat. He turned the repeal of the Corn Laws into a calming expression of class cooperation rather than an embittering victory of one class over another. In doing so, he preserved the reputation of the ruling classes, still predominantly landed, and of the existing institutions of state, for altruistic government. To that extent, his action was truly conservative. But his commitment to free trade, though acquired through pragmatic observation as well as intellectual analysis, had become doctrinaire, as he tactlessly confessed by paying public tribute to the leader of the Anti-Corn Law League, Richard Cobden. Peel had proposed Catholic emancipation reluctantly in 1829 "as a necessary expedient; he advocated the repeal of the Corn Laws as a desirable principle."[7]

With Whig support, the ministerial third of the Conservative party in the Commons, now called Peelites, had votes enough to enact the repeal bill. But within hours of its passage through the House of Lords, dissident Conservatives in the Commons joined forces with the Whigs to drive Peel's ministry out of office. At full strength, the dissidents comprised more than two thirds of the Conservative party in the Commons, virtually all the rank and file though scarcely anyone of ministerial caliber. The rebels rested their case upon two institutional commitments. The men who stepped forward to give the otherwise inarticulate Conservative squires a voice, Lord George Bentinck and Disraeli, dwelt upon commitment to party and upon the threat which Peel's betrayal of that commitment posed to the integrity of representative, Parliamentary government. Disraeli, politically the most acute of the rebels, was less concerned about the substantive matter of the Corn Laws. The sense of partisan, group loyalty among the dissidents ran deep, fortified by the canons of gentlemanly ethics which Bentinck embodied from his days as leader in the Jockey Club. But as a whole the dissidents, now called the Protectionist party, were even more deeply wedded to the privileges and values of the old landed order.

After 1846, Peel ceased to be a Conservative in any partisan, institutional sense. He reserved his deepest political antagonism for Protectionists rather than for Whigs, in spite of his low estimate of their administrative competence, or even for many Radicals, among some of whom he garnered great respect. Though he still wished to preserve the social, religious and constitutional order of the United Kingdom, his conception of that order and of the best ways to preserve it was hard to distinguish from that of the Whigs. He cooperated intimately with the Whig ministry until 1850, when he was thrown by his horse and killed. Most of his followers eventually became Liberals.

Never was the resilience of Conservative institutional commitments more apparent than in the middle years of the century, when they kept the party out of power yet intact. Conservatives' reluctance to modify their identification with land diminished the appeal of the party to the middle-class mercantile and industrial elements whose support had given Peel the margin of victory in 1841. Refusing to treat the repeal of the Corn Laws as an irreversible decision like Catholic emancipation and the Reform Act, Conservatives sought ways to restore agricultural protection until 1852. For another thirteen years, until the death of Lord Palmerston in 1865, they were the party of the landed interest in a much less diluted way than previously under Pitt and Peel or subsequently under Disraeli and Salisbury. Even Disraeli dismissed the ranks of English society beyond the landed classes as "leather and prunella." The price of this prejudice was nearly thirty years in the political wilderness, relieved by three Derby-Disraeli ministries with lifespans measured in months instead of years. The long stretches of time which Conservatives had to spend in Opposition made another of their institutional commitments, their commitment to their party, the more remarkable. Between the disruption of the Conservative party in 1846 and the victory of Gladstone's Liberals in the general election of 1868, no party commanded the support of a majority in the House of Commons. The Conservatives constituted not only the largest but the firmest of the minorities into which the Commons was divided. They were held at bay by alliances among the others: old Whigs, new Liberals, Peelites, Radicals, and the Irish. In spite of the hopelessness of restoring agricultural protection, in spite also of their suspicions of their leader in the Commons, Disraeli, Conservatives stuck to their party with dogged loyalty.

But the leaders of the party realized that, before it could restore itself as a serious contender for power, its commitments would have to become broader and more flexible; and they succeeded in making the change. No sooner had Peel left office that Disraeli began to canvass ways to loosen the Protectionist party's commitment to protection. The restoration of the term "Conservative" in place of "Protectionist" as the name of the party symbolized that aim. The experience of the first Derby-Disraeli ministry in 1852 demonstrated to the party that agricultural protection simply could not be restored. After the death of Palmerston, as Gladstone moved into the leadership of the Liberal party and alarmed a wide range of propertied interests with his love for crusades and his energy as a legislator, the Conservative party accommodated the alienated, and in doing so extended its commitment from land to all property.

Meanwhile, the party itself became a less inhibited instrument for government. As soon as it became clear that most Peelites were permanently alienated from the Conservative party, and that the only hope for replacing the Whigs in office lay in alliance with one of the other minorities in the Commons, if need be with some of the Radicals, Disraeli showed himself willing to work in that direction. But Lord Derby (as Lord Stanley had become), who was the leader of the party as a whole and the one to whom it gave its trust, foiled these initiatives: "if we are to be a Government," he instructed Disraeli, "we must be so by our own friends and in spite of all combinations, and not by purchasing a short-lived existence upon the forbearance of the Radical party."[8] In 1866–67, however, after two unhappy minority ministries, and now in a third, Derby determined to "take such a course as would convert, if possible, an existing minority into a practical majority."[9] It was in this frame of mind that, after gaining office by allying with apprehensive Liberals in the House of Commons to defeat a modest Reform bill which the Russell-Gladstone ministry proposed, the Derby-Disraeli ministry presided over the passage of the Reform Act of 1867 which gave Britain a predominantly working-class electorate. Apart from a small band of die-hards led by the future Lord Salisbury, the ministry carried its party along. This was partisan flexibility with a vengeance.

However vital to the pursuit of office, the broadening of the socio-economic interests of the party and the flexibility which Derby and Disraeli lent to its Parliamentary conduct diluted or debased the ethical ingredients in Conservative loyalties. Responsibility for enfranchising working men in 1867, the urban sanitary measures and the charter of trade union rights enacted under Disraeli a decade later, and the housing legislation of the 1880s and '90s demonstrated that the social mystique of Young England was still alive and had not been completely submerged by the consolidation of propertied interests in the Conservative party. But the behavior of the Parliamentary party in 1867 furnished materials for a disturbing commentary on the worth of Conservatives' devotion to their party. Instead of serving as a force to keep the leaders faithful to their followers, Conservative party loyalty turned the rank and file into putty in their leaders' hands. The stolid squires on the back benches were instinctively averse to the creation of popular government. But the intricacies and guesswork involved in extending the electorate obscured the principle at stake; back benchers enjoyed the dexterity with which Disraeli outmaneuvered Gladstone in the debates on the Reform bill; and they relished the extension of the Conservative ministry's life for another year. Disraeli's success deprived them of the courage of their convictions. During the 1870s, he inspired them with a new faith in empire. But on domestic issues, apart from the Church, they now scarcely knew where, if ever, to stand firm. After the death of Disraeli in 1881, they were impressed by the brash confidence with which Lord Randolph Churchill, in a bid to succeed Disraeli, preached a version of Gladstonian Liberalism under the name of Tory Democracy.

Lord Salisbury, who became prime minister and hence leader in 1885, reinvested Conservative party loyalty with moral spine. The events of 1867 had left him, for almost twenty years, so uncertain about the worth of the party that historians have tended to conclude that he was not a party man at all. But, in fact, he discerned and envisaged a greater practical value in the party, and he possessed a more highly developed appreciation of the moral relationships which it involved, than any other Conservative of the century. His anger in 1867 was a measure of his disappointed hopes. He allowed them to revive very slowly, and then deployed all his statecraft, under the difficult circumstances of alliance with the Liberal Unionists, to give effect to his hopes and to guard them against further violation.

Although the strains upon the order of British society were weaker in the second half of the century than in the first, Salisbury, an anxious, gloomy person, was as acutely concerned about the threat of social disintegration in his day as Peel had been about the earlier threat of social convulsion. But whereas Peel relied on unfettered, accommodating administration to ease the strains, Salisbury relied upon confident self-assertion by the Conservative party. The calmness which he hoped to bring back to English government could not be produced, so he argued, by satisfying the appetite for change: that craving would never cease. Equilibrium could be restored only when the forces resisting change were at least as vigorous as those supporting it. When the forces of resistance were shattered, as they had been by Peel's apostacies in 1829 and 1846, they were unable to ensure that the reforms under question or subsequent reforms were subjected to cautious consideration and were implemented in a balanced fashion. Deprive these forces of the will to resist, as Derby and Disraeli managed to do in 1867, and the result was even more diabolical. Then the party, unredeemed by any higher purpose, became nothing but a joint-stock company to gain and keep hold of office. Furthermore, a party and ministry which constantly tailored their policies to the moods of a majority in the House of Commons would leave Parliamentary government rudderless.

Salisbury's case for firm party government and for firm defense by the Conservative party of the interests which it held dear had an obviously mundane intent.[10] His own defense of the interests of property and of the Established Church was bluntly candid. His case was nonetheless permeated with ethical considerations. The heart of his indictment of Peel lay in the assertion that no amount of public gain could excuse the betrayal by Peel of those who had lifted him to power. He denounced Derby and Disraeli for draining away "the one ennobling element" which made party something better than mere faction, namely "that all the members of a party are enlisted in common to serve one great unselfish cause."[11] Salisbury also discerned a potentially redemptive moral force in the internal workings of party since 1832. The drying up of the resources of patronage and the extension of the electorate made parties dependent as never before upon the voluntary exertions of their supporters. Except for the very few who might be lifted into office by these exertions, the members of a party worked for no reward other than the victory of their common cause. If their leaders, once in office, betrayed that cause, the volunteer army might melt away. Even in the depths of his gloom after the passage of the second Reform bill, Salisbury allowed himself to hope that that danger might eventually give the opportunistic leaders of the Conservative party the courage of its members' convictions. He also drew comfort from recollection of the much earlier general election of 1784 when the voters registered emphatic disgust at the unholy alliance which Charles James Fox and Lord North had made in seeming violation of all of their previous principles and protestations. "There is no blindness," Salisbury commented in a memorable passage,

> so unaccountable as the blindness of English statesmen to the political value of a character. Living only in and for the House of Commons, moving in an atmosphere of constant intrigue, accustomed to look upon oratory as a mode of angling for political support and upon political professions as only baits of more or less attractiveness, they acquire a very peculiar code of ethics, and they are liable wholly to lose sight of the fact that there is a stiffer and less corrupted morality out of doors. They not only come to forget what is right, but they forget that there is any one who knows it. The educated thought of England, before the bar of whose opinion all political conduct must appear, measures the manoeuvres of politicians by no more lenient code than that which it applies to the affairs of private life. Ordinary men cannot easily bring themselves to pass over, as judicious tactics in a statesman, the conduct which in their next-door neighbours they would condemn as impudent insincerity. . . . A character for unselfish honesty is the only secure passport to the confidence of the English people.[12]

Though he joined Disraeli's Cabinet in 1874 and eventually received the old man's blessing to succeed him as leader in the Lords, Salisbury never trusted Disraeli's instincts in domestic policy. But the two men found a common bond in foreign policy. Disraeli's main impact upon the ethical sensibilities of the Conservative party was to confirm and, indeed, to exaggerate its aversion to the application of idealism to foreign affairs. Though Disraeli mesmerized his party in the last decade of his life and assumed mythic proportions from the moment he died, Conservatives never quite understood the nature of or trusted his commitment to their cherished interests. As his modern biographer, Robert Blake, has explained, "the ambivalent mixture of romance and irony in his outlook" kept contemporaries, and later historians, from knowing "what he was thinking about anything."[13] Even the concern for which he became most famous, to bridge the chasm between the "two nations" of rich and poor, proves upon examination to have been largely insubstantial.[14] But in their intense, almost incessant debate over foreign and imperial affairs between the Bulgarian massacres of 1876 and the general election of 1880, Disraeli and Gladstone unmistakably deepened the antagonistic identification of their respective parties with imperial necessity and British prestige as against movements of national liberation and the application of humanitarian moral standards overseas.

After a year of painful ambivalence, Salisbury came down decisively in December of 1877 on Disraeli's side and in 1878 became Foreign Secretary, a post which after 1885 he usually combined with the premiership. Both Salisbury and Gladstone were ardent high churchmen. But Salisbury believed that a statesman had no right to impose his moral or religious views upon the country except as a spokesman for the party or body of support which gave him his power. And he argued that the application of Christian sensitivities to non-Christian peoples, like the Afghans who held the northwestern approaches to India, was foolish. He gave a sardonic edge to his remarks on this theme. "The Afghan looks upon an Englishman in two lights," he told a north-country audience,

> —first, as a person who is an infidel, and next as a person who has money. In the first character he is anxious to kill him, in the second he is anxious to rifle him. . . . [Gladstone's] pulpit style of eloquence, admirable and beautiful as it is as a testimony of the moral feelings of the speaker, and the susceptibilities which he suspects in his audience, is in danger of leading the country very far astray if it induces you to think that the considerations which are true and just as applied to your civilized neighbours can safely be taken as a guide to policy on the frontiers which are threatened by barbarians.[15]

Nevertheless, he attempted to combine respect for the humanitarian and religious desires of Britain with pursuit of the national interest.

Until the turn of the century, there was no real tension between Salisbury's superficially cynical injunctions on foreign policy and his ear-

nest injunctions on domestic. He brought two principles of conduct to
the Foreign Office, the same two which he brought to the leadership of
the Conservative party. One was the obligation, whether of the spokesman for the country or the leader of the party, to reflect the views and
defend the interests of those whom he represented. In foreign affairs, he
likened this obligation to the responsibilities of a trustee. In domestic affairs, he pitched his demand higher, elevating the loyalty due from party
leader to followers to the level of a moral imperative. Salisbury's second
principle of conduct was to insist that the way in which one selected or
pursued a policy was more important than the policy itself. In foreign affairs, this principle was meant to defuse the moral debate between the
disciples of Gladstone and of Disraeli. In domestic affairs, he equated
the principle with what he termed "character," a demand that leaders act
with sufficient consistency to maintain public trust.

There was a paradoxical relationship between the language which
Salisbury used to explain the bearing of these principles upon their
spheres of political activity on the one hand, and their actual impact on
the other. In discussing foreign affairs, where he in fact reflected and
even shared some of the moral concerns popularly associated with Gladstone, Salisbury either eschewed ethical language or sought to explain
why the Sermon on the Mount was inapplicable. By contrast, he used
ethically charged language and strenuous moral argument to justify his
adherence to his two principles of behavior in domestic and Irish affairs,
where their ethical impact was much more dubious.

It is not difficult to account for this paradox. In foreign affairs, particularly after 1885, Salisbury sought to act along lines acceptable to both
political parties and hence free of the risk of enfeebling reversal when the
reins of government changed hands. The constituency to which, as Foreign Secretary, he felt obliged to appeal and reflect was national rather
than partisan. He went out of his way in the 1880s to point out, and in
the 1890s to maintain, the consensus on foreign policy among the leaders
on both sides. There was substantial ethical content to this consensus,
both in its conception of the empire and in its reaction to recurrent
massacres of Christian minorities in the Ottoman Empire. But to attempt
to define that ethical content might well endanger the consensus by reac-
tivating the ideological loyalties of 1876 to 1880. In order, on the other
hand, to apply his two principles to domestic and Irish affairs, Salisbury
had to defy the pattern of consensus at moments of crisis to which British
political leaders, particularly in his own party, had adhered, in 1829, in
1846, and in a sense in 1867. He had to fight the widespread agreement
that, however questionable the behavior of Peel and Disraeli as leaders

of their party might have been, the policies which they adopted in those years were good for the country or at least necessary for its tranquillity.

Whatever men thought of Peel's treatment of his party, he placed his stamp in 1846 upon the politics of the ensuing generation by reducing the effectiveness of party loyalty. In similar fashion, Salisbury's behavior over Ireland in 1885/6 placed his very different stamp upon British politics and Parliamentary conduct for the rest of the century. He managed to turn loyalty to followers into the controlling principle of late Victorian politics. It fashioned his policy in every sphere, confirmed him in the leadership of his party, ensured Conservative preponderance within the Unionist alliance, galvanized the bonds of party discipline, and made respect for the requirements of popular government unexpectedly Conservative in practice.

The chemistry of the process by which Salisbury arrived at the decision to make opposition to Home Rule the paramount policy of the Conservative party turns out, under examination, to be more complex than it soon came to seem. Still, all but one of its determining ingredients had to do with relations among Conservatives. In private, Salisbury talked about the limits which maintenance of the rank and file's trust placed upon the party leadership and particularly upon himself. In public, he promised to adhere to the traditions of the party in governing Ireland— though he did not say what those traditions were until the general election of 1885 was over. Then he defined them to mean preservation of the Act of Union between Great Britain and Ireland, the handiwork of Pitt, whose following Peel had shattered and Salisbury wished to reconstitute. The one Anglo-Irish relationship which Salisbury invested with moral importance amounted to another demand for loyalty, this time for loyalty from England to the minority in Ireland who had upheld the English ascendancy: "abandoning to your enemies those whom you have called upon to defend you and who have risked their all on your behalf," he told the first great Unionist audience at the Opera House on the Haymarket, "is an infamy below which it is impossible to go."[16]

Salisbury used his insistence upon respect for the hewers and carriers of the party's wood and water to intensify the party's conservatism and to maximize the Conservative party's weight within the Unionist alliance. When the Liberal Unionist Lord Hartington attempted in the spring of 1886 to rally all but doctrinaire Home Rule Liberals together with reasonable Conservatives into a centrist alliance for which he would be the natural leader, Salisbury outmaneuvered him. Through the notorious "manacles and Manitoba" speech to the National Union of Conservative Associations, Salisbury gave the policy of defending the Union with Ireland an aggressively Conservative guise and also emphasized the critical importance of the massed Conservative organizations in every constituency as compared to the small band of Liberal Unionists. Because Hartington was, for the moment, bound to Lord Salisbury in opposing Gladstone's Home Rule bill, Salisbury's speech burned Hartington's bridge with the main Liberal camp and reasserted Conservative leadership for the Unionist cause. With similar intent, in the deliberations of his Cabinets on domestic matters, Salisbury checked the preoccupation of Joseph Chamberlain, C. T. Ritchie and Arthur Balfour with program building, legislative construction, and administrative accomplishment—in short, with public policy—by voicing the concerns of institutions allied to or pivotal bodies of support within the Conservative party. Except when the Church of England was involved, Salisbury responded to conflicts among the interests supporting his party and its Liberal Unionist confederates as arguments in favor, if not of complete inaction, then of action which was inoffensive.

In order to protect the Established Church, however, he was ready to irritate other interests within the party. He pressed for a change in the law governing the collection of tithes in order to release the clergy of the Church of England from the odium of collecting their income by carrying off the goods of defaulting tenant farmers, even though the reform annoyed Conservative land owners by making them directly responsible for the payment of tithes. He astonished contemporaries by proposing what became free elementary education in order to rescue the Church of England's schools from their financial straits. The grant of free education ate up a budgetary surplus which urban men of property had hoped would be used to reduce the income tax; but their concern for the Church was livelier than the squires', and resistance to this proposal by Salisbury was correspondingly weaker than the resistance to his tithes bills.

Except in the ecclesiastical sphere, he preached and practiced party loyalty, and in doing so he fostered the growth of Parliamentary commitment to the Conservative and Liberal parties. By rejecting the consensual model over Home Rule, he helped to divide Parliament into two sharply opposed alliances to one or other of which virtually every Member had to subscribe. The pattern of voting, which Peel's action had helped to produce in the 1850s, of frequent cross-voting among moderates, was replaced by the late 1880s with a pattern of much greater party discipline endangered periodically, not by defections among moderates, but by abstentions among diehards.

There was, as A. B. Cooke and John Vincent have emphasized in *The Governing Passion* (1974), a great deal of self-interest mixed up with the moral rhetoric in 1885–86 for and against Home Rule. Salisbury and Gladstone arrived at their respective policies, by no means simply through contemplation of the ethical issues at stake or even of the governmental requirements of Ireland and the United Kingdom, but through a complicated game of personal as well as partisan chess in which each side had several kings striving to eliminate each other as well as to beat the opposing color. Both Salisbury and Gladstone used the Irish question to defeat internal rivals and to impose their leadership upon the Unionist and Home Rule alliances. This analysis, however unwelcome initially to Gladstonian historians, should give them even less difficulty than the drawings of sexual whips discovered in Gladstone's diaries. When Gladstone decided in 1868 to propose the disestablishment of the Irish Church, he knew that this motion stood a better chance than any other of uniting the Liberal party under his leadership; but this calculation was entirely compatible with belief that disestablishment was intrinsically just and good for the country. So too, the genuineness of his ethical case for Home Rule in 1886 was not vitiated by the political utility of the policy.

But what is good for the Gladstonian goose is good also for the Salisburian gander. Those who defend Gladstone's conscience against cynical attack should be willing to do the same for Lord Salisbury. Insistence upon attentiveness to sentiment among the rank and file was an obviously expedient precept for a new and insecure party leader confronted by the extraordinary unsettlement of politics in 1885. It also suited Salisbury's purposes to insist upon appreciation of his right wing's concerns, for he shared them. There is, in any case, an inherently Conservative bias in focusing upon the way a policy is implemented rather than upon the policy's abstract justice. These calculations do not, however, dispose of the congruent ethical issue. By investing party loyalty from leader to followers with binding moral force, Salisbury admittedly rejected Gladstone's attempt to raise the terms of ethical reference to relations between whole peoples. As far as the relations between the English and Irish peoples were concerned, Salisbury refused to do anything more than reflect his supporters' sensibilities. Indeed he did less. When he threw his government's support behind *The Times*'s effort to smear the Irish leader, Charles Stewart Parnell, with the Phoenix Park murders committed by Irish terrorists, he subjected the Conservative party to moral embarrassment. But the Irish question also tarnished Gladstone. He fell short of Salisbury's modest principles by refusing to take even Cabinet colleagues into his confidence in the critical winter months of 1885/6, to their intense indignation. The English debate on Home Rule was in part a debate between rival terms of ethical reference.

The ethical substance of Lord Salisbury's code becomes clearer in his demand that political leaders act with sufficient consistency to maintain public trust, the demand which he summed up in the word "character." He directed this injunction against the free-wheeling willingness of Lord Randolph Churchill, Joseph Chamberlain, and even his own nephew, Arthur Balfour, to canvass all possible policies and strategies with little regard for their previous course of conduct. In the summer of 1900, when Salisbury was resisting pressure from Chamberlain and Balfour for an early election before the improving fortunes of war reached their expected conclusion, he explained himself to a high-spirited member of his family: "You are like Joe, who again is like Randolph. You don't care the least for *character*. We could not dissolve with our work unfinished without loss of character."[17]

Lord Salisbury's code of conduct served him well until the turn of the century. His massive victory in the general election of 1895 discounted the code's partisan limitations by making the Conservative and Unionist alliance virtually the party of the nation. The quiescence of the Irish question and its rapid replacement after the election by foreign and imperial affairs as the dominant concern in British politics had a similar effect. But the prominence of foreign affairs, in which he was again deeply involved as Foreign Secretary as well as prime minister, put a strain on the integrity of his code. The quick growth of aggressive imperial sentiment among Conservatives and Liberal Unionists revealed a gulf, often overlooked in the 1880s, between Salisbury's sense of obligation as Conservative leader to his party on domestic and Irish matters and his sense of obligation as Foreign Secretary to the nation as a whole. He remained loyal to both obligations, but in their discrete spheres. By 1898, assertive imperialists on the Conservative and Unionist benches were responding to this distinction with impatience.

In the interests of bipartisan continuity in foreign policy, Salisbury knew that he himself had to reckon, and that he had to make foreign powers reckon, with Gladstonian moral and cultural susceptibilities, even when they left him personally cold. In the conflict between Greece and Turkey over Crete, for example, he worked out a string of proposals to the Concert of Europe to reconcile the powers' and his own anger at the bellicosity of Greece with the Hellenistic sympathies fostered among English statesmen by their classical education and particularly strong among Liberals, a set of sentiments which he admitted publicly that he did not share. He did not often speak up directly even about those moral concerns which moved him deeply. But Gladstone was not alone in sensing, quite rightly, that the recurrent massacre of Armenians in the Ottoman empire filled Salisbury with a revulsion similar to his own. Salisbury retained the friendship of the foremost high church agitators over both sets of Ottoman atrocities, Canon Liddon during the Bulgarian agitation of the 1870s, Canon MacColl over the Armenian massacres of the '90s. No matter how attentive to sentiment at home, Salisbury at the Foreign Office was more concerned with British interests abroad. But here too his reckoning was not completely divorced from Gladstone's. Salisbury despised Gladstone's reliance upon friendly opinion on the fringes of empire as a mainstay of British influence, and he had long advocated a "forward policy" on the western approaches to India against Gladstonian objections. But he shared some of the Gladstonian concern that territorial expansion overseas might overstrain the mother country's internal resources. Chamberlain, on the other hand, advocated expansion to consolidate British strength in face of intensifying competition from other great powers. The strain between Salisbury and the many Conservatives and Unionists for whom Chamberlain spoke surfaced in the spring of 1898 over China. The capture of Khartoum that autumn, and the outbreak next year of the Boer War, submerged the strain. But it reemerged, again over China, in the middle of 1900 as a result of the Boxer rebellion.

The reconstruction of the government after the general election in September opened the last chapter in the story of Salisbury's behavior toward party and country. In the final analysis, his ability to control foreign policy depended upon the consent of the Conservative and Unionist Cabinet. He lost the confidence of the Cabinet through his dilatory handling of the Boxer rebellion, and as a result he lost the Foreign Office. Reallocation of the Foreign Office could not, however, solve the problem. Foreign and imperial affairs could not be disposed of departmentally, if only because of the consuming importance of the Boer War. The enormous cost of the war, and the new awareness it created of the still greater costs which Britain would have to incur to enable it to hold its own in the event of war among the great powers on the Continent, broke through the rough distinction which Salisbury had drawn between domestic and foreign affairs. The demands of the armed services upon the Exchequer presaged an era of heavy expenditure, which in all likelihood would extend to domestic as well as to military objects. That prospect, as Salisbury saw it, bode ill for the owners of property and for the unfettered economy. The jingoistic fervor aroused over the Boer War in the general election of 1900 also disgusted him. In previous elections he had shattered the custom which precluded peers from campaigning after the issue of the writs. This time he sat the campaign out. The manifesto which, after much resistance, he was prevailed upon to write was deliberately depressing. He half hoped for defeat.

When, nevertheless, victory was heaped upon him, he ought, according to his code, to have gratified the wishes of the party at least in the domestic sphere. Instead, in the field of finance, he attempted to take the khaki out of the khaki election's verdict. He did so in partnership with the Chancellor of the Exchequer, his long-time colleague, Sir Michael Hicks Beach. As recently as January of 1900, Salisbury had held Treasury practice, with which Hicks Beach was associated, up to public criticism. But after the general election, against the wishes of his two most powerful colleagues Chamberlain and Balfour, Salisbury retained Hicks Beach as Chancellor. For the next year and a half, Salisbury and Hicks Beach attempted to keep down the estimates in face of what Salisbury called a "Jingo hurricane."[18]

There would, however, be nothing like a repetition of 1846. Salisbury's deepening exhaustion, the age of both men, and their ingrained aversion to individual heroics disabled them from any such attempt. Furthermore, though no longer in harmony with the will of his party, Salisbury still adhered to the pattern, which he had gently inculcated for a dozen years, of deference to the collective will of the Cabinet: he and Hicks Beach could not carry the Cabinet with them, and they retired. To that extent his code of political behavior was still intact.

In 1902, when Salisbury, the last Victorian prime minister, retired, the commitment of Conservatives to property and the Church was at least as strong as at any time in the preceding century. By giving Anglican elementary schools direct support from local taxes through the Education Act of that year, the party pressed beyond what even Salisbury thought prudent. By allowing the courts to scuttle the charter of trade union rights which Disraeli had bestowed a generation earlier, the party completed the transition in its allegiance from land, which had dominated the socio-political order at the beginning of the century, to capital, dominant at the end. And if the loyalty from leaders and followers to their party was coming under fresh strains, that in itself testified to some extent that men felt free to take the party and its accomplishments for granted.

Yet, however hard the shell of these commitments, their moral contents were draining away. The transition in allegiance from land to capital dried up one well-understood though rose-colored tradition of ethical responsibilities without replacing it with another. The Church of England had reached its peak of vitality in the middle of the nineteenth century, and while the statistics for religious observance remained high past the turn of the century, they fell precipitously and permanently over the first World War. The ethical commentary through which Lord Salisbury insisted upon loyalty to party as a moral imperative was already fading from memory by the time he retired and died. The Conservative conscience stood in need of a new formulation.

Notes

1. Anthony Trollope, *The Eustace Diamonds* (1902), I: 45.

2. See, e.g., R. A. Butler, *The Art of the Possible* (1971), p. 17.

3. See Linda J. Colley, "The Loyal Brotherhood and the Cocoa Tree: The London Organization of the Tory Party, 1727–1760," *Historical Journal* 20 (1) (1977): 77–96.

4. Norman Gash, *Mr. Secretary Peel* (1961), p. 226.

5. *Ibid.,* p. 515.

6. Norman Gash, *Sir Robert Peel* (1972), p. 419.

7. *Ibid.,* p. 553.

8. Robert Blake, *Disraeli* (1966), p. 343.

9. *Hansard,* 3rd ser., CLXXXVIII, 1783 (22 July 1867).

10. For a detailed exploration of Lord Salisbury's domestic statecraft from 1881 to 1902, see Peter Marsh, *The Discipline of Popular Government* (1978).

11. Salisbury, "The Conservative Surrender," *Quarterly Review* 246 (Oct. 1867), in Paul Smith, ed., *Lord Salisbury on Politics* (1972), p. 271.

12. Salisbury, *Essays: Biographical* (1905), pp. 85–86.

13. Blake, *Disraeli,* p. 153.

14. Paul Smith, *Disraelian Conservatism and Social Reform* (1967).

15. Reported in *The Times,* 13 Oct. 1881, 7c.

16. Reported in *The Times,* 15 Apr. 1886, 6e.

17. Lady Frances Balfour, *Ne Obliviscaris* (1930), II: 335.

18. Salisbury to Hicks Beach, 14 Sept. 1901, in Lady Victoria Hicks-Beach, *Life of Sir Michael Hicks-Beach (Earl St. Aldwyn)* (1932), II: 153.

SUGGESTED FURTHER READING

THE SOMETIMES INSPIRING, sometimes maddening insistence of the Victorians upon moral values in their attempts to control their society has drawn the writers of this volume together, and they hope that their interest will be infectious. The introductory chapter points out the great omissions in the ensuing coverage of the subject, partly in hopes of stimulating enquiry there: into the ethical framework in which the "have-nots" couched their demands, possibly also into the impact of sexual standards and behavior upon the assumptions and conduct of public politics. The book has, furthermore, scarcely touched the domain of ethical philosophy to which the most outstanding nineteenth-century British philosophers often devoted their efforts. Nor, except briefly for Trollope, does the book allude to the preoccupation with public as well as private morality so evident in the great literature of the century—the novels, poetry, and essays from which, more than from anything else, the continuing cultural importance of Victorian England is derived. This volume is presented in the belief that these gaps cannot be fathomed adequately without an understanding of the bearing of moral values upon the conduct of state. Still, even within their self-assigned limits, the preceding chapters are meant to stimulate as many queries as they answer.

Those who wish to explore the fields uncharted in this book would do well to take the advice of Lionel Madden on *How to Find out about the Victorian Period: A Guide to Sources of Information* (1970), and to make use of the bibliographical handbook of Josef L. Altholz, *Victorian England, 1837–1901* (1970). That handbook can be updated through the annual bibliography in each June's issue of *Victorian Studies,* an outstanding interdisciplinary quarterly on the period.

To acquire a fuller understanding of the conscience of the Victorian state, the enquirer should turn to at least one of the following works: Gertrude Himmelfarb, *Lord Acton: A Study in Conscience and Politics* (1952); Michael Howard, *War and the Liberal Conscience* (1978); E. M. Howse, *Saints in Politics: The "Clapham Sect" and the Growth of Freedom* (1952); Melvin Richter, *The Politics of Conscience: T. H. Green and his Age* (1964); and R. T. Shannon, *Gladstone and the Bulgarian Agitation, 1876* (1963).

Even beginning students should not hesitate to avail themselves of opportunities for direct encounter with the Victorians through their published writing and speeches. The most agreeable source of information on Macaulay is his own works, which, as they are frequently reprinted, are readily available in nineteenth-century editions. Especially recommended are his *Speeches* (especially those of 1831–32 on the Reform bill), his essays (especially those on Hallam, Mackintosh, Temple, and Bacon), and his letters, which are now available in a splendid edition by Thomas Pinney. Extracts from Macaulay's *History of England* are available in paperback, edited by H. R. Trevor Roper, who has also edited a selection of Macaulay's essays. Macaulay's uncompleted but important "History of France" is now available under the title *Napoleon and the Restoration of Louis XVIII,* edited by Joseph Hamburger (1977).

The only comprehensive work on nineteenth-century Whigs is Donald Southgate, *The Passing of the Whigs* (1962). Among the comparatively recent biographies of leading Victorian Whigs, David Cecil's *Melbourne* (1965) and John Prest's *Lord John Russell* (1972) stand out. The best biography of Macaulay is by John Clive, *Thomas Babington Macaulay—the Shaping of the Historian* (1973), which, however, deals only with the first half of Macaulay's life. Pinney in his edition of the *Letters* also provides useful biographical information. Lady Knutsford's *Zachary Macaulay* (1900) should also be mentioned. For comment on Macaulay's political outlook and its intellectual origins and implications, see Joseph Hamburger, *Macaulay and the Whig Tradition* (1977). Also see Vincent Starzinger, *Middlingness: Juste Milieu Political Theory in France and England, 1815–48* (1965), for a thought-provoking analysis, and John P. Kenyon's introduction to the Penguin edition of the Marquess of Halifax's *Collected Works* for illuminating comments about Macaulay in the context of an analysis of Halifax and the Trimming tradition.

On Whiggism and Whig ideas, see Walter Bagehot, "The First Edinburgh Review," in most editions of Bagehot's works; John Clive, *Scotch Reviewers: The Edinburgh Review, 1802–1815* (1957); and W. H. Auden's introduction to *Selected Writings of Sydney Smith* (1956). For an unsympathetic view, see Benjamin Disraeli's *Whigs and Whiggism* (1913). Caroline Robbins, in *The Eighteenth-Century Commonwealthman* (1959), investigates an important kind of Whiggism for which Macaulay had no affinity. For Whiggism in relation to historiography, see Herbert Butterfield's important but somewhat conflicting views in *The Whig Interpretation of History* (1951) and *The Englishman and His History* (1944). On Machiavellian themes see Felix Raab, *The English Face of Machiavelli* (1964) and Herbert Butterfield, *The Statecraft of Machiavelli* (1955).

There are not many good books on the Utilitarians, a surprising fact given their importance. But there are two classics, a good biography of Bentham, many studies of John Stuart Mill, and two fine monographs on the politics of the Utilitarians. The classics are John Stuart Mill's *Autobiography* (1873) and Elie Halevy's *The Growth of Philosophical Radicalism* (1928). The best biography of Bentham is Mary Mack, *Jeremy Bentham: An Odyssey of Ideas, 1748–1792* (1963), but it is incomplete, ending forty years before his death. The most recent biography of Bentham is by James Steintrager (1977). Biographical studies of John Stuart Mill are more numerous. The best is by Michael Packe, *The Life of John Stuart Mill* (1954). There are two able analyses of the politics of the two Mills and their followers, both by Joseph Hamburger: *James Mill and the Art of Revolution* (1963) and *Intellectuals in Politics: John Stuart Mill and the Philosophic Radicals* (1965). Those who wish to learn more about George Grote, John Arthur Roebuck, William Molesworth, Charles Buller, and T. Perronet Thompson, will find the following books useful: Martin L. Clarke, *George Grote* (1962); Robert Leader, *Life and Letters of John Arthur Roebuck* (1897); Harriet Grote, *The Philosophical Radicals of 1832: Comprising the Life of Sir William Molesworth* (1866); E. M. Wrong, *Charles Buller and Responsible Government* (1926); and L. G. Johnson, *General T. Perronet Thompson, 1783–1869* (1957).

Cold print fails to convey Gladstone's persuasive power with live audiences. In 1916 A. Tilney Bassett edited a single volume of Gladstone's major *Speeches* and appended an incomplete list of his other speeches inside and outside Parliament. *The Gladstone Diaries* are being published (1968–). Also important are *The Political Correspondence of Mr. Gladstone and Lord Granville*, edited by Agatha Ramm in four volumes (1952, 1962), covering the years 1868–86; Philip Guedalla's collection of Gladstone's official letters to the Queen (1933) and the main Gladstone-Palmerston correspondence (1928); and D. C. Lathbury's two-volume edition of Gladstone's *Correspondence on Church and Religion* (1910), which contains much more than the title implies.

John Morley's official, three-volume *Life* of Gladstone (1903) is still unsurpassed. There are readable modern biographies by Philip Magnus (1954) and E. J. Feuchtwanger (1975). S. G. Checkland's illuminating study (1971) of the Gladstone family ends at 1851. Vivid views from the inside of a Gladstone Cabinet and of Gladstone's private office can be found in Lord Kimberley's *Journal of Events during the Gladstone Ministry, 1868–74* (1958), edited by Ethel Drus, and in D. W. R. Bahlman's edition of *The Diary of Sir Edward Walter Hamilton* (1972), principal private secretary to Gladstone from 1880 to 1885.

Important monographs bearing on Gladstone's career include John Vincent, *The Formation of the Liberal Party, 1857–1868* (1866), and A. B. Cooke and John Vincent, *The Governing Passion: Cabinet Government and Party Politics in Britain, 1885–86* (1974); Michael K. Barker, *Gladstone and Radicalism: The Reconstruction of Liberal Policy in Britain, 1885–94* (1975); and D. A. Hamer, *Liberal Politics in the Age of Gladstone and Rosebery* (1972). Older works which are still of much value include W. E. Williams, *The Rise of Gladstone to the Leadership of the Liberal Party, 1859 to 1868* (1934); J. L. Hammond, *Gladstone and the Irish Nation* (1938); F. W. Hirst, *Gladstone as Financier and Economist* (1931); F. E. Hyde, *Gladstone at the Board of Trade* (1934); J. L. Hammond and M. R. D. Foot, *Gladstone and Liberalism (1952),* and R. W. Seton Watson, *Disraeli, Gladstone and the Eastern Question* (1935). H. J. Hanham, *Elections and Party Management: Politics in the Time of Disraeli and Gladstone* (1959), is a work of enduring importance.

The best general study of the religious history of the age is Owen Chadwick's

The Victorian Church, 2 volumes (1966–70). His argument that organized religion was strong and resilient throughout the century can be compared with that of Bryan Wilson in *Religion in Secular Society* (1966) that the decline of religion which became apparent after the first World War began in the late nineteenth century. Several recent works deal thoughtfully with the role of religion in Victorian society: E. R. Norman, *Church and Society in England, 1770–1970* (1976); A. D. Gilbert, *Religion in Industrial Society* (1977); W. R. Ward, *Religion and Society in England, 1790–1850* (1973); Stephen Yeo, *Religion and Voluntary Organizations in Crisis* (1977); Hugh McLeod, *Class and Religion in the Late Victorian City* (1974); and parts of Harold Perkin, *The Origins of Modern English Society* (1969).

There is no really good general history of Victorian Nonconformity. The best introduction is Erik Routley's *English Religious Dissent* (1960). George Kitson Clark's *The English Inheritance* (1950) is useful. The collections of documents by David Thompson, *Nonconformity in the Nineteenth Century* (1972), and by Ian Sellers and John Briggs, *Victorian Nonconformity* (1973), are also helpful starting points. Several novels deal with chapel life: Margaret Oliphant's *Salem Chapel* (1863), which is probably the most rewarding; and Elizabeth Gaskell, *Mary Barton* (1848) and *North and South* (1855). William Hale White, who wrote under the name of Mark Rutherford, was the most intellectually ambitious Nonconformist novelist: *The Autobiography of Mark Rutherford* (1881) and *Mark Rutherford's Deliverance* (1885) provide a fascinating picture of Nonconformist culture.

For the history of particular denominations, see R. Tudur Jones, *Congregationalism in England, 1662–1962* (1962); Albert Peel, *These Hundred Years: A History of the Congregational Union of England and Wales* (1931); Ernest Payne, *The Baptist Union* (1959); Elizabeth Isichei, *Victorian Quakers* (1970); Robert Currie, *Methodism Divided* (1968); and Bernard Semmel, *The Methodist Revolution* (1974), which explores the harmony of John Wesley's theology with the political and social changes that accompanied the industrial revolution. Willis B. Glover, *Evangelical Nonconformists and Higher Criticism in the Nineteenth Century* (1955), and John H. Rodgers, *The Theology of P. T. Forsyth* (1965), are the best of the very few studies which concentrate on Nonconformist thought.

More has been written on the political role of nineteenth-century Nonconformity: R. W. Davis, *Dissent in Politics, 1780–1830: The Political Life of William Smith, M.P.* (1971); Bernard Lord Manning, *The Protestant Dissenting Deputies* (1952); David Thompson, "The Liberation Society, 1844–1868," in *Pressure From Without in Early Victorian England,* edited by Patricia Hollis (1974); S. M. Ingham, "The Disestablishment Movement in England, 1868–74," *Journal of Religious History* 3 (1) (June 1964): 38–60; John F. Glaser, "English Nonconformity and the Decline of Liberalism," *American Historical Review* 63 (2) (Jan. 1958): 352–63; John Kent, "Hugh Price Hughes and the Nonconformist Conscience," in *Essays in Modern Church History,* edited by G. V. Bennett and J. D. Walsh (1966); and Stephen Koss, *Nonconformity in Modern British Politics* (1975).

The most useful general surveys of modern British imperialism are Ronald Hyam, *Britain's Imperial Century, 1815-1914* (1976); Ronald Hyam and Ged Martin, *Reappraisals in British Imperial History* (1975); Bernard Porter, *The Lion's Share* (1975); and David K. Fieldhouse, *Economics and Empire, 1830-1914* (1973).

Nineteenth-century British colonial policy is analyzed in William P. Morrell, *British Colonial Policy in the Age of Peel and Russell* (1930) and *British Colonial Policy in the Mid-Victorian Age* (1969); John W. Cell, *British Colonial Administration in the Mid-Nineteenth Century* (1970); C. C. Eldridge, *England's Mission: The Imperial Idea in the Age of Gladstone and Disraeli* (1973); Deryck Schreuder, *Gladstone and Kruger: Liberal Government and Colonial "Home Rule", 1880–85* (1969); Ronald E. Robinson and John Gallagher, *Africa and the Victorians* (1961), a controversial classic; and Robert V. Kubicek, *The Administration of Imperialism: Joseph Chamberlain at the Colonial Office* (1969).

There is good, provocative literature on the ideology of imperialism, its advocates, and critics: Archibald P. Thornton, *The Imperial Idea and Its Enemies* (1959), *Doctrines of Imperialism* (1965), and *The Habit of Authority: Paternalism in British History* (1966); Richard Koebner and H. D. Schmidt, *Imperialism: The Story and Significance of a Political Word, 1840–1960* (1964); Bernard Porter, *Critics of Empire: British Radical Attitudes to Colonialism in Africa, 1895–1914* (1968); and, as a guide to the Marxist critique, Michael Barratt-Brown, *The Economics of Imperialism* (1974).

On anti-slavery, in addition to those works discussed in chapter six, see Ford K. Brown, *Fathers of the Victorians: The Age of Wilberforce* (1961); Eric Williams, *Capitalism and Slavery* (1944); and Howard Temperley, *British Anti-slavery, 1833-1870* (1972). The best works on missionaries are Kenneth S. Latourette's multivolume *A History of the Expansion of Christianity* (1937–); Charles P. Groves, *The Planting of Christianity in Africa,* 4 volumes (1955–64); Roland Oliver, *The Missionary Factor in East Africa* (1952); H. Alan Cairns, *Prelude to Imperialism: British Reactions to Central African Society, 1840–1890* (1965); and Emmanuel A. Ayandele, *The Missionary Impact on Modern Nigeria, 1842-1914* (1966).

Racial ideology in a broader context can be studied in Philip D. Curtin, *The Image of Africa: British Ideas and Action, 1780–1850* (1964); Christine Bolt, *Victorian Attitudes toward Race* (1971); Gertrude Himmelfarb, *Darwin and the Darwinian Revolution* (1962); John W. Burrow, *Evolution and Society: A Study in Victorian Social Evolution* (1970); and Bernard Semmel, *The Governor Eyre Controversy* (1963). On blacks in Britain, see Kenneth L. Little, *Negroes in Britain: A Study in Racial Relations in English Society* (1948), and James Walvin, *Black and White: The Negro and English Society, 1555–1945* (1973).

On the Conservatives, Robert Blake has written a good introduction: *The Conservative Party from Peel to Churchill* (1970). Closer enquiries follow two often overlapping routes: monographs on shorter periods or themes, and biographies. The best of these on the last generation of Tories before the 1832 Reform Act are W. R. Brock, *Lord Liverpool and Liberal Toryism, 1820 to 1827,* 2nd ed.

(1967), and Norman Gash, *Mr. Secretary Peel: The Life of Sir Robert Peel to 1830* (1961), which may be supplemented by the much broader study by Keith Feiling of *The Second Tory Party, 1714-1832* (1938). Norman Gash has made the next generation, the age of Peel, his own through the second volume of the biography, *Sir Robert Peel: The Life of Sir Robert Peel after 1830* (1972), and a number of other books and articles, preeminently "Peel and the Party System," *Transactions of the Royal Historical Society*, 5th ser. 1 (1951): 47–69; *Politics in the Age of Peel* (1953); and *Reaction and Reconstruction in English Politics, 1832-1852* (1965). Critical Conservative perspectives on the achievement of Peel are presented by Benjamin Disraeli, *Lord George Bentinck* (1852); Charles Whibley, *Lord John Manners and His Friends,* 2 volumes (1925); Cecil Driver, *Tory Radical: The Life of Richard Oastler* (1946); and Robert Stewart, *The Politics of Protection: Lord Derby and the Protectionist Party, 1841-1852* (1971).

While Disraeli has mesmerized politicians in every generation, he has tended to elude the grasp of scholars, with three notable exceptions: Robert Blake, *Disraeli* (1966); Maurice Cowling, *1867: Disraeli, Gladstone and Revolution* (1967); and Paul Smith, *Disraelian Conservatism and Social Reform* (1967). Still the best biography of Lord Salisbury is by his daughter, Lady Gwendolen Cecil, *Life of Robert, Marquis of Salisbury,* 4 volumes (1921–32), though it stops in 1892. It may be supplemented through the incisive introduction in Paul Smith, ed., *Lord Salisbury on Politics: A Selection from his Articles in the Quarterly Review, 1860-1883* (1972), and Peter Marsh, *The Discipline of Popular Government: Lord Salisbury's Domestic Statecraft, 1881 to 1902* (1978). Two articles deal with ethical tensions in Salisbury's thought and politics: Elie Kedourie, "Tory ideologue: Salisbury as a Conservative intellectual," *Encounter* (June 1972): 45–53, and Peter Marsh, "Lord Salisbury and the Ottoman Massacres," *Journal of British Studies* 11 (2) (May 1972): 63–83. The practice of Tory Democracy is recounted in Harold E. Gorst, *The Fourth Party* (1906), and in two biographies of Lord Randolph Churchill, by Winston Churchill (1906) and by Robert Rhodes James (1959). The greatest work of late nineteenth-century Conservative thought, James Fitzjames Stephen's *Liberty, Equality, Fraternity,* has been edited by R. J. White (1967). Two books pierce contrasting enclaves of Conservative society at the turn of the century: Kenneth Rose, *Superior Person: A Portrait of Curzon and his Circle in Late Victorian England* (1969), and J. A. Bridges, *Reminiscences of a Country Politician* (1906).

INDEX

249

THE CONSCIENCE OF THE VICTORIAN STATE

was composed in ten point Compugraphic Times Roman and leaded two points
with display type also in Times Roman
by Metricomp Studios, Inc.;
printed on Warren's antique cream paper stock,
Smyth-sewn, and bound over boards in Columbia Vellum Natural
by Maple-Vail Book Manufacturing Group, Inc.;
and published by

SYRACUSE UNIVERSITY PRESS
SYRACUSE, NEW YORK 13210